IN!

COLLEGE ADMISSIONS
AND BEYOND

THE EXPERTS' PROVEN STRATEGY
FOR SUCCESS

"I'm worried about a monster under my bed
and I'm worried about college."

IN!

COLLEGE ADMISSIONS
AND BEYOND

THE EXPERTS' PROVEN STRATEGY
FOR SUCCESS

LILLIAN LUTERMAN

AND

JENNIFER BLOOM

ABBEVILLE PRESS PUBLISHERS
NEW YORK LONDON

TO RYAN AND OUR BOYS
—J. B.

TO GERRY AND OUR GIRLS
—L. L.

EDITOR: Jacqueline Decter
ASSOCIATE EDITOR: Austin Allen
PRODUCTION MANAGER: Louise Kurtz
DESIGNER: Celia Fuller
COVER DESIGN: Misha Beletsky

First Edition
10 9 8 7 6 5 4 3 2 1

For cartoon credits, see page 304.

Library of Congress Cataloging-in-Publication Data

Luterman, Lillian.
 In! college admissions and beyond : the experts' proven strategy for success / Lillian Luterman and Jennifer Bloom.
   p. cm.
 Includes bibliographical references and index.
  ISBN 978-0-7892-1062-3 (hardcover : alk. paper) -- ISBN 978-0-7892-1060-9 (pbk. : alk. paper) 1. Universities and colleges--United States--Admission. 2. College choice--United States. I. Bloom, Jennifer L. II. Title.
 LB2351.2.L88 2010
 378.1'610973--dc22

                                                            2010014039

For bulk and premium sales and for text adoption procedures, write to Customer Service Manager, Abbeville Press, 137 Varick Street, New York, NY 10013, or call 1-800-ARTBOOK.

Visit Abbeville Press online at www.abbeville.com.

Contents

Acknowledgments

So many students, family members, and friends were instrumental in helping us complete this project. Our thanks, first and foremost, to our students. It has been our privilege to work with you and guide you through the application process. Through you, we have learned so much.

We also want to thank Abbeville Press. We are especially grateful to Abbeville's publisher and our longtime friend, Bob Abrams. This book would not have existed without your continual encouragement and enthusiasm. To our editor, Jackie Decter, thank you for all your help. You were instrumental in every step of this process and we are so grateful. To Austin Allen, thank you for helping us to edit and polish our text. Thanks also to Michaelann Millrood, Briana Green, Erin Dress, Misha Beletsky, Celia Fuller, and Susan Costello. And a heartfelt thank you to our publicist, Sandi Mendelson, and her whole team for their support and sound advice.

We would also like to thank individual students who made concrete contributions to this book: Jake Brodlie, Eli Brodlie, Alyson Ryder Burks, Austin Conti, Alexa Disciullo, Lizzie Ellis, Nicole Fallick, Justin Goldstein, Ari Golub, Alex Hamill, Katie Lee, Rachel Neporent, and Philippa Pavia. Thank you!

Jessica Luterman Naeve, thank you for all your help and advice, provided just when we needed it most. Your suggestions were always spot on and we loved your idea for the title as soon as we heard it. Milena Alberti Perez, thank you for your invaluable guidance and recommendations. To Hannah Yang, Amanda Pustilnik, and so many friends who read chapters and drafts and kept us excited about the book, thank you.

Finally, to our husbands.

Ryan, thank you for encouraging me in my decision to change careers and for always being my best sounding board. I still remember the evening you helped me draft the outline of this book—even though you thought I was crazy to start writing a book while working and pregnant. You are my biggest supporter and I love you.

Gerry, my husband and Jennifer and Jessica's dad, thank you for so many things—encouraging me to start my business so many years ago, constantly singing my praises to everyone who would listen, being so proud of all my accomplishments and milestones, and always being there for me in every way. I couldn't have done it without you.

We are forever grateful.
Jennifer Bloom
Lillian Luterman

Introduction

The Genesis of Our Educational Consultancy

We are a mother (Lillian)-daughter (Jennifer) team of educational consultants. While writing this book, we were often reminded of Jennifer's college application process. Although we couldn't have known it at the time, that experience turned out to be the genesis of our consulting service.

We first began thinking about Jennifer's college prospects in her sophomore year of high school. Even back then, the selectivity ratio was daunting. Everyone kept calling college admissions a "crap shoot," which sounded precarious and intimidating.

As a Canadian, Lillian had applied to one college—late on a school night, after TV and homework. It never occurred to her to apply to more than one school. But by the time Jennifer was approaching college age, we lived in the ultra-competitive Northeast. College was a defining status symbol, a brand plastered on sweatshirts, hats, and rear windshields. College lists ran to double digits in length, with separate columns for "safeties," "probables," and "reaches." We decided that rather than avoid the system, we would learn it.

What we have learned since that experience, in more than two decades working with hundreds of students and speaking with numerous admissions officers, is that the college-admissions process actually isn't a crap shoot. As with preparation for any other activity—from a sports tournament to a job interview—following a smart, step-by-step strategy makes success far more likely. Over the years, we have refined our own proven strategy, which we now call "be alike but spike." The reasons for "being alike"—that is, performing at least as well as other top applicants, specifically in the academic arena—are simple. First, admissions officers don't want to admit students who can't succeed in the classroom. Four years of academic struggle isn't fair to the student and reflects poorly on the college. The second reason is less "altruistic." Each year there is intense pressure on college administrators to boost or maintain their school's rank on the *U.S. News & World Report* lists ("Top Universities," "Best Small Colleges," and so on). The academic performance statistics of incoming students heavily influence these rankings. Thus, while accepting candidates with below-average GPAs and SAT scores does happen, it's rare. Today, colleges simply expect applicants to fit in.

As we will show, however, *just* fitting in with other top students isn't enough; admissions officers routinely claim that more than 80 percent of applicants fall within their desired metrics. Successful applicants also have to stand out, or "spike," in some specific area. Contrary to an old myth, selective colleges don't desire well-rounded *students* as much as well-rounded *classes*. Of course, colleges don't want their students to be completely one-dimensional, but they do want each student to contribute a special attribute or skill to the college community. They want a superb musician, a star athlete, a master mathematician, and a brilliant dancer. By combining these kinds of students, admissions officers strive to create a vibrant, diverse, and multidisciplinary campus community. The well-rounded student may do each of these activities, but through lack of focus probably won't end up doing any of them really, really well.

With this in mind, we knew that Jennifer needed to stand out from the thousands of applicants competing with her. We thought back to areas in which Jennifer had always excelled. Once we identified this interest— something Jennifer *chose* to do when she didn't *need* to do anything—she went through a process very similar to the one we describe in our book.

Like the students in our case studies, she was incredibly lucky to have parents who helped her cultivate her interest, which happened to be art. Through a process we now call "layering," we sought out art-related summer programs, internships, jobs, and volunteer opportunities. Each opportunity led to and built on the others. By Jennifer's senior year, she had developed her interest in the arts into an area of true distinction.

While Jennifer was developing and layering her passion, she was also making sure that her grades and standardized test scores compared well with those of other students applying. When she applied to college, she was competitive in all respects and outstanding in one. Receiving acceptances from the schools she applied to was both exciting and rewarding.

It's common to hear people tell you to do what you love. And it makes sense: the only way you're going to be great at something is if you genuinely love practicing and perfecting it. This book shows you how to create opportunities to do what you love—or at least what you're interested in (as we'll describe later, high school students often tell us that they only *love* video games or hanging out with their friends, so at first we brainstorm activities they *like*.) At the same time, this book shows you how to match other top applicants' academic performance. (The "be alike" half of our strategy shouldn't be confused with social conformity, let alone mediocrity. What you're conforming to is simply the standards set by the colleges you want to attend.) While we can't promise Princeton-level GPAs and SAT averages, we can provide strategies for maximizing your ability within the high school system.

What *In!* Covers

In! covers all aspects of the college application process, explaining everything from course selection to creating a college list to essay writing and interview preparation. Following our strategy, we have organized the book into four parts:

our Day
9:00 - circle time
10:00 - art fun
11:00 - snack
12:00 - S.A.T. prep

B. Smaller

Part I: "Be Alike." This section shows you how to match—if not outdo—admitted applicants' performance in certain key areas. In the chapters devoted to academic achievement, standardized testing, and in-school leadership, you will learn everything you need to do for your academic record to equal or surpass that of other successful candidates at the colleges to which you are applying.

Part II: "Spike." The second section of this book is about *not* being alike. While successful applicants must perform on a par with other students applying to similar colleges, they must also work to become highly distinctive—like a spike on a graph—in one area. (Remember, it's often the "well-rounded student," an ideal that many applicants strive toward, who gets rejected.) In this section, we show you how to create that distinction by isolating a passion and layering it, showcasing it in many different ways and under many different circumstances.

Part III: "Pulling It All Together: Being Alike and Spiking on the College Application." As we tell our students, your college application has an important job to do: it's four or five pages that must represent some seventeen years of your life. Part III first explains how to prepare to apply—by creating a working college list based on your preferences and visiting those colleges. It then illustrates how to create an application— activity charts, essays, letters of recommendation, interviews, and supplementary materials—that instantly and effectively shows admissions officers that you will be both a comfortable fit and a distinctive asset at their college.

Part IV: "College and Beyond." The final part of *In!* demonstrates that the skills you develop in your college application process have long-lasting benefits and direct applicability to post-college life. From exploring a passion to acing an interview, these skills will not only get you into your top-choice school but also lay the groundwork for real-world success.

How to Use This Book

There are two ways to use *In!* First, and ideally, you can read it from end to end. Used this way, it provides a strategy—no matter how early or late in the process you begin—for getting into the school of your dreams.

The second way to use this book is as a reference for specific topics. Need help with letters of recommendation? Check out Chapter 10, "Letters of Recommendation." Confused about which classes to take? See Chapter 1, "Academic Achievement." You get the picture.

Note: The part that we most strongly recommend reading from start to finish is Part II, "Spike" (Chapters 4 and 5). In it, you'll learn, through brainstorming and case studies, how to figure out what you're interested in and fully develop that interest. You'll see how small, simple steps can, over time, add up to a big impact.

Parents' Role

We realize that just as parents are generally the first to inquire about our educational service, they are also likely to be the purchasers of this book. Although it is written primarily for students, we know that few students have the time to think about a comprehensive college strategy while studying for standardized tests, engaging in extracurriculars, completing classroom assignments, and yes, squeezing in some fun. At the same time, we are well aware that being a parent is tricky. While we all understand that college is a major family expense and the university your child will attend often has long-lasting implications, parents still need to walk the fine line between being involved and not *too* involved, being helpful and not *too* helpful. Interference can backfire. Here is some advice we've shared with families:

First, trust your instincts. As a parent, you've gotten this far!

Expect the college application process to be an extension of your existing relationship. How have you worked with your child in the past? Has it been a close partnership, or have you helped from behind the scenes? Whatever the dynamic, it will probably continue (with a few bumps) in much the same fashion.

Many parents worry about getting too involved. While we understand this concern—especially in light of the media coverage given to the "helicopter parent" phenomenon—we'd also ask you to consider the findings of the March 2007 College Board study. Over 1,700 students who recently completed the college application process were asked about parental involvement in that process. Their findings? More than 95 percent said their parents were "involved to some degree" or "very involved" in their college application process. Of that 95 percent, more than 60 percent were very happy with their parents' level of involvement. However, 30 percent wished their parents had been *more* involved. This figure rises to 40 percent among students with lower SAT scores and household incomes. Only 6 percent wished their parents had been *less* involved.[*]

---

[*] "High school students want parents to be more involved in college planning," CollegeBoard studentPOLL, vol. 6, issue 1, 2007, http://www.collegeboard.com/about/news_info/report.html.

The takeaway lesson? Parental over-involvement may be less of an issue than previously assumed. Again, trust your instincts: even though your kids may nag, complain, or scream, chances are they are secretly grateful for your support and glad that they're not confronting this stressful and time-consuming process on their own.

Finally, although students are often grateful for parental support, keep in mind that colleges want to learn about your child, not you. We often tell parents that their job is that of an unpaid intern: to schedule, organize, proofread, review, and plan. While you should never write your child's essay, you can check for spelling errors or grammar mistakes. While you should never accompany your child into an interview, you can schedule her interview and make sure she arrives on time. Is there a question about tour and information session dates? That's a call you can make. A question about course requirements for a bio major versus a pre-med major? That's a call your son or daughter should make. (For more on this topic, see pages 150–52).

How Is Our Book on College Admissions Different?

In! differs from others of its kind in a few important ways. First, while many other books on college admissions explain (with varying degrees of success) how students can make the most of individual components of the application—for example, essays, standardized test scores, or interviews—no other book helps students combine all these elements into a more comprehensive and more effective strategy. For example, we don't just show you how to create an outstanding activity chart; we explain how to create a chart that reveals to admissions officers the ways in which you are both comparable to and distinct from other applicants. Given the intense competition surrounding college admissions, it's not enough to create a successful application piecemeal; the pieces must function together as a seamless whole.

Second, our book shows students how to identify and cultivate an area of interest that will make their application unique. Many students arrive at our offices convinced that they are exactly the same as all their friends, with no unique hobbies or interests. After a little digging, however, genuine interests emerge. Yet even after isolating these interests, many students aren't sure how to explore and expand them, so that they evolve from hobbies into passions. By providing case studies, examples, and resource lists, we explain how to cultivate the activity that makes you stand out.

Third, and most importantly, *In!* shows how small steps can add up to large accomplishments. Passions are not created in giant leaps, but rather through small, thoughtful steps in a specific direction. Students are always surprised at how seemingly trivial activities can lead to opportunities they might never have expected—and how this process can lay the foundation for a lifetime of creative exploration.

Finally, unlike most books about "getting in," our story doesn't end at high school graduation and acceptance into college. Exploring a passion through varied channels is not just a strategy that gets you into college. It's something our most successful students do again and again throughout their college, postgraduate, and professional careers. As in college admissions, equaling your professional peers in the basics is expected. At the same time, developing a special talent or niche is almost always a prerequisite for professional success, whether you're a pro football player or a tax lawyer. Similarly, interviewing well, creating a strong "activity chart" or résumé, obtaining positive recommendations, and maximizing a financial-aid package are all skills that matter after college. Perhaps the only form that makes a financial-aid form look simple is a mortgage application.

Rather than viewing college admissions as something to be dealt with as quickly and painlessly as possible, we see it both as an opportunity and as a crucial stage in any young person's development. It's an important opportunity to mature, expand your horizons, and discover what makes you tick. We have repeated our college-preparation process with hundreds of families all over the country and the world; it works. Not only does *In!* "get you in," but it also gives you the tools and confidence you'll need for future success.

About Us

A graduate of McGill University, **Lillian Luterman** has been advising students on college and boarding school admissions since 1989, but has been involved in education throughout her career. Having a master's degree in speech pathology and counseling, Lillian has worked with students of all levels and backgrounds, from those with learning disabilities to gifted students aiming for the top-tier colleges. She lives with her husband in Westport, Connecticut.

A graduate of Harvard College with a master's degree from Cambridge University (U.K.) and an MBA from Harvard Business School, **Jennifer Bloom** began working with her mother in 2005. Previously she spent more than ten years in marketing and advertising. She has worked for companies such as American Express and Ogilvy & Mather, creating and launching new services as well as award-winning advertising campaigns. She lives with her family in New York City.

Together, Luterman and Bloom founded Entryway Inc., providing premier counseling and specialized workshops.

"Hello, I'm Nesbit. I'm three, and I'm right on track."

Be Alike

Throughout this book, we'll be repeating the mantralike phrase "be alike but spike." All this phrase means is that the students who get into top colleges are "alike" in certain key ways—that is, they all meet certain minimum standards of academic excellence, test performance, and extracurricular leadership involvement—but also "spike," or excel, in other, more distinctive ways. Distinguishing between the two categories is important, because there are areas in which "spiking," or standing out, in the eyes of admissions officers is very difficult; simply comparing favorably is the name of the game. It may surprise some readers to learn that it's nearly impossible to stand out through academic achievement, standardized test scores, or in-school leadership alone.

But think about it a little more and it makes sense. It's like your mom always said: you *have* to go to school, get good grades, take standardized tests, and participate in a few extracurriculars. Colleges aren't going to award you extra points for doing that—especially when you're competing against kids who have performed equally well in the same areas. In fact, *not* meeting these basic criteria may put you out of the running for an acceptance at your top-choice school. Admissions officers at selective colleges admit that *more than 80 percent of applicants* meet the minimum "fit in" criteria of admitted students. What colleges will *really* pay attention to is evidence of outstanding intellectual curiosity—a true love of "learning for learning's sake," particularly as expressed outside of classes... but take a deep breath, we'll get there.

Even if they won't set you apart, your grades, standardized test scores, and in-school leadership activities *will* be the foundation on which the rest of your application stands, so they're a natural place to start our step-by-step breakdown of the college admissions process. Part I of this book consists of three chapters: "Academic Achievement," "Standardized Tests," and "In-School Leadership Activities." While being like other students in these three areas won't guarantee that your application sails through admissions, it will ensure that nothing—no glaring weaknesses or omissions—will stop it cold, either.

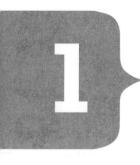

Academic Achievement

Overview

In this chapter you'll learn:

- The role of academics in the college admissions process
- Which courses to take to prepare for college
- How to improve your grades or make up for poor past performance
- What a High School Profile is and how to review and understand it
- How parents can help their child's academic performance

What Is an Academic Record?

Your academic record consists of the type and level of courses you've taken and the grades you've earned in them. Again, unless you're a super-genius who has taken college-level courses throughout high school, it's hard to "spike" on the basis of this record alone. The high school curriculum is a fairly standard one: World History, Physics, Geometry... you're one of thousands, if not millions, of students taking similar courses at any one time.

So what should your academic record do for you? Very simply, it should show that you are able to fit into a particular college and handle the curriculum. In this way, you'll meet the school's academic standards and be at least as good as or "like" other students attending the school. Your record should also show that you've challenged yourself—wisely (see "Advanced vs. Regular Courses" on page 23).

"Where do you get off saying my kid is grade level?"

What Courses Do Colleges Expect Me to Take?

First and foremost, many colleges recommend that you take four years in each of the five key high school subjects:

- English
- Math
- Social Studies (History)
- Science
- Foreign Language

Our advice is to stick to this curriculum if at all possible. Don't assume that just because your high school allows students to drop foreign language and science during senior year, colleges will endorse that recommendation. In many cases, they won't. If you decide that you just can't sit through one more year of Spanish, check what your top-choice colleges "recommend" before you drop it. Hint: these aren't really "recommendations." Assume that what a college recommends, it actually requires! The most competitive schools will want to see that you've fulfilled all of their recommendations and done so in the most competitive classes that your high school offers.

ADVANCED VS. REGULAR COURSES

Your academic record is not just about your grades; it's also about the courses you get them in. In general, you should take the most rigorous classes you can handle. The most competitive colleges will expect you to take the most competitive classes your high school offers in most subjects. That said, if you're struggling under your course load, you may be taking too many advanced-level courses. It's okay to choose your advanced or honors courses selectively. Get to know what you're best at and challenge yourself in those areas. Identify your weaknesses and consider your overall workload (even the most well-rounded students can see their grades slip as a result of burnout).

NO LOOPHOLES

As a general rule, never assume that competitive colleges will respect any academic loopholes your high school might provide. One of our students, a bright girl we first met during her sophomore year, had gotten poor grades as a freshman. When we asked her why, she explained that her lax performance that year didn't count because her high school averaged only sophomore-through-senior-year grades in computing GPA. That may have been true of her high school, but many colleges will recompute GPAs to average in freshman-year grades, so slacking off that year is a bad idea. Likewise, don't try to cheat the system by taking elective or easy courses that deliver easy A's. Even though some high schools compute only an unweighted GPA, many colleges will recalculate a weighted GPA—that is, one that factors in the difficulty level of each course.

BE CONSISTENT

Another rule of thumb: colleges reward consistency. Don't start taking Spanish during freshman year only to switch to French during sophomore year. Stick with your chosen language. If you're passionate about

WHAT IF MY HIGH SCHOOL DOESN'T OFFER ACCELERATED/HONORS/ADVANCED PLACEMENT/ INTERNATIONAL BACCALAUREATE CLASSES?

Will you be penalized? Absolutely not. Because of your High School Profile (explained later in this chapter), admissions officers are aware of which advanced courses are available to you. Just try to take the most difficult courses *your* high school offers.

a language for which your high school doesn't offer four years' worth of courses, you may want to get creative and seek out unusual options.

DON'T SACRIFICE ACADEMICS FOR ELECTIVES

Finally, don't sacrifice academic courses for semi-academics. Don't take Psychology instead of a basic science like Biology, Chemistry, or Physics. Use your time in high school to acquire a strong foundation in standard academic courses. Once you've fulfilled those basics, then feel free to explore electives.

WHEN SHOULD I SWITCH UP OR DOWN A LEVEL?

If your grades fall below a B- in an AP class, consider switching down a level to a less competitive course. Don't assume that the weighted GPA will rectify this low grade. If you're scoring at the A or A+ level in a normal-level course, you may be invited to take the accelerated course the following year. Switch only if you can maintain a B or B- level in the advanced course; it's not worth switching if you can't. Although colleges always like to see that you're challenging yourself academically, remember that it's also wise to be realistic about your strengths and weaknesses.

For example, we had a student who attended a high school where she did not have to qualify to take AP classes (for a detailed explanation of AP and IB courses and tests, see pages 48–52). She had gotten

GOING THE EXTRA MILE

A student we worked with studied Latin for two years in his private middle school and then took Latin during his freshman and sophomore years. There were no other Latin courses offered in his school, so we suggested that during his junior year he do an independent study with his teacher in an area of Latin that interested him. We also suggested that as a senior, he ask his freshman-year Latin teacher if he could be an aide for the freshman class. He followed both suggestions. When his guidance counselor wrote his letter of recommendation for college, she noted the "extra mile" he had gone in continuing to pursue Latin. In another letter of recommendation, his Latin teacher was able to describe him as someone who truly distinguished himself in class. He was accepted at his top-choice school.

a B- in her regular U.S. History class. As a junior, she opted to take AP World History, against our recommendation, and scored C's on tests and papers in the first quarter. We advised her to drop down to a lower level of History. She did and began to score in the B+/A- range. Although we encourage students to take the most competitive courses offered by their schools, it's important for colleges to see that the student knows what her capabilities are. Getting C's is not impressive to colleges, even if it is in AP courses.

Achieving consistently high grades in advanced courses is ideal. However, schools will also look favorably on students who show a steady upward grade trend. Students often will begin high school without the focus and maturity that high school classes demand. Only by sophomore and sometimes junior year will they develop these qualities. Colleges understand this and will factor it into their considerations, so if your grades as a fourteen-year-old freshman weren't all that they could have been, don't despair.

The Million-Dollar Question: How Can I Raise My Grades?

- Master the Basics. Be disciplined. Come prepared. Don't be late. Ask questions. Do your homework. Fundamental stuff—but until you've taken these simple steps, you can ignore all further advice. Extracurricular activities and hanging out with friends, while important, should never interfere with schoolwork.

- Show teachers that you're interested in their class material by contributing out-of-class sources. Did you read an op-ed column that examines the makeup of the Supreme Court, something you are studying this week in your U.S. History class? Did the Science section of the *New York Times* explore the biology of termites—a topic you just covered? Clip the article; e-mail the story; share with the class.

- Contribute to discussions in class. Try to help other students learn. A perceptive comment is wonderful in its own right, but to a teacher, it's even better if it helps other students understand a point more clearly.

- Focus your test and quiz preparation on what teachers spend time reviewing. If a teacher takes time to review a particular problem or concept, chances are you'll be tested on it.

- Seek out extra help. If you don't understand what a teacher covers in class, it's your responsibility—whether or not you like the teacher—to ask for help before or after class.

- Make room in your schedule for free periods. We often recommend that students choose their courses so they can schedule in a free period each day, especially during their junior and senior years. Use these free periods to talk to your teachers and get extra help wherever needed.

- Get in the habit of handing in "final" papers three days in advance. Ask your teacher to review your rough draft (remember, it's not really a rough draft—it's the best work you can do prior to the review). Listen to her comments and incorporate them. Not only will this improve your grade, but you'll learn a lot in the process.

"I'll pencil you in for recess."

- If you're struggling with a class and "in-school help" isn't helping, or if the teacher just isn't available enough to make a difference, consider hiring a coach for that class. If at all possible, try to find someone who is familiar with your school curriculum.

What Is a High School Profile?

The High School Profile is a report that's available from your guidance office upon request. It will accompany your transcript and be sent to all of your prospective colleges. It is a matter of public record, and although few students do this, you should ask your guidance office to see a copy. Its main job is to put your transcript (the classes you took, the grades you received) into context with respect to your class. For example:

Here is a sample High School Profile from a competitive college preparatory high school:

SAMPLE HIGH SCHOOL PROFILE

School
A comprehensive four-year public high school.
Enrollment: 1,800
Average class size: 25
Faculty: 184, including 11 counselors
Accreditation: Regional Association of Schools and Colleges

Graduation requirements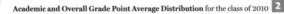

English	4.0
Math	3.0
Social Studies	3.5
Science	2.0
World Language	2.0
Arts	1.5
Physical Ed	3.0
Electives	6.0

CREDITS REQUIRED   25.0

Statistics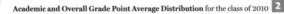

Class of 2010: 411 students

Based on six semesters
   highest academic GPA: 4.6486
   lowest academic GPA: 0.31
   highest overall GPA: 4.2222
   lowest overall GPA: 0.8864
   mean academic GPA: 2.9865
   mean overall GPA: 3.1982

Class of 2009: 418 students

SAT average scores
   Critical Reading: 596
   Math: 608
   Writing: 605
   Percentage taking: 96%

Students attending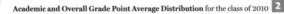
   4-year colleges: 90.4%
   2-year colleges: 3.5%
   PG, Voc. other ed: 1.6%

TOTAL ATTENDING   95.5%

Employment: 2.3%
Military: 0%
Other: 1.9%

National Merit Scholar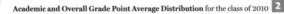
finalists: 6

National Merit Commended Students: 33

Grade Point Average is calculated only on courses taken at this high school

Academic Grade Point Average is based on the arithmetic average (total grade points divided by credits taken) of grades earned in English, world language, mathematics, science, and social studies, weighted by instructional levels*

	A+	A	A-	B+	B	B-	C+	C	C-	D+	D	D-	F
AP	5.00	4.67	4.33	4.00	3.67	3.33	3.00	2.67	2.33	2.00	1.67	1.33	0.00
HONORS	4.67	4.33	4.00	3.67	3.33	3.00	2.67	2.33	2.00	1.67	1.33	1.00	0.00
A level	4.33	4.00	3.67	3.33	3.00	2.67	2.33	2.00	1.67	1.33	1.00	0.67	0.00
B level	4.00	3.67	3.33	3.00	2.67	2.33	2.00	1.67	1.33	1.00	0.67	0.33	0.00
C level	3.67	3.33	3.00	2.67	2.33	2.00	1.67	1.33	1.00	0.67	0.33	0.16	0.00

* All advanced placement classes including electives receive AP points in calculating academic GPA.
* All "A" level course are considered advanced college preparatory. Both "B" and "C" levels are college preparatory. Course level placement is primarily by teacher recommendation.

Overall Grade Point Average is based on the unweighted arithmetic average of grades earned in all courses using numerical grade values as follows:

A+	A	A-	B+	B	B-	C+	C	C-	D+	D	D-	F
4.33	4.0	3.67	3.33	3.0	2.67	2.33	2.0	1.67	1.33	1.0	.67	0.00

Academic and Overall Grade Point Average Distribution for the class of 2010

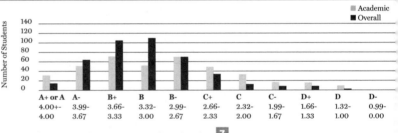

Legend: ▨ Academic ■ Overall

	A+ or A 4.00+-4.00	A- 3.99-3.67	B+ 3.66-3.33	B 3.32-3.00	B- 2.99-2.67	C+ 2.66-2.33	C 2.32-2.00	C- 1.99-1.67	D+ 1.66-1.33	D 1.32-1.00	D- 0.99-0.00

(y-axis: Number of Students — 0, 20, 40, 60, 80, 100, 120, 140)

Advanced Placement at a glance for 2009 in grades 10 through 12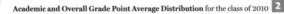

AP courses offered: 21
Total students taking AP test: 445

Number of AP tests taken: 910
Number of scores 3 or better: 841

Honors and Advanced Placement Offerings for the class of 2009/2010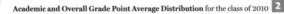

English	Math	Science	Social Studies	World Language
English 1 Honors	Geometry *Honors*	Biology Honors	Western Humanities Honors	Spanish 2, 3, 4, 5 *Honors*
English 2 Honors	Algebra II *Honors*	Chemistry *Honors*		
		Physics Honors	U.S. History Honors	AP Spanish Language
Grade 11	Pre-Calculus *Honors*	AP Biology	AP U.S. History	AP Spanish Literature
AP Language & Composition	Calculus *Honors*	AP Chemistry	AP Modern World History	French 2, 3, 4, 5 *Honors*
	AP Calculus AB	AP Physics B		
Grade 12	AP Calculus BC	AP Physics C	AP U.S. Government & Politics	AP French Language
AP English Literature	AP Statistics	AP Environmental Science	AP Macro/Micro-economics	German 2, 3, 4 *Honors*
	AP Multivariable Calculus (AB, BC)		AP European	AP German Language
				Latin 2, 3, 4 *Honors*
				Mandarin Chinese 1, 2, 3, 4 *Honors*

Some of the main sections of the High School Profile are explained below:

1 This chart explains how your weighted and unweighted GPAs are calculated. It also reveals the different course levels this high school offers (AP through C Level).

2 This chart reveals the high school's grade distribution, putting your grades in context for the admissions officer. At some high schools, the average grade is closer to a C, while at this high school, the average grade is closer to a B+/B.

3 This chart explains which courses were available for students to take.

Are you taking the most rigorous courses your high school offers? Don't be fooled into thinking that an admissions officer won't know that your high school offers advanced courses, if you chose not to take them.

On the flip side, if your high school does not offer honors or AP courses, you will not be penalized for not taking them.

Finally, your High School Profile will explain to admissions officers that there was a reason you didn't take Latin 5 Honors. It simply was not offered.

4 What are your high school's requirements for graduation? Have you simply fulfilled them to graduate or have you gone above and beyond the base requirements?

5 This high school reveals students' average GPA and SAT scores. How do yours compare? An underprivileged student from an under-resourced school who has SAT scores in the low 600s will be viewed more leniently than a student who attended this school, where the *average* SAT is a 600 and many of the residents are described as college graduates in professional and business careers.

6 Revealing the number of National Merit Scholar Finalists and Commended Students, based on students' PSAT scores, puts this achievement into context. At this high school, 39 students won this impressive award.

7 Note the total number of students taking AP (Advanced Placement) tests. In this high school, 445 students took 910 AP tests; there were 841 3's or better (out of a possible score of 5). Taking AP classes and tests at this high school is not as unusual as it would be at a less competitive high school, and this information will be taken into consideration by admissions officers.

8 How many students from this high school attend college? This statistic is very revealing to admissions officers. Did you attend a privileged high school, such as this one, where 90 percent of students attend a 4-year college, and attending college is essentially expected? Or did you attend a high school where keeping an academic focus was much more difficult? Your transcript and application will be reviewed accordingly.

- An admissions officer may view your transcript to see that you received As in every class you took.
  - The High School Profile will, however, reveal that you took the least difficult classes your high school offered.
- An admissions officer may wonder why you took only two years of high school Latin.
  - The High School Profile will reveal that the high school offers only two years of that language. There were no more advanced Latin courses offered.
- An admissions officer may wonder why a student with 700+ SAT scores has only a B-level grade point average (GPA).
  - The High School Profile will reveal that the mean GPA at this rigorous high school is closer to a C, making the student's B average much more impressive.

For these reasons and many more, the High School Profile is an important component of your college application.

If your high school profile doesn't clear up academic issues that you think are confusing, consider including a very succinct (1–2 line) explanation in your application—or even better, ask your guidance counselor to do so.

Make sure that your academic record is not only clear but correct. Inaccuracies do exist. You might even check to ensure that teachers are accurate in calculating midterm and end-of-year grades. We've found that despite honest efforts, teachers do make mistakes!

I Messed Up. Now What?

Was your poor performance limited to one or two classes? If so, you might be able to retake those classes. This doesn't mean that your GPA will immediately rise, but you will be able to demonstrate to colleges that this grade isn't representative of your capabilities. Unless you failed, you probably won't be able to repeat the class in your high school. Look for summer classes at local community colleges and summer school.

When you want to improve your high school record, you might consider taking a gap year. Sometimes this involves study overseas. There are international schools all over Europe, and some will admit American students for a year of additional study after high school. For example, Oxford Advanced Studies Program offers a postgraduate (PG) year for international students. Other students—especially those from overseas—consider a postgraduate year at an American prep school to improve their English and their chance of admittance to an American college. This extra year of study, if financially feasible, not only gives students another year of experiences from which to draw and therefore make themselves more attractive candidates but can also significantly expand their world view. See below for more information on gap years, postgraduate years, and study abroad, and the Resources section for a selection of gap year and study-abroad programs.

Gap Year, Postgraduate Year, and Study Abroad

GAP YEAR

Many students ask us about the possibility of taking a gap year. This question usually arises because students—for a variety of reasons—are not sure they want to go directly to college. Our students often use a gap year to expand and continue activities within their area of interest or pursue a postgraduate year or a thirteenth-grade equivalent (see below) at a high school offering this option. If they choose to apply (or re-apply) to colleges, they may end up doing so with an even stronger application.

In other cases, students are burned out and feel they could benefit from a year off before they begin college. High school today is a truly rigorous experience, and each year at college is costly. Many parents want to make sure that students do not rush blindly into that next step.

We always tell families that while a gap year can be a wonderful idea, it almost always requires extensive planning to ensure that the time is spent wisely and productively. Organizing a gap year is often far more

HOW CAN PARENTS HELP THEIR KIDS SUCCEED?

As parents, you have many ways to support your high schoolers academically and reinforce their study process. For example:

- Try to minimize disruptions; for example, turn off the TV if they want to study at the kitchen table.
- Help them with their homework if the work is on a topic you remember. Even if it's not, you can still test them on material.
- Encourage them to approach teachers before or after school if they need extra help.
- Provide balanced discipline. For example, you can go out with your friends *after* finishing your homework.
- Don't become so distraught over a poor test or paper that your child never shows you another bad grade again.
- If your child does get a poor grade, strategize with her about how she can raise her score next time. Let her know you're in this together.
- Determine whether you need to hire outside tutors for your kids. Sometimes an outside tutor or peer tutor can explain a subject in a way you and the teacher cannot.
- Is your child anxious, overworked, and overwhelmed? Should she drop a course or an after-school sport? Does her workload allow her enough time for rest, free time, and fun? Help your child negotiate these issues and make these decisions.
- If your child is continually struggling, realize that there may be some unknown factor at play. Is she eating or sleeping enough? Could she

complicated than sending in a deposit and moving to a college campus: you must create both your extracurricular and academic program on your own. Because your past experiences may be limited (as you've just graduated from high school), many internship and work opportunities may prove difficult to qualify for. That said, a number of our students

"It's a lot of pressure on me not to pressure him."

be suffering from a learning disorder? According to the Learning Disabilities Association of America, between 4 and 6 percent of all students are classified as having a learning disability.[*] Distressingly, approximately 35 percent of all high school dropouts are those with learning disabilities, twice the rate of students without such disabilities.[**]

---

[*] Learning Disabilities Association of America Web site http://www.ldanatl.org/aboutld/teachers/index.asp.

[**] Linda Broatch. "Is There Life After High School? A Primer for Teens With Learning Disorders," GreatSchools.org, http://www.greatschools.org/LD/school-learning/life-after-high-school.gs?content=909.

have spent wonderful, productive gap years exploring an interest. Their experiences have included working with a service organization in India, interning at the United Nations, working on an organic farm (exchanging labor for room and board), creating an independent documentary, and studying Italian architecture in Italy. In many cases, these activities were extensions of their high school spikes (see Chapter 4, "Spike"), pursued with a focus that is difficult to achieve during a typical school year.

Perhaps you have already applied to college and are considering a gap year. A question we are often asked at this stage is whether colleges will allow you to defer an acceptance for a year. Colleges typically grant deferral on a case-by-case basis. Check with your specific school about its policy. If it does permit deferral, we always recommend letting colleges know how you plan to spend that year. If you do defer your acceptance, you will need to put down a deposit; if you put down a deposit and decide to change your college choice after your gap year, you will forfeit that deposit. Note that some colleges are strongly in favor of a gap year. Princeton, for example, announced in 2008 that it will help accepted students structure a precollegiate gap year in a culturally unfamiliar context. Often this involves community service overseas: teaching English, working in a health clinic, creating art with children in an orphanage, etc.[*] Harvard has also encouraged its students to pursue a gap year prior to arriving on campus.

See Resources on pages 273–74, 276, 289–90 for books and organizations that will help you plan your gap year.

Postgraduate Year

One special kind of gap year is a postgraduate (PG) year. If, for any number of reasons (for example, sickness, lack of motivation, extensive athletic commitments), a student has not done as well in high school as he is capable of doing, has not taken challenging courses, and is motivated to improve his grades and overall GPA, a PG year can provide substantial benefits. PG years are often offered at private boarding and prep schools. It is possible to enroll in challenging courses at these schools, do well the first semester, and reapply to college with a more competitive

---

[*] "Creation of international 'bridge program' endorsed." Princeton University Web site, press release, July 15, 2008, http://www.princeton.edu/main/news/archive/S21/60/67K74/index.xml?section=newsreleases.

application. However, this is an expensive proposition—often as expensive as a year away at college. Also note that students may have difficulty doing extremely well their first semester while adjusting to a new environment and living away from home. Nevertheless, for students who wish to improve their high school record, can afford to pay for the experience, and are willing to enter college a year later than expected, a PG year may be the answer.

Study Abroad

Gap years often involve studying abroad. We caution families to be mindful of the relative lack of control and the "element of the unknown" associated with study-abroad programs, including the living situations these programs provide. Despite careful research, a former student of ours had to cut short his gap year in Italy because members of his host family kept offering him various, shall we say, illegal substances. (At least he learned the Italian words for all of them.) Stories like this are rare, but be sure to learn as much as possible about any program you're considering before committing to it. Once you have committed, communicate with your host family before leaving home. Know and prepare for the environment you'll be joining. Consider well-established programs and check references. Always check with your high school guidance office to see if the credits you will be earning during the gap year are transferable. Well-established international schools generally have the facilities for helping you with this as well. See Resources for a list of reputable study-abroad programs.

A Final Warning: "Senior Slide"

We all know what happens at the end of senior year. You're into your top-choice college. Enjoying yourself. Life is good. Yes, having your grades drop from an A to a B in a couple of classes is to be expected. But anything more drastic—a C or D—may result in a warning from your college (academic probation before you even begin!) or worse. Every year offers of admission are revoked because of severe senior slide. Yes, really!

We had a student who was accepted early in her senior year at the University of Michigan under their rolling admissions program. After she received a low midterm grade in Chemistry (C), she was contacted by Michigan and told that if she didn't raise her grade, her acceptance would be revoked. Alarmed but motivated, she managed to raise her grade to a B+ by the end of the term. Crisis averted.

Colleges assume that you'll maintain your current grade levels, so don't flirt with disaster by throwing academics out the window after you've been admitted. Keep the grades reasonably high, and have a great senior spring.

Standardized Tests

Overview

In this chapter you'll learn:

- Why standardized tests are controversial—but still important
- What the major tests are like and how to prepare for them
- Which tests to take and which scores to submit to schools
- What to do on the day of the test
- How the tests fit into your overall admissions strategy
- General timeline for taking standardized tests

Standardized Tests: The Controversy!

Standardized tests are not anyone's favorite part of life, and for a lot of people involved in education they are a favorite punching bag. Just a few of the criticisms commonly leveled at the tests include:

- They reflect preparation, not innate intelligence or IQ.
- They don't really predict how well a student will do in college.
- Their content is biased, for example against poor and minority students.
- They reflect one morning's performance, as opposed to a GPA, which reflects four years' worth of work and study.

Even the history of the SAT's name reflects the controversy. Originally, SAT stood for "Scholastic Aptitude Test." However, there was concern that the test didn't test aptitude, so the name was changed to "Scholastic Assessment Test." But some people argued that it didn't truly assess scholastic performance either, so now it's just the SAT. That's right: the letters *don't stand for anything.*

But before you dismiss standardized tests, realize that they are still required by most colleges and make up an important part of the application. If a school requires them, you'll need to prepare properly and try to do as well as you can. We'll go so far as to say that when applying for admission to the most prestigious colleges, it is difficult to overcome poor standardized test scores.

If the tests are so controversial, why should they be administered? There are several reasons. First, a number of colleges use something called an Academic Index, or AI (see "So What's an Academic Index?" on page 40). In some cases, standardized test scores make up two-thirds of the input for your calculated AI. Admissions officers use this index

THE SAT: WHO REQUIRES IT (AND WHO DOESN'T)?

Over the years, many schools have questioned the validity of the SAT. Much has been written on this subject and today some 760 four-year colleges don't require the test. These schools include Bates, Hampshire, Bowdoin, Middlebury, Connecticut College, and more. For a list of these schools and more on this debate, see www. fairtest.org. If your standardized test scores are significantly different from your GPA, these schools are well worth considering.

as a main determinant of acceptance. Second, college administrations publish standardized test scores as a proxy for the (ideally, improving) quality of first-year students. Third, these scores are an important factor in the well-known *U.S. News & World Report* rankings, and no school wants its ranking to go down.

"You're kidding! You count S.A.T.s?"

SO WHAT'S AN ACADEMIC INDEX?

An Academic Index (AI) is used by many selective colleges as a way of indexing or standardizing students' academic performance across thousands of high schools. The Academic Index is typically made up of three criteria: Grades/Class Rank, Subject Tests, and SAT/ACT scores. If the ACT score is used instead of both the SAT and Subject Tests, then the ACT score will make up two-thirds of the AI. Note that the AI does not include AP or IB tests (see pages 48–53) and that, most important, grades count for only one-third of the score. While much has been written about the Academic Index, we mention it mainly to discourage you from ignoring your standardized test scores, as their large contribution to the AI make low scores difficult to overcome.

Finally, standardized tests are still valued because, quite simply, they are the only national standard by which to compare students' academic achievement. From the perspective of an admissions officer, comparing students on a national basis is extremely difficult. Grades, recommendations, essays—all are specific to a given high school. Many high schools have even started suppressing student rank. Standardized tests, however, are a standard measure of student performance, from New York to Honolulu.

Standardized Tests and the "Be Alike but Spike" Strategy

Unless you fall into a special category of desirable applicants, assume that your scores must fall within the average range for admitted students. This means that your scores must lie between (or above) the 25th–75th percentile of other admitted applicants to that specific school. However, comparing well with other students will not guarantee admission. At the super-selective schools, even a perfect score will not guarantee admission. Some schools, like Harvard, boast about how many "perfect score"

SHOULD YOU SEND YOUR SAT SCORES WHEN SENDING THEM IS OPTIONAL?

Send your SAT scores only if they will help your application. How do you know whether they'll help? First, compare your SAT percentile to your GPA percentile. Are your SATs significantly more impressive? (For example, is your GPA percentile average at 75 while your SAT percentile is a 90?) Second, investigate whether the college publishes SAT averages of admitted students. Does your score fall into or rise above the 25th–75th percentile? If you answered yes to either question, go ahead and submit the scores. Otherwise, take the option to withhold them.

applicants they reject. Yet while a perfect score doesn't always mean you're automatically admitted, a score below the 25th percentile usually *does* mean that you'll need to be a "special case" to gain admission. Special cases include legacies, star athletes, recruited minorities, and students with an unusually special or attractive talent.

If you're sensing that it's very hard to stand out, or "spike," with standardized test scores even in the best of cases, you're right. Nearly always, good scores will help satisfy the "be alike" side of the equation by demonstrating that you compare favorably with your most academically gifted peers. As elaborate test prep becomes more and more the norm, high achievement on standardized tests has begun to be expected of those seeking admission to top schools—not a mark of distinction that will open doors by itself.

Grades, Scores, and "Not Testing Well"

As professionals, we can't tell you how many times we hear of "brilliant students who don't test well." Sometimes these students have test anxiety. Sometimes a very bright student will see ambiguities in the multiple-choice questions and can make arguments for more than one right answer. For whatever reason, it's true that there are some very bright students who have a hard time with standardized tests. Although we're empathetic, our advice to these students is always to try to learn how to take the SATs. Most selective colleges don't have to choose between students with good grades *or* high test scores; they have plenty of applicants with *both*. The idea that sterling grades can "overcome" subpar test scores at a college that requires them is by and large a myth. Also, an inability to perform well under test pressure is not exactly an asset in college. College will be filled with many stressful exams; it's not going to help you to say that you can't handle the stress. Besides, brilliance is often *defined* by performance under pressure. We once worked with a boy whose mom called him both an exceptional student and an exceptional tennis player. Yet, as skilled as he may have been in tennis practice, he did poorly in tennis tournaments, and as bright as he may have been in theory, he "didn't test well." As in sports, the name of the game in standardized testing is converting your abstract potential into concrete achievement—because schools, unlike moms, won't take your brilliance as an article of faith.

At the same time, the last thing colleges want is a class of students with high standardized test scores and low grades. Colleges perceive this type of student as one who is unwilling or unable to live up to his potential. Colleges, like your future employers, see past performance as indicative of future performance and expect the same low grades to continue in college. They also see the SAT as a single day's performance, as opposed to your grades, which represent four solid years of work. If you have high SATs and low grades, be prepared to write an application essay (most often an optional or supplemental essay) explaining why your grades are low (for example, illness, heavy extracurricular involvement, family circumstances), conveying how you have matured and now understand the importance of schoolwork and academic achievement, and pointing out that your grades have (hopefully) improved over time (see Chapter 9, "Essays," for more advice on this topic).

Grades vs. Test Scores: Two Case Studies

In one extreme case, we worked with a student with Asperger's syndrome who scored in the mid-to-high 700s on the verbal and math sections of the SAT but did extremely poorly in his classes. His average grade in high school was a C or D, and he had even failed some subjects, usually because he did not get assignments in on time. We advised this student to attend a small, pre-professional college that specialized in graphic design, an area that he had a talent for and was passionate about. Regardless of your strengths and weaknesses, the most important thing is finding a college that's right for you.

In another case, we worked with a student who had a relatively strong GPA of 3.7 but SAT scores in the low 500s, even after concentrated effort and tutoring. She had a very strong work ethic and teachers liked and respected her. In order for this student not to "fall through the cracks," we felt her best option was to apply to colleges that did not require SAT scores. She was ultimately accepted by Middlebury, which is just such a college.

Which Test(s) Should I Take?

The tests each school requires are in flux. Some colleges require SAT and Subject Tests or ACT with the optional Writing Section and Subject Tests. Others may require just the SAT or ACT. Some may require only Subject Tests or AP Tests. Check the colleges' Web sites, as these requirements can change on a yearly basis. Also inquire as to whether a specific Subject Test is required.

THE RUNDOWN: EVERYTHING YOU NEED TO KNOW ABOUT THE MAJOR TESTS

SAT

While imperfect, this test is a key component of college applications. Some schools consider it a fairly accurate predictor of first-year performance. Each school weighs this test slightly differently. The test is currently made up of critical reading, math, and writing sections, with each section scored between 200 and 800 points. These scores are then added together to come up with a total score ranging between 600 and 2400. Guessing on the SAT is generally discouraged unless at least two of the answers can be eliminated as wrong, as a quarter point is deducted for each incorrect answer. Some colleges (engineering schools, for example) look more closely at math scores, while verbal scores are more important for students planning to study the humanities. Some schools place less importance on the writing section than on the critical reading and math sections. Our advice is to weigh the writing section as strongly as the others and allow plenty of time for preparation (see "How to Prepare" on pages 54–56).

NATIONAL MERIT® SCHOLARSHIP PROGRAM

Of the 1.5 million juniors who take the PSAT, about 50,000 (top one-half of one percent in each state) with the highest PSAT scores qualify for recognition in the National Merit® Scholarship Program. Of these students, about 34,000 are notified in September that they are "Commended Students" and do not continue in the competition. The remaining students progress on a state-representational basis (the highest scorers in each state) through semifinalist to finalist status. Of the finalists, the Board selects approximately 8,200 as winners of Merit Scholarship awards. (Note: It is the PSAT, *not* the SAT, that qualifies you for this competition.) For more information on the National Merit Scholarship program, see their Web site, http://www.nationalmerit.org/nmsp.php.

Qualifying as a National Merit Scholar semifinalist is certainly a distinctive achievement—but not a "get in free" card for colleges. Still, if you feel you have a chance at becoming a National Merit Scholar, do preparation work prior to the PSAT test.

PSAT

Simply a preparatory test for the SAT. The PSAT is administered only in October and typically taken by juniors, although in some schools, sophomores are encouraged to take the test as well. Scores range from 20 to 80. Add a "0" to the end of PSAT scores to convert them to SAT score equivalents (60 turns into a 600). We advise you to review your answers on the PSAT test as a way of outlining your SAT preparation strategy.

SAT SUBJECT TESTS

Many colleges require or recommend that students take two Subject Tests as part of the admissions package. At the time of publication, Harvard, Georgetown, and Princeton require three Subject Tests. Even if a college merely recommends (and doesn't require) them, be aware that your application package is being compared with those of students who have taken the recommended number of Subject Tests (and done well on them!).

Subject Tests are offered in the following areas: Literature, U.S. History, World History, Math Level 1 (consisting of algebra, geometry,

A NOTE ON THE MATH SUBJECT TESTS

If you are applying to a selective college and have had the appropriate math course, plan to take Math Level 2 rather than Math Level 1, as it is a more challenging test and more appropriate to advanced students' junior-year course load (typically Pre-Calculus, though of course there are even more advanced students who take Pre-Calculus as sophomores; AP Calculus [AB or BC] as juniors; and AP Statistics or Multivariable Calculus as seniors). Also, the statistical curve of the Math Level 2 test is generally said to be more forgiving of errors. Recently, a student of ours left six questions blank and got three questions wrong on the Math Level 2 subject test and received a score in the low 700s.

trigonometry, algebraic functions, statistics, and other miscellaneous items), Math Level 2 (consisting of algebra, geometry, trigonometry, statistics, functions, and other miscellaneous items), Biology E/M (based on ecology or molecular biology), Chemistry, Physics, Chinese with Listening, French, French with Listening, German, German with Listening, Modern Hebrew, Italian, Japanese with Listening, Korean with Listening, Latin, Spanish, and Spanish with Listening.

Most of the above are curriculum-based tests, usually taken in June at the completion of the relevant academic course. A few of the Subject Tests are not curriculum based. These "floater" tests—Literature, for example—can be taken at any time of the year. Other examples of tests that can be considered "floaters" are the language Subject Tests, designed for students who happen to speak those languages fluently at home. Students who are native speakers of a language often do best in the "language with listening" Subject Tests, which are offered only in November.

We often advise students to take the SAT Subject Test in areas they intend to pursue in college. Take the Chemistry and Biology Subject

CANCELING YOUR TEST SCORES

Perhaps you became ill before or during the test, or you felt that you weren't properly prepared when you saw the test questions. For the SAT and Subject Tests, you are allowed to cancel either at the test center or before the following Wednesday. For the ACT, you can cancel only while you are at the test center. Once you leave, you are not longer permitted to cancel your ACT.

Note: You must cancel the scores for all tests you took or registered for on that day, and the registration fees will not be refunded. For the most up-to-date policies regarding scoring and canceling options, check the test Web sites (see Resources section for links).

AVERAGE SUBJECT TEST SCORES

As counterintuitive as it may seem, average Subject Test scores vary from test to test. This is because the group of students that takes each test is different. For example, in 2009 the College Board reported that the average Chinese with Listening test score was an almost perfect 763. This shouldn't lead you to conclude that the Chinese test is slam-dunk easy; it's just that most of the students who take it are completely fluent in the language. See CollegeBoard.com for more on this topic.

English		Language Tests	
Literature	580	Chinese with Listening	763
History and Social Sciences		French	618
United States History	599	French with Listening	637
World History	589	German	616
Mathematics		German with Listening	609
Mathematics Level 1	599	Modern Hebrew	650
Mathematics Level 2	648	Italian	667
Sciences		Japanese with Listening	689
Biology-Ecological	598	Korean with Listening	763
Biology-Molecular	641	Latin	618
Chemistry	638	Spanish	646
Physics	655	Spanish with Listening	652

Tests if you plan to be a pre-med major. If you plan to be a French literature major, take the French and Literature Subject Tests. If you're applying to a specific school within a college—say, the Cornell College of Engineering—the Math Level 2 and Chemistry or Physics Subject Tests may be required. But be careful: if your scores don't measure up to your passion for, and commitment to, the major, colleges may be concerned about your level of future success in that area.

You cannot take the SAT and Subject Tests on the same date. Each Subject Test lasts one hour and, like the SAT, scores range between 200 and 800. You can take up to three Subject Tests at one time, although ideally students should not take more than one Subject Test at a sitting. If absolutely necessary, take two at one time, but don't take three if you can possibly avoid it. Taking three tests at one sitting will make studying three times as strenuous, and it will also limit your flexibility in canceling: if you choose to cancel one of the scores afterward, you must cancel the scores for all the tests you took at that sitting.

ACT

Fast becoming just as popular as the SAT, this test is less focused on aptitude and more focused on students' academic knowledge of English, math, science, reading, and sometimes writing (the writing section is optional). Many students prefer this test to the SAT and find it less "tricky." Some admissions officers also prefer it, considering it more closely correlated to school curricula (see "SAT or ACT?" on the facing page) No points are deducted for incorrect answers, so guessing is encouraged. Scores for each section range from 1 to 36, with 36 being the highest. The scores from each section—English, Math, Reading, Science, and the optional Writing Test—are averaged to create an overall score that is also between 1 and 36. Just as the PSAT is the preparation test for the SAT, the PLAN Assessment is the preparation exam for the ACT. It is identical to the ACT in every way, except that the scores do not count toward college admission. The PLAN is typically taken in the fall of tenth grade—a year earlier than the PSAT.

AP (ADVANCED PLACEMENT)

If you take AP courses, you will be expected to take the corresponding AP exams at the end of the courses. AP tests are very highly regarded; they are seen by the most selective colleges as the most accurate predictor of first-year performance. Each test has a score range of 1–5; a score of 3, 4, or 5 may provide you with college-level credits. However, each

SAT OR ACT?

Many students these days are choosing the ACT over the SAT. There are a number of reasons why the ACT might be a better option for some. For example, the ACT:

- Is more closely correlated to the high school curriculum.
- Requires little memorization—all formulas are provided and vocabulary is not tested.
- Tests science for those who are excellent science students.
- Doesn't subtract points for incorrect answers.
- Is generally less "tricky." We believe that on the SAT there are often two good answers, with one just a little bit better than the other. The ACT is generally more straightforward.

We worked with a student who scored in the low 700s on both his verbal and math SAT sections, but scored a perfect 36 on the ACT, resulting in his winning merit scholarships. That said, if you are applying to a highly exclusive school, and live on one of the coasts—where the SAT remains the most prevalent test—there is still a minuscule preference for the SAT. Schools will expect you to take this test and excel.

Finally, it's important to understand that both the ACT and SAT are graded on a curve, and thus test "relative" performance. In deciding which test to take, it is therefore also important to determine which one you are likely to score higher on *in relation to your peers*. Are you better than most at remembering formulas and vocabulary words and deciphering tricky multiple-choice questions? Then it may make sense for you to take the SAT.

college differs in its policy toward granting credit. Some selective colleges see a score of 3 as average performance and will grant credit only for 4's or 5's. AP tests in less common subjects, such as Geography and Psychology, are generally seen as less challenging by colleges than tests

SCORE CHOICE AND SUPER-SCORING

WHAT IS "SCORE CHOICE"?

Score Choice is simply the ability to send certain scores, rather than all your scores, to colleges.

The ACT has always operated on a score-choice basis. That is, students who take the ACT have always had the ability to choose which scores (by test date) they wanted colleges to see. Prior to March 2009, the SAT did not recognize score choice. That is, if a student sent his SAT scores to Top Choice U, they would see scores from *all* of his SAT attempts. In March 2009, however, the SAT and Subject Tests adopted a score-choice policy, so you can now decide which scores you want colleges to see.

That being said, some colleges have not adopted a score-choice policy and still want to view *every* ACT, SAT, and/or Subject Test attempt made by a candidate. As with super-scoring, colleges' policies on this topic change from year to year. Check the colleges on your list for their latest guidelines.

Note:

- Scores from an entire ACT or SAT must be sent. You *cannot* choose to send just your math score from one test and reading comprehension from another.
- Subject Test scores can be chosen by individual test, rather than test date. For example, if you took U.S. History and Literature on the same test date, you can choose to send Literature and not U.S. History.

in more "traditional" subjects, such as Physics, English, and Chemistry. Foreign language AP (and SAT Subject) tests are generally seen as extremely challenging, as many fluent students take these tests and may disrupt the curve. AP Tests are administered in May.

(IB) INTERNATIONAL BACCALAUREATE

The IB program was developed to provide a consistent educational standard for high-achieving students, regardless of where they

WHAT IS "SUPER-SCORING"?

Much has been written about this recent practice as it applies to both the SAT and ACT. Some colleges—when they receive multiple ACT or SAT tests from students—select the *highest* sub-scores from each test. For example, Julie takes the SAT twice. On the first test, she scores Math 700, Critical Reading 650, and Writing 600. On the second test she scores Math 680, Critical Reading 700, and Writing 650. She sends both scores to Top Choice U. If Top Choice U's admissions office super-scores, they would calculate her super-scored SAT as the highest sub-score from each test; in other words, her new final score would be: Math 700, Critical Reading 700, and Writing 650, resulting in a final score of 2050. Many colleges claim this is why they want to see every SAT and ACT score and are opposed to score choice; they themselves can then select and combine the highest sub-scores from every test the student has taken, resulting in a higher overall score for the student.

Note: Not all colleges super-score. To make matters even more confusing, some admissions offices super-score the SAT but not the ACT, and vice versa. The list of colleges that do super-score is changing, so check all of the colleges you're interested in for their most up-to-date policies.

studied. Today, we often recommend seeking out IB courses if a student is seriously considering attending college abroad, where the IB curriculum is widely recognized and highly regarded. Many high schools all over the United States, both public and private, offer the IB Curriculum (go to www.ibo.org for a complete list). To earn the IB diploma, students must complete the following program at an accredited school.

The IB program consists of:

- Six academic courses:
    1. Language A (native language)
    2. Language B (a modern language)
    3. Individuals and Societies (e.g., history, economics, geography)
    4. Experimental Science (e.g., biology, chemistry, physics)
    5. Mathematics and Computer Science
    6. The Arts (e.g., art, music, classical language)

Note: At some high schools you have the option of completing individual IB courses without completing the entire IB program.

- Theory of Knowledge, a critical-thinking course that constitutes an integrated approach to learning in which students make connections among the different academic areas.
- Extended 4,000-word essay based on independent research.
- CAS—150 hours of service divided equally among three categories: creativity, action, and service. Activities are chosen to promote

"How are her scores?"

TEST REGISTRATION DOS AND DON'TS

Don't forget to register for the tests on time! You must do this approximately four to five weeks in advance of the test date to avoid paying a late fee. Note that the SAT is available in different states at different times. Contact your child's guidance office if you are unsure of how to register. You want your child to be able to take the test in a location that is comfortable, familiar, and convenient, although it's possible that your child may *not* want to take the test at his own high school, preferring to take it anonymously at a neighboring school. Whatever the case, registering well in advance of the deadline is essential. Taking the test standby, that is, in place of students who don't show up for the test, is often possible; however, don't rely on this approach. Find out where the exam will be given and what your child needs to bring in terms of identification, pencils, calculators, snacks for the break periods in the test, and so on. Note that only in cases of religious commitments can your child take the exam on a Sunday morning instead of Saturday.

personal growth and world awareness and balance the purely academic nature of the program.

Testing is done in May of junior and senior years. Three of the subjects are tested at the higher level (these may qualify for college credit), and three are tested at the subsidiary (lower) level. International examiners assess exams and the most selective colleges view strong IB exam scores very favorably.

Note: Exams are graded from 1 to 7, with 7 being the highest. A passing exam score is 4, while 5 is typically required by selective colleges for credit. If you choose not to send your scores for a given AP or IB exam, some colleges may assume you did poorly.

For more information about this program, see the Resources section (page 274).

TOEFL (TEST OF ENGLISH AS A FOREIGN LANGUAGE)

The TOEFL is designed for non-native speakers as a test of their proficiency in English. Many colleges in the U.S. and Canada require this test of international students who are applying from non-English-speaking countries. They will generally accept the SAT verbal score as an alternative evaluation of proficiency. If eligible, you may take the TOEFL to supplement a low verbal score even if it is not required. Today, most students take the Internet-based test (iBT) rather than the paper or computer versions. Scores fall between 0 and 120; there are also scaled scores (between 1 and 30) for each of four sections: Listening, Writing, Speaking, and Reading. This four-hour test cannot be taken more than once a week. Scores are valid for two years, although colleges typically consider the most recent score.

How to Prepare

Although in the olden days many students took the SAT without preparation, today this approach is viewed as irresponsible—not to mention unintelligent (and the test is, after all, about showing off your smarts). Here are some tips on getting ready.

1. We believe in leaving yourself at least six months to prepare. This means that if you plan to take the May SAT, you must begin preparing in the beginning of the preceding December. That may seem like a lot of time, but it's not when you consider what's involved. We have been told by some tutors that there are approximately 50 different types of math problems on the SAT. And there are approximately 1,000 vocabulary words you should try to master. On the other hand, don't start preparing too early; you might peak too soon and arrive at the test burned out.

2. Take practice exams. This is by far the best way to prepare (with one exception; see #3). For the three months leading up to the exam, plan to take one full test each week. If possible, do this on Saturday mornings, under realistic testing conditions. Correct the exam and determine why you made the mistakes you did.

3. The best way to prepare for the verbal sections is to begin reading from an early age. Of course, this is easier said than done. But if a student is an avid reader, we can almost guarantee that he will have little trouble with the verbal portions of the SAT. Even if that student isn't you (yet), start reading well-written books and publications as soon as possible to prepare for the test. Some of our favorites are the *New York Times* (especially op-ed pieces), the *Wall Street Journal* (especially the front page), the *Washington Post*, the *New Yorker* and *Time*. Mark words that you don't understand and look them up. Continue studying and memorizing them as you would the words you missed on a practice test.

Note that not all SAT vocabulary words are esoteric; some are "simple" words with less common definitions. We had a very bright student who memorized practically every long word in the dictionary, then came away from the test laughing because she had been stumped by *stand*, as in "stand of trees." (She could afford to laugh; she had still scored extremely well.) Context is crucial, and reading, not memorization, is the only way to improve this aspect of your vocabulary comprehension.

4. Purchase an SAT vocabulary book, create your own flashcards, and learn the words. The process of making flashcards is a great memorization strategy, and the same words are repeated again and again on the test.

5. Many of our students benefit from a tutor. A talented tutor provides a strategy for approaching the test and fosters discipline with regard to preparation. Knowing that your parents are paying for the tutor can also encourage work and study. (See more on comparing tutoring options below.) Some students also take one of the numerous standardized test–preparation classes. Although these are not as intensive as one-on-one sessions, some students thrive on the camaraderie and competition a classroom environment provides.

Some students think (or some of their parents tell us) that they're too advanced to need tutoring. We don't doubt their brilliance, but even the world's best athletes use coaches to improve. A good tutor can teach the finer points of test strategy as well as fill any "gaps" that the student's school curriculum may not have covered (for example, algebra skills). That said, tutoring is most beneficial for students whose practice test scores fall in the 500–700 range for any given section. Students whose practice scores fall in the mid-700s can improve their performance still further with tutoring, but they won't be getting quite as much bang for their buck, as their incremental improvement will be less dramatic.

6. If necessary, retake the test. Many students improve their scores with retakes. Often students find that the critical reading section is easier for them on one test date while the math section is easier for them on another. Colleges may select the highest math, critical reading, and writing scores from all the tests you have taken—the practice known as super-scoring—and combine them to come up with your overall score. But don't tempt fate. If your SAT scores reflect your best practice test scores, move on! Under very few circumstances should you take the SAT more than three times. And although colleges generally consider only the top scores, they do see all your attempts if they are among the growing list of schools that don't accept score choice (see pages 50–51 for an explanation of super-scoring and score choice).

Which Test-Preparation Option Should I Use?

The answer to that question depends on the answer to this one: How do you learn best? One on one? In a small group? In a larger classroom setting? All of these options provide familiarity with the test format and questions, discipline in studying, and a strategy for answering questions; each option simply caters to a different learning style. Whichever you choose, most tutors firmly believe this is a test that can be learned.

INDIVIDUAL TUTORS

Individual tutors customize the preparation process so that you can work on areas you need the most help with and don't have to waste time on areas you already know. But individual tutors can be very expensive; they

*"I'll pay you double what my parents
are giving you not to tutor me."*

generally charge by the hour. Still, many parents rationalize the cost by seeing it in the context of the cost of a four-year private college (between $160 and $220K, the last time we checked). Some families decide that individual tutoring is worth the money if it can give their child a better shot at getting into his top-choice schools.

Individual tutors generally come from two sources:

1. Word-of-mouth recommendations. In this case, you have a good idea of whom you are hiring. Often this person also has a proven record, having been used by a trusted friend. Sometimes the tutor is a current or former teacher, sometimes simply a former high scorer with prestigious academic credentials. Make sure the tutors are very familiar with the questions and strategies that pertain to the tests themselves, not just the academic subjects as they are taught in school. Also, to

get the most for your money, make sure the tutor isn't simply proctoring the practice exams. Plan to do the exams on your own time and review incorrect answers together.

2. Some test-prep companies offer individual tutoring and have a consistently high standard of performance with excellent tutors and low instructor turnover. Reputation is extremely important in evaluating which company to hire, as you are hiring the firm and not an individual person. Larger companies also offer the benefit of being able to "switch" tutors if you feel that the one assigned to you isn't teaching material in the way you can best understand. In addition, large companies may also provide weekly test-taking sessions under real testing conditions—a true benefit for those who recognize that they don't have the discipline to duplicate these testing conditions at home.

CLASSROOM TUTORING

You may also hire a test-prep company that offers preparation sessions in a classroom environment. Here again, word of mouth and personal recommendations are very important. Keep in mind that in the classroom, you are learning what the class learns and the tutors are not able to customize the material to each individual's needs. However, there are some excellent classroom-tutoring companies available. Our advice is to pick a convenient test-prep company and find out which tutor within that company has the most popular classes. The law of numbers doesn't lie and the most packed classes are usually packed because they have the best teachers. Large classes are less expensive and carry one fixed price. The better companies often have guarantees if your test results don't improve by a certain number of points.

SELF-STUDY

Although many students do benefit from some tutoring, some students are able to prepare for standardized tests on their own. They are typically disciplined and able to set aside preparation time each week. There are many excellent test-prep manuals available to guide your progress.

Note: Even for students who do get tutoring, self-study is a critical component of preparation.

On the Day of the Test

- Sleep. A lot. Not just the night before, but the few previous nights as well. Some of our students admit to experiencing terrible insomnia the night before the test, and that's okay, as long as you get plenty of sleep on the three nights beforehand.
- Know where you're going. If you're unsure, make the trip the day before. Leave yourself plenty of time to arrive.
- Know what to bring to the test (water, food, ID, pencils, calculator with extra batteries, and so on). Earplugs are strongly recommended. We once had a student who was given a separate room in which to take the test because of a special time dispensation; unfortunately, it was the room right next to the lawn where the marching band was practicing. Most testing rooms will

HOW CAN YOU HELP YOUR CHILD PREPARE FOR STANDARDIZED TESTS?

Students will differ in the extent to which they welcome or resist your help, and as always, you'll want to strike a balance between pressuring them too much and too little. Support your child's study process as much as possible and always offer help if he or she is struggling. Break out index cards of vocabulary words during car, plane, or train trips. (College visits are a natural time to do this.) Help come up with fun mnemonic devices. The time before dinner can become a daily vocabulary game show; you might even offer prizes for right answers to 25, 50, or 75 words. A Starbucks or iTunes gift card can incentivize even the most jaded teenager.

"My parents never talk to me about S-E-X—
all they talk about is S-A-Ts."

be a lot quieter than that one, but screening out unwanted noise can always help you focus.

- Know what to expect. If you've taken enough full practice tests under realistic testing conditions, you should be all set in this regard.
- Finally, mark those answer bubbles carefully! Mark one out of order and all the rest of your answers will be "off." This is the oldest piece of SAT advice in the book.

Now That I Have My Score, Where Can I Get In?

Each year, most high school guidance offices compile GPA, SAT, and Subject Test scores for each student. They list colleges alphabetically along with the number of students who were accepted, rejected, or wait-listed at each college that year (without using the students' names, of course). Families can access this information online or find it at the high school guidance office; it is usually provided by Naviance or another software program (see page 108 for more on these programs). The information can be invaluable, as you can compare these statistics against your

GETTING ACCOMMODATIONS FOR A LEARNING DISABILITY DESIGNATION

Students with different types of learning disabilities may be eligible for special accommodations when taking the SAT or ACT. Obtaining them usually requires special testing by a psychologist as well as recommendation by the high school. Often, the student must attest that similar accommodations, such as extended time, were made by the high school when the student took exams. Typical examples of accommodations offered are use of a calculator, use of a computer for typing, one-and-a-half time, or double time, depending on the type of disability.

GENERAL TIMELINE/GUIDELINE FOR STANDARDIZED TESTS

Students and parents often ask for a standardized-test timeline. Although it is difficult to provide a timeline that will be applicable to all students, the list below serves as a general guideline for standardized-test options, based on grade level and curriculum. Choose the test and timing appropriate to your curriculum, preparation schedule, and requirements/recommendations of the colleges on your list.

9TH GRADE FALL: PLAN (very optional—a pre-PLAN)

9TH GRADE SPRING: Subject Tests appropriate to class curriculum

10TH GRADE FALL: PLAN (the pre-ACT)

10TH GRADE FALL: PSAT (very optional—a pre-PSAT)

10TH GRADE SPRING: Subject Tests appropriate to class curriculum

10TH GRADE SPRING: AP Tests appropriate to class curriculum

11TH GRADE FALL: PSAT

11TH GRADE NOVEMBER: Listening language tests for native speakers of a language

11TH GRADE FALL/SPRING: Math Level 1, Math Level 2, Language, Literature Subject Tests

11TH GRADE SPRING: SAT (March/May/June) / ACT (April/June)

11TH GRADE SPRING: Subject Tests appropriate to class curriculum

11TH GRADE SPRING: AP Tests appropriate to class curriculum

12TH GRADE FALL: Math Level 1, Math Level 2, Language, Literature Subject Tests

12TH GRADE FALL: SAT/ACT

12TH GRADE SPRING: AP Tests appropriate to class curriculum

own to get an idea of where you might gain admission. Don't take the information at face value, however, as it doesn't convey the whole story. For example, was the student a legacy, a sports star, a highly sought-after first violinist, a recruited minority? These designations can make a significant difference in overcoming lower test scores and in boosting your overall chances of admission (see Chapter 6, "Researching and Creating a Working College List," for more on this topic).

Remember to Register

A number of years ago, one of our students had spent several months diligently preparing for the SATs. He had a tutor who worked exclusively with him, and he was fully ready to take the test in May of his junior year. At around 9 P.M. the Friday night before the test, we got a frantic call. "How do I get hold of a registration ticket?" he asked. We instructed him to check the packet that was sent after he registered. "After I what?" Then we understood: neither he nor his parents had remembered to register for the test, despite our frequent reminders to do so during the course of that year. Although we finally found a location in New York City where he could take the test as a walk-in the next morning, he obviously could have eliminated a great deal of last-minute stress by registering on time. Imagine the thought of all that preparation going for nothing. There are also rare instances when you just can't take the SATs: during the huge blizzard in Buffalo in 2006, for example, which forced cancellation of the test there. But snowstorms, floods, or even locusts shouldn't prevent you from actually registering for the test!

3 In-School Leadership Activities

Overview

In this chapter you'll learn:

- Why in-school leadership activities are an essential qualification for any college applicant.
- How to pursue in-school leadership activities successfully.

We'll be discussing extracurricular activities in depth in Part II, "Spike," because it's your pursuits outside the classroom that really help you stand out on a college application. But there is a group of extracurriculars that belongs here in the "Be Alike" part of the book. These are in-school activities that have the potential to demonstrate your leadership ability—an essential component, along with your academic achievement and test scores, of "being like" other applicants.

We always tell families that many, many years ago (when we applied to college), being captain of the tennis team, or class president, or editor of the yearbook, or holding any other in-school leadership position, was enough to make a student stand out. Today that's no longer the case. In fact, like academic excellence, in-school leadership positions are *expected* at the most competitive colleges. Rather than making your application exceptional, these positions simply indicate that you fit in with other qualified candidates. That doesn't mean you shouldn't pursue these activities—you should. It just means that they aren't distinctive enough to comprise your entire extracurricular involvement.

We strongly recommend getting involved within your high school. Pursue activities outside of your extracurricular specialty, and follow these three important guidelines:

Strive for In-School Leadership Positions

Ideally, these in-school activities will lie *outside* your spike area. They can be in any other extracurricular area: student government, French club, athletics…the list is endless and the only condition is that the activity should be of interest to you. Get involved early and strive to earn a leadership position by senior year.

Peter, a past student of ours, loved photography—it was his spike (for more on developing a spike, see Chapter 4). Although he was exploring photography extensively outside of school, we encouraged him to get involved *within* his school as well. We learned that he was really interested in his school newspaper, and even though the activities associated with it didn't necessarily involve photography, we recommended that he branch out and join it anyway. His freshman year responsibilities weren't particularly interesting: collecting and entering data and editing the articles others contributed. But the faculty advisor and senior co-editors in chief noted his dedication, and the following year he was promoted to associate editor. That year, Peter again proved to be a reliable team player. He even submitted several articles to the paper, some of which were accepted for publication. By junior year he had been promoted once again, to entertainment editor, and had even created an additional niche for himself as the official newspaper photographer, thereby incorporating his spike area into his leadership position. By senior year he had been named one of two co-editors in chief.

Peter's progression clearly demonstrates both teamwork and leadership. He performed successfully at every stage, making sound decisions and increasing his level of responsibility, all while finding new

"Andy plays perfectly well with others—
it's others who don't play well with Andy."

ways to contribute ideas and work independently. Peter became a valued member of the paper and was promoted accordingly until, by his senior year, he had reached the top position of editor in chief. He was able to get an additional letter of recommendation from the paper's faculty advisor, who by this time knew him well. While colleges were very impressed with Peter's independent passion for photography, they also noted his steadfast dedication, teamwork, and leadership within his high school.

Some students mistakenly believe that pursuing *only* out-of-school activities is okay. Why be part of the French club when you can intern at a museum? Why write for the high school newspaper when you've had your articles published in your town newspaper?

Although we encourage all students to explore opportunities in their community, we feel that in-school participation is *also* crucial. Leading and, perhaps even more important, participating as a member of a team are essential skills. As we emphasize throughout the book, college admissions officers believe that past performance is indicative of future performance. Your participation and leadership *within* your high school will anticipate your active contribution to life on your college campus.

Don't Get Pigeonholed

Colleges tend to be wary of students who seem too single-minded too early on. Remember, although they may want that focused first violinist or debater, they also want a balanced person—someone who will be an interesting roommate and dining hall companion.

While we advise pursuing a focused interest, the most successful and compelling applicants can't be pigeonholed. Remember, you're young; focusing your interests too narrowly can seem artificial and unhealthy. By participating in one or two other non-related extracurriculars within your high school, you'll broaden your perspective and experience.

As you will see in the example below, as well as in the case studies in Part II (see pages 77–80, 84–93), the most successful students we've worked with had a clear and distinctive passion but also pursued areas outside of these defined interests.

We recently worked with Anna, a brilliant student who was also a passionate poet. Whereas Anna's list of out-of-school activities was lengthy, impressive, and focused on her love of poetry, her in-school extracurriculars were nonexistent. Although we didn't want her to join *every* high school club (for the record, we would never advise that), we did want her to be a part of her high school community and explore areas outside of her passion. Anna was initially resistant. As an additional point, we showed her the activity chart she would prepare for college (see Chapter 8, "Preparing the Activity Chart and Completing the Written Application," and the sample activity chart on page 138), otherwise known as your college résumé; we didn't want her in-school extracurriculars category to be blank or for her to appear too one-dimensional in the eyes of admissions officers. Most important, we believed that branching out would be a positive experience for Anna. After much brainstorming, Anna mentioned that she loved teaching younger students. Great, we told her, because there's a club at your high school that does just that. Anna joined the Tutoring Club as a sophomore and loved it. Through her tutoring sessions with middle school students, she even became friends with high school students she had never met before. By Anna's senior year, she had become the club's vice president and was responsible for planning all of its tutoring sessions with local middle schools. As a result of Anna's involvement in the Tutoring Club, she was able to get an outstanding letter of recommendation from the club's faculty advisor, who was also her social studies teacher. Getting a letter of recommendation from a teacher who knows you from many different perspectives can be invaluable.

Quality Over Quantity

It seems as though every student today has limited time. Our advice is to beware of spreading yourself too thin by joining every possible club or team. When you're investigating extracurriculars, focus on a few activities that you'll really enjoy and in which you could potentially advance to a leadership position. Even in clubs you don't lead, demonstrating that you've made a contribution as part of the organization signals genuine interest and initiative.

Finally, don't wait until the spring of your junior year to start accumulating extracurriculars. Joining a long list of clubs to pad your activity chart is completely transparent to colleges and will backfire. Also, the later you join a club in your high school, the less opportunity you'll have to rise to a leadership position by senior year. Even if you start early, filling your application with activities that show little leadership ability (or serious interest) will count against you. Just as you don't want to get pegged as a "one-trick pony," you don't want to be a "jack of all trades, master of none."

HIGH SCHOOL ATHLETICS

There is no doubt that high school sports are a wonderful way to demonstrate teamwork and leadership. For many students, athletics are one of the peaks of their high school experience. However, for many juniors and seniors, there never seem to be enough hours in a day, and this can be doubly true for student-athletes. Daily (sometimes twice-daily) practices, home games, time-intensive travel to away games—all of these can interfere with academics and other extracurricular commitments. For some students, this time commitment is beneficial; the sports season requires them to develop excellent time-management skills, and their grades actually improve during the season. For others, athletic commitments cause their grades to drop—sometimes precipitously. Our advice to these students is: remember that most high school athletes will not be recruited as college athletes, and that as much as you love your team, your grades still count more. (Even for recruited athletes, grades are an important criterion for getting recruited.) Coaches may disagree, but we recommend never biting off more than you can chew. For some students this may mean *not* participating in a varsity sport each season, and instead continuing to play only those varsity sports that they are truly passionate about. Others may decide that club-level sports are more realistic due to their other commitments. Determine what feels right to you.

PART

II ▶ Spike

The first part of this book focused on fitting in—that is, making sure your choice of courses, grades, standardized test scores, and in-school leadership activities are at least as strong as (if not stronger than) those of other qualified applicants. Doing so will ensure that you meet the first hurdle in college admissions. However, as we mentioned earlier, admissions officers report that 80 percent of applicants meet these basic criteria. So who gets admitted out of this 80 percent? Successful applicants can't just be *alike*; they also need to *spike*. They need some distinctive quality or achievement that makes them stand out like a spike on a graph, convincing admissions officers that they will be valuable contributors to the college campus, essential ingredients of a well-rounded class. Part II is about figuring out what your passion is, and is not, and then building that passion into an area of distinctiveness. In the next two chapters we will demonstrate how to identify a passion and develop it into a spike. Part III will explain how best to represent that spike on your college applications.

Your spike can be almost anything (with a few exceptions*) that distinguishes you from the thousands of other students applying to the same school at the same time. Is your position as editor of *High School News* a spike? Although this position is impressive, there are thousands of other editors of similar school newspapers applying to similar colleges each year. The same can be said for football team captain, yearbook editor, and many other high school positions. A spike is an interest that truly separates you from the pack and makes you memorable to an admissions officer who has just finished reading a hundred applications from well-qualified students. In almost all instances, a spike isn't just one or two activities, but rather a number of activities that build upon each other so that the whole becomes greater than the sum of the parts. For example, if you play softball very well, that alone isn't a spike; but if you're a top softball player who *also* collects and restores old softball equipment, uses that equipment

---

* Illegal, unethical, inappropriate, or legally ambiguous activities—such as card counting at casinos or creating a Web site for pirated music—may be distinguishing, but they won't be impressive to admissions officers.

to teach softball at an under-resourced middle school, and so on, *then* the interdisciplinary collage of activities, centered around a passion, has become a spike.

As we discussed in Chapter 3, "traditional" in-school activities—the tennis team, the yearbook, the school newspaper—are an important component of your record; you should pursue them and seek out leadership roles within them. However, to create a truly outstanding application, you are *also* required to identify and develop opportunities that are distinctive, memorable, and yours alone.

Creating Your Spike

Overview

In this chapter you'll learn:

- Strategies and brainstorming techniques to determine what your interests are
- What an area of distinctiveness *is* and *is not*
- How other students transformed interests into spikes

Getting Started: What Are Your Interests?

A spike is almost always based on a student's interests. During our first meeting with a student, we try to determine what he or she is interested in—or better yet, passionate about. The problem is, very few students believe they have a passion. Sure, we've worked with Intel finalists who seem like they were born in a biogenetics lab. Or that gifted athlete who has excelled on the soccer field. These lucky few have a readily identifiable passion, but for the remaining 99 percent, figuring out their passion is half the battle.

Many students believe that they don't have any interests, never mind passions. When we first meet with a student, we're afraid even to utter that dreaded "P" word. But every student—you included!—has interests, even if it takes some careful thinking to identify them. Many students also feel

*"What we have here is technically impressive, Jason,
but regrettably lacking in passion."*

that they are just like everyone else. Wrong again: you are different from everyone else, even if it requires some time to think of how to explain why.

What do you like doing when you don't have to do anything? This is what you need to ask yourself first, although even that question is difficult for most students to answer. Below is a list of many activities and interests. It is not meant to be comprehensive but rather to give you an idea of the broad range of possibilities and to spark your imagination.

HOBBIES AND INTERESTS

Note: We have avoided making this list too specific. It's your job to determine your particular interest within these broad categories.

- Animals
- Anthropology
- Archaeology/Excavation
- Architectural History
- Architecture/Urban Design
- Astronomy/Aerospace
- Advertising/Public Relations (Publicity)
- Biology/Genetics
- Boating/Sailing

- Business/Finance/Investing
- Cars (repairing, restoring, building)
- Chess
- Community Service/Legal Advocacy
- Computers (programming, building, teaching, Web development, etc.)
- Construction
- Cooking
- Creative Writing
- Dance (performance, choreography)
- Debate
- Ecology/Conservation/ Environmentalism
- Engineering
- Farming
- Fashion
- Film Production/Documentary Filmmaking/Screenwriting
- Garden and Landscape Design
- Genetics
- Geography/Weather
- Government
- Hiking
- Interior Design
- International Relations
- Journalism
- Languages
- Literacy
- Literature
- Marine Biology
- Math/Problem Solving
- Media/Communications
- Medicine/Medical Research
- Mentoring/Teaching
- Music (composing/songwriting, playing an instrument/singing)
- Philosophy
- Piloting
- Poetry
- Psychology
- Radio
- Religion
- Restoration (furniture, old houses, and so on)
- Special Needs/Disabled Children and Adults
- Sports (participant/coach/ referee)
- Seniors/Working with the Elderly
- Space Travel
- Technology
- Television (production, screenwriting, anchoring)
- Theater (acting, producing, directing, writing, set design)
- Travel
- Veterinary Medicine
- Video Game Design and Development
- Visual Arts (Painting, Photography, Sculpture, Graphic Design)
- Wildlife

BRAINSTORMING

Here are some questions you can ask yourself as you brainstorm spike ideas.

- What are you best at in school?
- What causes move/inspire you?
- What club or activity do you most look forward to attending?
- What magazines do you always look at or buy?
- What online sites are you drawn to?
- What do you want to be when you grow up?
- And most basic of all: What do you really enjoy doing?

Answer as many of these questions as possible. Which answers came to you quickly? Why?

No one knows *you* better than *you*. Think about what makes you different from everyone else you know.

Keep in mind that interests can disguise themselves; sometimes you might not even think of them as interests. You might assume, for example, that interests have to be voluntary—but sometimes they're imposed on you.

- Do you need to take care of a younger sibling? A grandparent? A handicapped sibling?
- Do you have an unusual medical condition?
- Do you support yourself and/or members of your family through your own income?
- Have you lived in other countries or immigrated to the U.S. or your current country of residence?

Many of our students have created passions out of these "obligations," turning lemons into lemonade. After all, dealing with any one of these frequently stressful situations demands maturity, responsibility, and determination, particularly if you use your experiences to help others as well (see Julie's case study below). Even if you didn't actively "choose" these duties as passions, your creativity and investment of time and energy can reinvent them as such.

What a Passion Is and Is Not

So you've done a full inventory and you've figured out your passion. Drum roll... you enjoy hanging out with your friends.

We hate to disappoint, but hanging out with friends, partying, sleeping, playing video games, and watching sports are not passions. In fact, anything passive isn't likely to be impressive to admissions officers. You may enjoy these activities, and we're not telling you to avoid them, but unless you're designing and developing the video games, or actually playing the sports you like watching on TV, or organizing parties for local charities, the activity is not likely to develop into a passion that is viewed as attractive and distinctive by admissions officers.

Four Student Case Studies

Below are four examples of students whom we've worked with over the years. We chose these particular cases—out of hundreds of others—because they represent four very different types of students applying to very different types of colleges. All began with varying levels of extracurricular interests. One or two insisted they had *no* interests. Others had activities they absolutely loved doing outside of school. Several didn't realize their interest could be developed into a passion that would make their college application truly distinctive. Taken together, these four students present a broad cross-section of college applicants.

Note: In this chapter we will recount how these students *selected* an interest. In the next chapter we will show how they developed that interest into a distinctive passion.

JAKE

Jake was a typical high school freshman. Nothing interested him. He didn't play sports or belong to any clubs. He was an average student, not keen on any single subject. We spoke with Jake at length to determine what he was interested in, but he couldn't think of anything—besides hanging out with friends, watching TV, and playing video games. Finally, we asked what he did when he came home from school each day. Jake didn't hesitate: he always took care of his dog—walked him, brushed him, played with him. It was Jake's way of spending "down time"—what he chose to do when he didn't have to do anything. In other words, animals were his interest. Bingo! This small, seemingly insignificant detail was the springboard to what would become his spike—his distinctive pursuit—in his college applications and beyond.

JULIE

Julie was a smart, outgoing student. Like other students, however, she seemed to have nothing in her background that truly differentiated her. During our first meeting we saw her checking her insulin pump, and she told us she had diabetes. Although her parents had always encouraged her to be open about it, she admitted that it was something she sometimes tried to hide. But lately her perspective had been changing. She recognized that diabetes was a part of her, and she wasn't going to try to deny or be ashamed of her illness. We suggested that maybe others felt just as she had. Was there a Web site devoted to diabetic teenagers, featuring coping tactics specific to teens—such as how to wear a pump with a bikini or prom dress? It turned out that there wasn't. Julie had never thought of diabetes as a positive area of differentiation.

DANIEL

Some students actually create an interest for themselves. Daniel was a strong student but not significantly involved in any extracurricular activities. He played sports and was a member of some school clubs, but did nothing that would have distinguished his application from thousands of others—especially as he was aiming for the Ivy League. Then one day, when he was visiting his grandmother at her assisted-living facility, he decided he wanted to teach her how to use e-mail and surf the Web. This took place in 1998—before most grandparents knew how to turn on a computer, much less use a search engine! He wanted to write to his grandmother using e-mail and help her read newspapers from her native country in Europe. Soon he realized that many, many other grandparents wanted to learn the same skill. His interest was in using technology to assist the elderly and the PC Senior project was born—an idea that was ripe for the time and that grew in ways he never could have predicted.

AMY

Amy was a strong student, involved in sports and in-school extracurriculars, but when we brainstormed with her about what she truly enjoyed, she thought back to awards she had won in summer camp and activities she was effortlessly drawn to, and it occurred to her that they always involved art. That's your area of differentiation, we told her. Our job was to help her *extend* that distinguishing interest beyond her high school art classes into summer programs, internships, and jobs—all culminating in a town-wide art exhibition. Throughout this process, Amy also eliminated activities she didn't enjoy so that she had enough time to really explore her passion.

In the next chapter, you will see how these initial sparks turned into distinctive spikes—truly impressive, eye-catching accomplishments—on each of these students' college applications. But first, a few quick notes:

First, none of the interests we describe above was developed into a spike or area of distinctiveness overnight. Each required months or, in most cases, years of focused effort. Through small steps and individual achievements "layered" one on top of another, these students created applications that distinguished them from thousands of others and earned them spots at their top-choice colleges.

Second, none of the four stories above is meant to serve as an outline or guide. Rather, each presents a specific and distinct candidate. Your job is to take these ideas and figure out how to adapt them to a project that is representative of, and specific to, *you*. In the process, you will also learn a tremendous amount about yourself and your interests.

Finally, remember that you could also be the ninety-ninth application that your admissions officer at Top Choice University picks up to read, and you'll need to do all that you can to emerge as an impressive and unique candidate, not merely a number.

Layering Your Passion

Overview

In this chapter you'll learn:

- How to pursue your main interest through a variety of activities, building a strong record of achievement in "layers"
- How four real-world students used the layering process to build successful college applications
- How the skills you develop through layering can last through college and beyond

Build On Your Interests

After plenty of careful thought, you've pinpointed an interest, maybe even a passion—in other words, a potential spike. Now what?

The next step is to explore that area of interest. You can do this in many different ways: in school, out of school, through employment and summer programs. It really doesn't matter how you start—just don't be afraid to start small. (Putting too much pressure on yourself to create something "big" at the outset is a recipe for indefinite procrastination!) School is the first place most students look; if you're interested in French, for example, joining the French club is a great start. But that's just what it is—a start. We encourage our students to move beyond the limits of their high school to explore their interest through far more unconventional avenues.

Here are some questions to ask yourself as you begin exploring:

- Is there a job, paid or unpaid, that would allow you to explore your area of interest more fully?
- Could you learn more about your interest as an employee or intern or volunteer in a company? A hospital? A day-care center? A vet's office? A museum?
- Could you adapt your interest so that it's accessible to children? Is there a local Big Brother, Big Sister, or Boy or Girl Scout organization, or a children's community center through which you might be able to work?
- Could you create a program for senior citizens or geriatric residents around your area of interest? (Note: Teaching your passion to seniors or children may mean teaching the most basic version of a sport, craft, computer program, and so on. That's okay. Showing others the fundamentals of something you're advanced at has its own rewards.)
- Is there a summer program that could help you further develop your interest? A course taught at a university, near home or abroad? Could you explore your interest through local community colleges or summer courses at other colleges? (See Resources, pages 276–90, for an extensive list of summer programs in different disciplines.)
- Could you sell your service to neighbors, family, or friends?
- Could you create a Web site or online video about your interest? (Note that as college applications have become almost entirely electronic, having an online resource to which you can direct admissions officers is often an advantage.)
- Is there a need for an organization or Web site that centralizes information and resources about your interest?

Start with one opportunity and see where it leads, while keeping your eyes peeled for others. Don't shy away from avenues that are creative and

"I didn't do anything on my summer vacation—
should I write about what I bought?"

entrepreneurial; as you will see in our case studies, these often have the biggest impact and garner the most success.

Why are we asking you to consider all of these off-the-beaten-path ideas? Again, pretend for a moment that you're an admissions officer. You're evaluating two students with similar backgrounds, test scores, and grades. One student loves French and is a member of her high school's French club; the other loves French and has taught preliminary French to children at a local community center, created an online community for other high school Francophiles, spent summers in France living with a French family, and interned (for fun) in a bakery to learn how to bake French bread. Which student do you think is more interesting? Which do you imagine has stronger letters of recommendation? Which student would be more fun and compelling to present to other admissions officers as a potential candidate? Which do you envision making a more concrete impact on your college campus?

It is important not to concentrate all of your efforts on one activity, but to explore your interest through a variety of small activities—adding one activity, then another, and another, taking a slightly different approach each time. We call this process *layering*. Successful layering will ensure that by the time you are a high school senior, you will have created a record of achievement that shows real depth in one area—an area that has become your passion. This record will look like no one else's and paint a picture of you that is both compelling and unique.

Case Studies

JAKE

As you might remember from the last chapter, Jake came to us with no apparent interests. He was just a freshman when we first met and was slowly adjusting to high school life. His grades ranged from average to above average and his extracurricular activities were minimal. After much probing, we realized that what he really loved was taking care of his dog—walking, playing with, and grooming him each day.

After pinpointing this as Jake's interest, we asked him, "Why not create a business doing what you love?" We helped Jake and his family come up with the catchy name Pampered Pooch, and in no time some of his neighbors hired Jake to walk their dogs. Soon he was not only walking the dogs but grooming and training them. He posted his Pampered Pooch flyers all over the neighborhood, and the business quickly became so popular that he had to employ two other boys in the neighborhood just to maintain his service.

That year, Jake also realized that his love for animals was not limited to his own dogs. He (not his parents!) called one of his mom's friends, a local veterinarian. Jake began helping out in her office as an unpaid intern. He would continue working there for the next two years, shadowing the vet and cultivating his fascination with many different kinds of animals. The winter of his freshman year, he began investigating summer programs. He found and applied for an internship for high school students at a local maritime center and his application was accepted. He learned a lot from the program, most of all that he loved studying all kinds of animals, especially dolphins.

When he returned to school for sophomore year, Jake continued running Pampered Pooch and volunteering with the vet. That winter, he looked into other summer programs that would allow him to learn more about dolphin behavior. After much detective work, he discovered a program in Hawaii where he could study human-dolphin communication.

Again Jake applied and was accepted, and the summer he spent in the program cemented his passion for the subject.

Upon returning home for junior year, Jake became interested in the therapeutic benefits of playing with animals. He began another program that provided "pet therapy" to geriatric patients in local nursing homes. Jake brought animals into the nursing home and spent time helping seniors take care of and play with them. That winter he again explored summer programs that would allow him to keep investigating human-dolphin communication. Jake found and successfully applied to a program at a research facility in South Africa.

Although Jake had clearly developed a passion in the area of animals, dolphins in particular, he wasn't one-dimensional. He also loved playing the cello, and did so in his school's chamber orchestra, in his high school orchestra, and in the pit orchestra of theater productions.

Some takeaway lessons:

- Never rest on your laurels—keep creating and developing ideas. Jake went from developing Pampered Pooch in his freshman and sophomore years to founding and running a therapeutic pet program in his junior and senior years. Each summer, he investigated and attended different summer programs rather than returning to the same lab or campus.

- Catchy names (Pampered Pooch) are a great way to coin and communicate an idea or program.

- Winter is an ideal time to explore summer programs. Don't wait until the spring or early summer—many programs require application submissions in February or early March.
- Jake didn't attend any programs "with his friends." Rather, he was confident enough to set his own path.
- International experience is always a plus, especially as the world is becoming more interconnected. Universities often want students who have had experiences outside the U.S.
- Even though many of the programs in which Jake participated weren't free, none of his programs were teen tours or vacations. We never advise "purchasing" a summer experience with no goal other than to have fun with friends. If you decide you *must* go on a teen tour, try to limit it to a few weeks of your summer and combine it with another activity.

EPILOGUE: Jake went on to major in animal behavior and zoology at Cornell. His plan is to study marine biology in graduate school, following his life's passion.

JULIE

We began working with Julie in the spring of her sophomore year. She was a strong student who came from a relatively homogeneous community. She was aware that from the outside she looked like every other strong student in her high school. Yet, as she checked her insulin pump during our first meeting, she admitted that she always knew what made her different. Julie had lived with Type 1 diabetes for much of her life. As we mentioned in the last chapter, she had initially tried to figure out ways to disguise her illness. Gradually, however, with the support of her family, her perspective was changing, especially when it came to being an athlete with diabetes. It was sometimes problematic to play junior varsity and varsity sports because she had to remove her pump when she was on the field, but in the end she was quite proud of her athletic accomplishments. We were impressed that she had decided to highlight, rather than ignore or hide, her diabetes, and we felt that she was truly an outstanding model for others.

In our first meeting, we discussed how she had always been involved in the Juvenile Diabetes Research Foundation, fundraising for its annual Walk for the Cure. Clearly, this was a cause close to her heart. She had created her own team for Walk for the Cure—The A-Team—and emerged as a top fundraiser for the event. By the end of high school she had raised several hundred thousand dollars, an amazing accomplishment for anyone, no less a student.

Julie had also begun babysitting for two diabetic children, and would continue to do so throughout high school. The experience encouraged her to find a position as a counselor at a camp for children with Type 1 diabetes. She completed an intensive training course during the school year and began working with campers over the summer.

Upon her return to school, we discussed other ways in which Julie could learn and educate others about diabetes. In our conversation, she admitted how frustrating it was to find a place to position her pump when wearing certain kinds of clothing. We asked if there was a Web site devoted to discussing these specific teen diabetes issues. No site that she knew of. "That's something you can create," we told her. She loved the idea and began to take courses on Web site development, ultimately launching a site for which she was the designer, programmer, and major contributor.

Julie's site consisted primarily of a chat room in which pressing teen issues could be raised, addressed, and answered. (Where to put that pump while wearing a prom dress or bathing suit? How to be diabetic and play varsity sports? How to explain your illness to your boyfriend or girlfriend?) It also featured links to Julie's favorite diabetes sites and a page devoted to visitors' most frequently asked questions. Finally she was able to get links to her Web site posted on the sites of her own diabetes specialist, other doctors, and the National Diabetes Organization, driving major traffic to her own site.

Many diabetics began to hear about her Web site, and she became a role model for others. As a senior, she was asked to sit on the board of her local elementary school to study the effects of illness and handicaps on students. Julie also mentored and coached a handicapped Little League baseball player in her town's league.

Throughout this time, Julie continued to play sports. During her senior year, she became a varsity captain in both lacrosse and soccer, and both teams went on to be state champions. That fall, the local paper did a story on Julie, highlighting some of her amazing accomplishments as team captain, top fundraiser, Web site creator, and more. In the article's photograph, she is wearing shorts and a T-shirt—with her insulin pump front and center.

Some takeaway lessons:

■ Never ignore smaller opportunities. For example, Julie's work with a handicapped student in Little League was a real testament to her character. You don't need to be head or creator of a huge organization all the time!

■ Don't worry about combining disparate passions. Some kids might have thought that varsity sports and diabetes have nothing in common. However, it was partly Julie's frustration with the challenge of playing varsity sports as a diabetic that made her want to create a Web site in the first place.

■ The Internet is an amazing resource. If you have a passion, create a blog or Web site, or online video about it!

■ If you plan on being a camp counselor, don't work at just any camp. If possible, find one whose focus is meaningful to you.

EPILOGUE: Julie was accepted by her top-choice college. As a student there, she enjoys playing intramural sports and has continued to expand her interest in diabetes education and research.

DANIEL

Daniel was a good student, but he was not very active outside of high school athletics. He had joined some high school clubs, but did little that would distinguish his application in the ultra-competitive Ivy League schools he was shooting for. During one of his trips to visit his grandmother, he discovered that she wanted to learn how to use the computers in her assisted-living facility. He thought it would be great if she could e-mail her grandchildren and read newspapers in her native language, which she missed a great deal. With that observation, Daniel discovered his "interest."

Daniel taught his grandmother how to surf the Internet, bookmark her favorite sites, and register for and use her own e-mail account. While doing this, he saw that other seniors at the facility were interested in learning the same skills. He spoke to the director of the center and offered to conduct courses for the other seniors. The courses weren't fancy or complicated—they had titles like "What's a PC?"; "Internet 101"; and "E-mail 101." The director told him that other senior centers were also interested in these courses. He agreed to lead similar courses in other senior communities and began to learn what worked and didn't work when teaching technology to seniors. He found that teaching seniors was fundamentally the same as tutoring his fellow students. (However, there were also some differences: Don't rush through any steps. Large type is crucial. Don't take any piece of knowledge for granted. And speak loudly.)

Based on his work, Daniel created course manuals. To accomplish this, he applied for grants from local civic organizations: United Way, Lions Club, and Rotary Club of America. As we told Daniel, the amount he was asking for—be it $25, $50, or $100—didn't really matter. What mattered was that applying for and receiving this money validated his efforts, demonstrating initiative and community endorsement. Once he had created the manuals, he sent them to senior centers all over the country, as well as to national organizations such as Girl Scouts and Boy Scouts of America. A national organization added PC Senior to their list of activities—and with that single step, PC Senior instantly became a national program. Daniel also created a PC Senior club at his school, establishing a link between the local senior center and the public high school. Through this club, Daniel was able to transition the leadership of his program to a younger set of students.

Like most of our students, Daniel created a terrific program that he explored in many different ways. But he was definitely not a one-dimensional student. He loved playing sports and became a lacrosse captain in his senior year. The summer before his junior year, he wanted real-world experience, so he interned at a company that created computer networks for financial organizations, thereby pursuing his interest in computers along a far more sophisticated path.

Some takeaway lessons:

- Apply for grants. United Way, Rotary organizations, or even your local Y might offer small grants to assist high school students with projects they want to support. Applying for grants (even those in the $50–100 range) demonstrates organization, discipline, and (assuming you are successful) public support and validation for your program or service.

- Start a high school club related to your program only *after* the program is fully developed. If you start it too early, it may cease to be your project and become your high school's, and you may lose control of how it's run. That said, high school clubs are a useful way to prepare a transition of leadership to younger students.

- Don't shy away from working with seniors. Most of our students rush to work with children; seniors are a relatively overlooked age group, so there is often less competition for opportunities to work with them.

- Daniel is a good example of someone who *created* a passion—that is, saw a need and, on his own initiative, created a program to fill it.

EPILOGUE: Daniel attended Princeton and continued to expand PC Senior throughout college. Along with intramural sports, the program was the main extracurricular he cited when applying to Harvard Business School, where he is currently a student.

AMY

As we saw in the last chapter, Amy was a strong student who had always loved art. It was something that had come effortlessly to her. Even as a sixth grader, she had begun a business called Arty Parties, which organized art-themed birthday parties for younger children. Yet as a sophomore in high school, she did little outside of the typical high school drawing classes.

We brainstormed ideas that would allow her to expand her interest. We thought of all the places within her community that were associated with art. She recalled that there was an art museum a few towns over. After a few phone calls (made by Amy, not her parents), she entered a training program and became a volunteer docent at that museum. They didn't need her to come more than once a month, which was fine with Amy (the quality, not the quantity, of the experience is what counts, especially when you are layering activities). She enjoyed the docent position and during the winter began looking into summer art programs. She narrowed her choice to two art schools—Parsons in New York City and the Rhode Island School of Design (RISD)—and applied to both.

After further research, Amy decided on RISD. Her summer there helped her build her art portfolio as well as determine that she wanted to attend a liberal arts college, not an art school.

Upon returning home from RISD, Amy contacted her favorite middle school art teacher, who was now leading art classes for disadvantaged children at a local community center. She asked Amy to help out, and Amy jumped at the chance. She worked for her art teacher once a week, helping younger students with art projects. That winter, she again applied to and was accepted by an art school—this time an overseas program in France—where she spent the summer studying art history as well as painting and drawing. Although she created many additional works for her portfolio, she also discovered that she loved studying art history as much as (or more than) creating it.

She returned home from that summer only to find that her public school art classes were being severely cut. There was a fierce battle in her community over the cost of education. Unfortunately, the arts were seen as an unnecessary indulgence. Amy was outraged. Although she already sat on her student government board, she wanted to do more. We met and brainstormed ways to combat this injustice—and to showcase the amazing sculpture, drawing, painting, and photography being created in her high school. We came up with the idea of staging a town-wide high school art show. After an enormous amount of work (and lots of unpaid help from parents and friends!), Amy launched the show with tremendous success. Her town's mayor and state's congressmen recognized the project, and Amy put in place a transition team of students so the exhibition could continue to take place after she had graduated.

Amy's spike was clearly art, and she explored it from a wide variety of angles: community service, employment, summer programs, and in-school and out-of-school extracurriculars. She pursued both small and large programs—entrepreneurial efforts she created herself and programs that had been previously established. But the sum of her efforts was much greater than the individual steps involved—and had a tremendous impact on her application.

Some takeaway lessons:

- Lots of colleges offer pre-college art programs to high school students, but the best and most prestigious programs—the ones that will help you build the strongest portfolios—are typically at schools that specialize in your interest or passion (Parsons and RISD for Amy, for example). Even if you don't plan to attend an art school, consider enrolling for the summer if you have an artistic bent.

- Summers are a great time to explore your interests, and sometimes figuring out what you don't want is as important as figuring out what you do want.

- If possible, do the calling yourself! Taking the initiative in this way demonstrates (and builds) more maturity than having a parent do the work for you. If you're interested in an internship, volunteer opportunity, or summer course, pick up the phone or send an e-mail.

- You don't need to do an activity every day in order to include it on your activity chart. Amy's internship at the museum was only one day per month, but it was still interesting and important. Just be sure to note your time commitment for each activity on the chart. See Chapter 8 for more information on the activity chart.

- Combine traditional programs (such as the pre-college program at RISD that Amy attended) with intensely creative and entrepreneurial ones (such as her art show). Together, these create a healthy and (to admissions departments) eye-catching balance.

EPILOGUE: Amy continued to study art at Yale, in addition to earning a liberal arts degree. She also founded an art magazine at Yale and, after graduating, won a prestigious scholarship to study art at Oxford. Today, she is using art as the basis for creating an entrepreneurial start-up within a larger financial services organization.

Amy, Jake, Julie, and Daniel all developed impressive and creative programs. Their college applications both fit in and stood out; they were like their peers while at the same time spiking in one distinct area. And although the short-term benefits of their programs were clear from the admissions process—all four got into their top-choice schools—they have all acknowledged that the real benefits went far beyond "just" getting into college.

All four students found something they were interested in, and a couple even discovered a lifelong passion. Several discovered entrepreneurial ways to explore an interest, ways that required imagination and initiative. All four created programs from scratch, not only proving to themselves that they were capable of such a feat but also building the confidence and skill set necessary to reproduce that creative process in college and beyond. As much as we take pride in helping students "win" at college admissions, we feel truly successful when our students develop new skills and create original programs while exploring passions. The skills and creativity they discover in themselves can last a lifetime. We will explore this dynamic further in the last part of the book, "College and Beyond."

Pulling It All Together

Being Alike and Spiking on the College Application

Picture this: It's eleven P.M. and this is the fourth consecutive night of an admissions officer's application review. She decides she'll look at just one more application before she heads to bed. The application she reaches for is yours…

In Part III we will help you create an application that shows admissions officers—instantly, clearly, and even at eleven o'clock at night—what makes you both a natural fit and a terrific "catch" for their school. We'll help you show them that you are *like* other students on their campus in all the basic ways (your ability to hold your own in classes, for example), but that you also contribute an outstanding *spike*—a unique interest or passion—to their next freshman class. To start, we'll explain how to develop a list of prospective colleges and what to accomplish when you visit each school. Then we'll describe, step by step, how to implement your be-alike-but-spike strategy on the college application—including your activity chart, essays, letters of recommendation, interviews, and the application form itself. Remember, you have about four pages to represent seventeen years of your life; each aspect of your application has an important job to do. Here's how to get the job done.

Researching and Creating a Working College List

Overview

In this chapter you'll learn:

- How to weigh independent rankings against your personal criteria for colleges
- How to research colleges and determine which ones are right for you
- How to create a college list made up of safeties, probables, and reaches
- When to apply and how to use the different admissions options to your advantage

Independent Rankings vs. Personal Preferences

Every student and parent has been guilty of it: looking at a ranking, comparing one school to another based on its placement in some arbitrary list. Some students have determined they will not look at schools ranked below #45. Others want to look only at colleges that fall in the top ten. While we understand the desire of students to go to the best school they can get into, we always try to qualify and clarify the word *best*. The college you attend should be the best one for *you*. Rankings don't take into consideration your interests, proposed major, desire for a rural or urban setting, or hatred (or adoration) of Greek life. Here are some important considerations to keep in mind when looking at rankings:

- Rankings fluctuate. Keep in mind that what is at the "top" today may not be tomorrow. Don't pick a college because it's ranked three spots higher than your other top choice. The positions may be reversed next year!

- Rankings are inherently flawed because of the subjectivity involved in comparing one school to another. How one newspaper or magazine weighs the importance of library size versus alumni giving (both criteria in calculating rankings) may not match your preferences; *you might not even care much about either criterion.* Think about what's most important to you—not to the *U.S. News & World Report* or *Financial Times* rankers.

- Rankings are not customized; they don't always factor in the criteria that are relevant to your college decision. For example, rankings don't differentiate between colleges with strong and weak (or nonexistent) departments for a given subject. If you want to study business, be aware that even though Harvard may be a top school, it doesn't offer undergraduate business courses. Do you want to study theater? Yale's Theater Department is world renowned, while Princeton doesn't even offer this major.

■ Rankings are flawed because some colleges cater more to improving their rankings than others. For example, one school may accept a world-class musician with significantly lower SAT scores, while another school, conscious of the effect of the lower SAT scores on their ranking, may not.

■ Most important, rankings can't tell you whether you'll be happy at the school. If you despise fraternities, it's a good idea not to enroll at a college in which 80 percent of the freshman class pledges—no matter what that college's ranking. Do you love the intensity of a buzzing city? You won't be happy at even the highest-ranked school if it happens to be located in the middle of nowhere.

All of that said, rank should be *one* factor to take into consideration. At top-ranked schools, the endowment may be larger, allowing better access to facilities, scholarships, and professors. The alumni and recruiting network may also stretch farther outside of the schools' immediate geographic area—making it easier, for example, to get a job or internship in New York City if you attend college in St. Louis. But again, don't rely on rankings alone. Here are some other important factors to consider:

■ **Academic department and course offerings.** These differ widely from school to school. Consider your academic strengths and weaknesses and research which schools have strong programs and professors in the areas that most interest you.

■ **Campus location.** Do you love being in the middle of a huge city with little differentiation between the city and the campus? Or does the idea of walking to classes alongside cows make your heart soar?

Note: Colleges in or near cities have the advantage of restaurants, jazz clubs, and cultural events happening off campus, whereas more isolated schools may have few of these off-campus distractions. At such schools, activities are mainly campus centered.

RATING COLLEGES BASED ON CORE CURRICULUMS

A recent study by the nonprofit American Council of Trustees and Alumni (ACTA) rated colleges based on their commitment to a core curriculum of courses that the council considers essential to a well-rounded, competitive education. This curriculum comprises "general education" requirements in seven key subject areas: composition, literature, foreign language at the intermediate level, U.S. government or history, economics, math, and natural or physical science. The Web site whatwilltheylearn.com examines the general education course offerings at more than seven hundred four-year institutions and finds that all but sixteen fall short of requiring all seven subject areas. The winners of the study? Among them, Baylor University, City University of New York–Brooklyn College, Texas A&M University, the United States Air Force Academy, the United States Military Academy, the University of Arkansas, and St. Thomas Aquinas. The goal of the study was to give families greater insight into what a four-year college education actually delivers.

Note: Generally speaking, in addition to recruiting at the top-ranked colleges, companies are much more likely to recruit where it's convenient. For example, while many Wall Street firms recruit on campus at #31-ranked NYU, the majority of Wall Street firms do not recruit on campus at #30-ranked Brandeis or #32-ranked College of William and Mary. If you're passionate about a specific company or industry, consider a college in or near the city in which it's located.*

■ **Size.** Do you relish the idea of going to a school that's the size of a small city, or do you yearn to know the name of everyone in your freshman class? Whereas the first experience may be more

---

* "Best Colleges 2010: National Universities Rankings," *U.S. News & World Report*, online edition; February 12, 2010; http://colleges.usnews.rankingsandreviews.com/best-colleges/national-universities-rankings.

anonymous than the second, large schools often try to create smaller schools within larger ones (for example, the Michigan Honors Program). Larger schools are more likely to have nationally ranked sports teams and enthusiastically attended games. Also note that school size may affect the range of academic departments and courses offered within those departments. It may also reflect itself in class size, with larger schools initially offering a greater number of large lecture classes and small liberal arts colleges offering more small seminars. That's not to say you won't get small classes at a large state school; it just may not happen until your junior year. These are all generalities, but keep them in mind.

- **Distance from home.** Getting home can be costly, whether it's for that couch-potato weekend, your birthday, or a holiday. In addition to travel expenses, your distance from home may affect you on a daily basis as you encounter a three-hour time difference when you call home. Whereas some students love the idea of living on a different coast from their families, others prefer to stay within a two- or three-hour car or train ride from home.

- **Public vs. private.** Public schools will often draw many more in-state students—sometimes close to 50 percent of the class. While this appeals to some students, others want a more "diverse" student body. Cost is also a big consideration. The cost difference between public and private is substantial, even for out-of-state residents.

- **Greek life.** Some of our students abhor the very idea of fraternities, while others are intent on finding a campus with a strong Greek life. Look for the percentage of students who pledge when evaluating your college list. Note: Our experience has shown that for even the most enthusiastic Greek-life die-hards, the appeal of fraternities and sororities sometimes drops by junior or senior year. So no matter how high your initial enthusiasm about pledging, make sure a campus has other social outlets.

- **Political orientation.** While many campuses are solidly liberal— with students protesting and planning sit-ins—others are much

"It was a party school."

more conservative. Think about where you'd feel the most comfortable. Sometimes you need to visit a campus to get a true feeling for a school's political orientation. Look at the number and diversity of school organizations, the tone of campus publications, even the dominant religious affiliation (if there is one) among the students.

- **Cost of living.** As almost everyone knows, the cost of living is very different in different parts of the U.S. A thousand dollars per month can get you a house in Knoxville and only half of a tiny one-room apartment in Manhattan. Above and beyond the cost of tuition, consider these differences when creating a list.
- **Pre-professional vs. liberal arts schools.** Do you want to get an undergraduate marketing degree? A degree in finance or communications? A mechanical engineering degree? A degree in graphic design? Many schools offer these pre-professional options; others do not. Do your homework when creating your list.

LOOKING BEYOND BRAND NAMES

Just as we advise students not to base their choices entirely upon *U.S. News & World Report* rankings when creating a college list, we also encourage parents and students to look beyond brand-name colleges. Sure, everyone has heard of Harvard, but that doesn't necessarily mean that it's the best place for everyone. Much has been written on this topic, and we often recommend the Web site http://www.ctcl.com/, based on Loren Pope's book *Colleges That Change Lives*. For example, most students don't know that Juniata College in central Pennsylvania has an average class size of fifteen students and a ratio of two faculty advisors for each student. Or that recent graduates of Rhodes College in Memphis, Tennessee, have earned prestigious Fulbright, Watson, and Rhodes scholarships. Don't neglect colleges like these that aren't on the tip of everyone's tongue. They may not have huge marketing budgets, but they do have great academics, small class size, and excellent professors, and they offer students a highly customized and personalized educational experience.

We could go on and on. You can see why a one-size-fits-all list really fits no one. Understand what you want and create a list accordingly.

It's also worth bearing in mind that you will change over four years of college. You want a school that will change with you. For example, off-campus social options may not be important to you as a freshman when you are getting to know the other kids in your class, but you may welcome their availability as a senior. For more on this, see Chapter 7, "How to Visit Colleges."

Researching Schools

The best way to research schools is always to visit them. But there are many other ways to gather more information:

FALLING IN LOVE WITH A SCHOOL

When researching schools, keep in mind that you may fall "accidentally in love." We worked with a student who only wanted to attend a Big 10 sports-focused school with football games every Saturday. We encouraged him to look at an academically focused school—Washington University in St. Louis—just to make sure his instincts were right. He arrived at the school for a visit and changed his mind completely. Another student was sure from the start that Cornell was for her; she loved the size and spirit of the school. She was accepted there, but also at Williams—a much smaller, more isolated school. She visited Williams and fell in love. We encourage all students to visit the colleges they are considering. What you think you know about yourself—and the type of school you "absolutely" want to attend—may change.

- **Web sites.** These can be an amazing resource, providing course information, professor bios, publication links, videos, and much more. Their main downside is that they don't provide the most balanced account of the school.
- **Speaking to alumni.** This can be a great way to supplement objective information with personal perceptions. On the plus side, you'll get a real-world account of the pros and cons of a college; on the minus side, the alum's viewpoint may be out of date and in any case is just one person's opinion—not a statistically significant sample!
- **College guidebooks.** These are useful compilations of data and hard facts, though they are quickly being replaced by college Web sites and third-party sites (see below).
- **Third-party Web sites.** These are an excellent place to start searching for facts. An example, at the time of publication, is Unigo (www.unigo.com), which provides general school information, quick

links to school newspapers and publications, and input from a wide range of students. It will help you get an overall feeling for a school and its student-satisfaction level.

- ■ **College fairs and high school visits.** These are not substitutes for seeing a college with your own eyes, but they're an efficient way to become introduced to a wide range of schools. Representatives are typically admissions officers, so events of this kind provide an opportunity to introduce yourself and make a good impression.

Note: See Selected Bibliography and Resources for a full list of useful college research books and Web sites.

Again, the best way to get a feeling for a school—its courses, professors, students, and overall atmosphere—is to visit. There really isn't any substitute. Even better is spending the night. It's time-consuming and often expensive, but before you commit to one college (via Early Decision, say), take this step to ensure that you're making the right choice (see Chapter 7, "How to Visit Colleges").

Creating a List

Many students (and their parents) rush to prepare a final college list, but there is no need to plan too early—in fact, doing so can be counterproductive. Wait until you have taken the PSATs and have a sense of your GPA and class rank, preferably in your junior year. Sooner than that and your list may be based on wishful thinking, not valid information. (Of course, as with every step of the admissions process, you don't want to wait until the last minute, either.)

Your list of potential colleges should contain three to four schools in each of three categories: Safety, Probable, and Reach. Subject to the assumptions below, here's how we define these categories:

- ■ **Safety.** Your SAT/ACT scores and GPA should equal or surpass those of the top 25 percent of admitted students. Based strictly on these metrics, you should be admitted to this school.

"If he was really intelligent, he wouldn't limit his applications to East Coast schools."

- **Probable.** Your SAT/ACT scores and GPA rankings are in the top half of admitted students. You have a good chance of admittance.
- **Reach.** Your SAT/ACT scores and GPA rankings are in the bottom half of admitted students.

Note that these categorizations assume:
- You are not a legacy.
- You don't compete (athletically, musically, mathematically) on a national or world-class level.
- You have good grades and distinctive extracurriculars.
- You have not been arrested, your guidance counselor loves you, and all your letters of recommendation are very positive.

Depending on the school and various other circumstances, factors such as recruited-minority/legacy status may also affect these categories. In general, however, they provide a sound rule of thumb on which to base your list.

YOUR GUIDANCE COUNSELOR

At some point, typically in the spring of your junior year (but not sooner—the senior class will have priority until then), your guidance counselor will begin to discuss colleges with you, determining what kind of schools interest you most and why. Based on your GPA, curriculum difficulty level, standardized-test scores, and out-of-class activities, he or she will help you refine your list of safeties, probables, and reaches. Later, in the fall of your senior year, your guidance counselor will write you a key letter of recommendation (see more on this topic in Chapter 10). A few things to keep in mind:

1. As we also advise in Chapter 10, get to know your guidance counselor. Stop by her office, say hello, and let her know what you've been up to both inside and outside of classes. Even if your guidance counselor just arrived at your high school during your senior year (unfortunately, this does happen), you should still try to form a relationship with her.

2. Understand the important role that your guidance counselor plays in your college application process. Not only does she work with you to finalize your college list and write that key letter of recommendation, she is also the main contact for any admissions officer with questions about your application. That's right—the admissions officer at Top Choice University may call your guidance counselor if she has any questions about your application.

3. At some high schools, you guidance counselor may ask you to fill out an information sheet (providing personal data, a list of activities, and so forth) that will form the basis of her letter of recommendation. Don't blow this off. Think through the questions carefully, and be

both thorough and thoughtful in your responses. Your guidance counselor recommendation is an important part of your application (see Chapter 10).

4. Finally, be aware that although your guidance counselor has your best interests at heart, she is employed by your high school, not by you or your parents. A big part of her job is to consider how the high school as a whole, not merely the individual student, does in college admissions each year. She has to work hard to maintain and even improve the high school's standing in the community, and one of the ways she can do this is to ensure that all of her students get admitted into a college. It may not be the college that is your "ultimate reach first choice" or even a college that is your perfect fit; instead, it may be a college that balances the overall plan the guidance counselor has for the high school. Whether or not all students are admitted by, and go on to attend, four-year-colleges affects many matters of local interest, including the high school's educational budget and real estate values in your town or city.

Note: In private schools, the guidance counselor must ensure that the alumni, as well as the school administration, are pleased with the students' overall performance in terms of college acceptances. This can impact not only alumni generosity in supporting the high school but also the number and quality of future applicants to the school.

So always remember that it's your guidance counselor's job to consider each of her advisees in relation to the others she is responsible for that year, and to come up with a balance of colleges that makes sense for the high school overall, and hopefully, though not necessarily, for you.

SOFTWARE FOR CREATING A COLLEGE LIST

Today, many guidance counselors use computer software to compile an anonymous database of students' GPAs, standardized-test scores, and record of college admissions. With this information, guidance counselors can compare current students' GPAs and test scores against those of past students' and assess chances of college admissions. Often, this software is supplied by Naviance. The information can be enormously useful, as it can help you confirm safety, probable, and reach schools based on other students in your high school. However, these tools have their drawbacks, including:

1. They don't factor in class difficulty.
2. They don't factor in any non-academic variables: extracurricular involvement, legacy status, minority status, recruited-athlete status, and so on. Take these factors into consideration when compiling your list.

We probably don't need to warn you about the dangers of applying to all reaches and no safeties—being punished by the College Gods for your hubris, getting turned down everywhere, and so forth—but you don't want to err in the opposite direction either. Getting in everywhere you apply is not necessarily a badge of genius; in fact, it's probably a sign that you've aimed too low. We once worked with a student who believed that he had stress and anxiety problems so serious that they would hinder his performance as a college student. Although we encouraged him to apply to a few reaches, he chose to apply only to safeties and probables. He ended up being accepted everywhere he applied. Use the guidelines above to create a realistic list and remember to cover all your bases.

WHEN DON'T THESE PREDICTIONS WORK?

Kids can sometimes "fall through the cracks" when there is nothing distinctive about their application (see the "Spike" part of this book to avoid this fate). We had a student come to us after her Early Decision application had been deferred by a school that should have been a probable for her in terms of her SAT scores and GPA. After talking to her about her extracurriculars and out-of-school activities, we realized that the picture she painted on her college application was very different from the one apparent to us. On her college application, nothing stood out and she'd shown no apparent leadership. Students are often too modest on their applications—this is one time when it's okay to boast! We helped her understand how to group her activities and describe her accomplishments, which were very real, and what to emphasize with regard to her commitment and leadership. We encouraged her to include out-of-school activities that she hadn't thought were important, such as regularly reading classics for her own enjoyment and starting an online book group with friends from different parts of the country. She was eventually accepted by the school that had deferred her. (For more on application self-presentation, see Chapters 8–12).

When Safeties Aren't Safeties

If you make safety schools feel like safety schools, they often won't accept you. Everyone needs to feel wanted. Here's how to make a safety feel like a reach:

- **Be specific.** Show the school that you know what makes it special and unique. When you write about why you want to attend that school, be prepared to name professors you want to study with, classes you want to take, majors that fascinate you, and internships that may be available through that school.

Note: After all this research, you may discover that the school is much more interesting to you than you had originally thought!

- **Visit and interview.** Nothing shows a school that you consider it a safety more than if you never visit, especially if the school is within driving distance of your home. If possible, stay and audit a class.

- **Start your essay fresh.** Don't take an essay you've already written for another application and adapt it to this school, especially if it just doesn't answer the given question. An application screams "safety school" to an admissions department when your essay doesn't address what they're asking.

- **Ask a trusted person to proofread** your application for careless mistakes, such as including the name of a different college in your essay.

Deciding When to Apply: Navigating Early Action, Early Decision, and Regular and Rolling Admissions

The variety of admissions options now offered by colleges can seem confusing, but once you understand how they work, it's easy to combine them into a smart and timely admissions strategy. Let's start with some definitions:

EARLY ACTION (EA)

If you apply Early Action, you get to hear early from the school, but you have until the spring to make your decision. This option is primarily offered by selective schools and can be useful if you have to compare financial-aid packages. Many schools have "single-choice Early Action," meaning that you can apply to only *one* school EA (and you cannot apply to another school Early Decision). There is some debate as to whether EA gives you an advantage in the application cycle (typically the percentage of students accepted via EA is higher, but often, so is the quality of applicant). Many admissions officers admit that this option does not deliver the same benefit to students as Early Decision.

EARLY DECISION (ED)

Applying to a college ED means entering into a binding agreement to attend that college if admitted. In other words, you must be sure when you apply that the ED school is your first choice! This requires careful thinking; many students are not ready to make this commitment in the fall of their senior year. (ED applications are generally due on November 1 or November 15, and decisions are made by December 15.) If you choose to apply ED, you can do so to only one school. This application option delivers the greatest admissions advantage for students; studies have shown the benefit to be the equivalent of a 100–150 point SAT score increase. At some colleges, applying ED can increase your chances of being accepted by as much as 33 percent.* More and more colleges have begun incorporating ED policies, including "ED1"—traditional ED—and a variant, "ED2" (see below). Doing so helps increase their yield rates (see "Yield Rates" on page 112) and makes the schools appear more selective, thereby increasing their rankings in publications such as *U.S. News & World Report*. Admissions officers like ED, as it helps them plan their class more accurately. (If they accept a pianist and a soccer star through ED, they know they're getting a pianist and soccer star.)

Note, too, that if you are accepted ED at a school to which you've applied for financial aid, you are bound to accept that school's aid package rather than evaluate a variety of offers.

Schools either accept, reject, or defer EA/ED1 applicants. Deferred applicants are then evaluated in the larger Regular Admissions pool. Some schools do not reject anyone who has applied EA or ED, preferring to look at all students in the larger admissions pool. Others would rather not have

---

* "The Early Decision Racket," *The Atlantic*, online edition, September 2001, http://www.the-atlantic.com/doc/200109/fallows. See also "Colleges Where Applying Early Decision Helps," *U.S. News & World Report*, online edition, posted September 30, 2009; http://www.usnews.com/education/articles/2009/09/30/colleges-where-applying-early-decision-helps.html.

YIELD RATES

Why is it important to commit to attend a college? It's a valid question. The percentage of accepted students who decide to attend the school is called the yield rate. Yield rates are very meaningful to colleges. They are closely tracked by college administrators and powerful alumni. Most important, yield rates figure heavily in the *U.S. News & World Report* rankings. For example, in 2009 Harvard's yield rate was 76 percent, Georgetown's was 47 percent, and George Washington's was 34 percent, according to the colleges' Web sites. According to 2010 *U.S. News & World Report* rankings, Harvard was ranked 1st, Georgetown, 23rd, and George Washington 53rd. For better or worse, schools are always trying to increase their standing on this metric. Yield rates are one reason why the Early Decision process is so attractive to schools: applicants who are accepted through ED have a 100 percent yield rate.

REJECTION VS. DEFERRAL

Contrary to conventional wisdom, it's sometimes better to get rejected than deferred, as rejection allows you to plan your revised college list more accurately. Many colleges prefer to let students down slowly, especially if they are legacy children or siblings of alumni. Although we understand the sentiment, this policy tends to build false hope. Our advice is: if you're deferred, expect your chances of acceptance to be slim. We're not saying you might not be pleasantly surprised; rather, you should hope for the best and plan for the worst. (For deferral strategies, see the appendix "Deferral and Waitlist Strategies" on pages 263–67.)

students hold out false hope for an acceptance and will reject those they are sure will not meet admissions criteria. If either your EA or ED1 application does get deferred, it's helpful to know the admissions office policies.

Many schools have also created an "ED2" category. Although deadlines vary, schools with ED2 often follow the same calendars as regular decision: applications due in January/early February, The responses, however, typically arrive only four weeks later, in February/early March. This option is best for students who have a clear first choice but may not have been prepared to apply in time for the ED1 date. Many students resort to ED2 when they are rejected or deferred by their ED1 first choice and have a clear second choice. Because acceptance of ED2, like ED1, is binding, it also delivers a clear advantage to applicants, although it, too, requires students to accept the college's financial-aid package, if applicable.

REGULAR ADMISSIONS

This term refers to the standard admissions cycle, in which candidates typically submit their applications the January before they hope to enroll and hear from the college in early April. Admissions officers review all applications before making a decision on individual candidates. Accordingly, candidates applying through the Regular Admissions process will be able to hear from all schools they applied to Regular Admission, and compare all financial-aid packages, before having to make a decision (typically by May 1).

ROLLING ADMISSIONS

Under this option, typically used by larger public universities, applicants will be reviewed on an ongoing basis as their applications arrive in the admissions office. Don't fret if your application doesn't arrive at the admissions office by Labor Day. Not only does it take weeks for your transcript and letters of recommendation to arrive and your application to be complete, but most admissions officers are out of the office

HOUSING CONSIDERATIONS

In colleges where housing is very limited (city schools, for example), or even where some of the housing has been renovated and some has not, it may be to your advantage to make a decision on attendance as early as possible, because rooms are usually assigned on a first-come-first-served basis. We know some students who applied under Rolling Admissions in October, were accepted in November, and immediately sent a deposit to ensure housing—even though their decision wasn't due until May 1 of the following year. Contact the college admissions office as soon as you have been accepted to determine their housing policy.

promoting the school during September and October and only begin evaluating applications in mid-to-late October. Generally, however, it is advantageous to get applications in as early in the cycle as possible, as admissions officers have more flexibility during this time with regard to whom they can accept. (Later in their acceptance cycle, a lower SAT score or GPA may be harder to accept, as it may adversely affect the SAT/GPA average of the incoming class.)

We often advise our students to apply to a Rolling Admissions school early in the application cycle. You will get a response in four to eight weeks and ideally have an acceptance in your back pocket by December; moreover, you typically don't need to notify the school of your decision until May 1.

Note: Many of these Rolling Admissions schools are responding to the influx of applicants and the relative ease of getting accepted by making their applications more difficult and specific to their school—in other words, they don't want students mindlessly filing applications. If a student is on the cusp, for instance, some schools will choose not to respond right away. They may want to see a student's first-semester grades before making a decision. But many students get into a terrific school this way, and avoid having to apply to many safeties through Regular Admissions.

Combining Options

Now let's take all of these admissions options, keeping in mind the pros and cons of each, and synthesize them into an overall application strategy. Here's what we advise:

1. Apply to 1–2 Rolling Admissions schools in October. Ideally you will get an acceptance to one and will have a safety in your back pocket.
2. Choose an ED1 or EA option. ED clearly gives you the greatest advantage. Aim for a *realistic* reach school and apply.
3. Once your ED1/EA school application is submitted, begin filling out your ED2 choice. Aim for a reach/probable. Complete the applications for any outstanding Rolling Admissions schools.
4. After you've submitted your ED2 and Rolling Admissions applications, begin filling out the rest of your applications. Keep your fingers crossed and wait for the mail!

Note: If you get into your ED1 or ED2 choice, remember to withdraw all other applications. For deferrals, see the appendix "Deferral and Waitlist Strategies."

How to Visit Colleges

Overview

In this chapter you'll learn:

- Why visits are a crucial step in the college search process
- How to plan a successful college visit
- What to look for—and what to ignore—as you visit colleges

Seeing for Yourself

We once had a student who had her heart set on getting into Duke. Along with its high academic reputation, the school had everything she wanted: Southern location, strong school spirit and athletic programs, active Greek life, and more. But once we got to know her, we convinced her to apply to Dartmouth as well, and after making the kind of face usually reserved for biology-class dissections, she agreed to travel there for an overnight visit. We got a phone call from her within a few hours of her arrival. "This is it," she said. She felt completely at home—and ended up matriculating and having a wonderful four years there.

The lesson? There's nothing like seeing things for yourself. As persuasive as reputation and promotional materials can be, visiting schools is the best—and often the only—way to learn what makes them distinctive. While the brochures and Web sites of many colleges may appear similar, visiting them will show you that they are really very different. Use your visits to gather information and, in the process, begin to formulate what is best for you. You'll quickly be able to assess how the schools view *themselves*, and through your applications, essays, and interviews, you'll be able to *show* the schools that you know what makes them unique. Colleges want to understand you and want *you* to understand *them*.

Your goal while visiting is to imagine yourself as a student at the college. Separate from your parents for at least part of your visit and chat not only with your assigned tour guide but also with other students. When you speak with them, find out whether this college was their first choice. Are they happy with their decision? Even the most satisfied student might want to change something about the school. Find out what that is. Check out the study spaces in the library, visit the gym. Do students appear happy? Is there a laid-back pulse or a buzzing energy? How are the students dressed? Sweaters and skirts or tie-dye T-shirts and jeans?

Although you'll want to spend most of your visit deciding what you like about the school, at least part of the time should be focused on determining what the *college* values. Keep track of these impressions; they will be useful when writing application essays and during interviews, and will demonstrate to the college that you understand and appreciate its approach. Most important, gaining an understanding of a school's culture and values will help you accurately position your application so that it both fits in with and stands out from your peers' applications.

Planning Your Visits

We almost always advise students to visit a broad range of schools initially: big and small, urban and rural, religious and secular, party schools and academically rigorous schools. To limit the expense, we suggest restricting your visits to local schools. You don't want to blow your entire college visit budget on this early phase of evaluation.

Although we encourage visiting colleges as early in the process as possible, there are also advantages to holding off. Your time will become

LETTING THEM CHOOSE

In most cases, students are not able to choose their high school. College may be the first time students can actually decide what they like—and more important, don't like—in a school. Try not to impose too many early restrictions on which colleges they should consider. This strategy may backfire, and they may choose a college *just because* it's not one of your recommendations. (Seventeen-year-olds have been known to have the occasional rebellious streak.) Although the college admissions process is often a tension-filled time, try not to create a standoff and allow a student's defiance to cloud decisions. Instead, speak broadly about criteria for selecting a college and allow your child to remain in the driver's seat. The choice of college should be up to your son or daughter, not you.

extremely tight, with finals, AP exams, SATs, Subject Tests, and so forth, but you will have more information available to you if you wait. Once you know your scores on those standardized tests, you will be able to compile your list of potential schools more accurately and reasonably. Consequently, your impressions on college visits will be better informed, which, in turn, will help in answering short-answer essay questions on applications (see Chapter 9, "Essays"). During your visit, you may also be able to interview, audit a class, and speak to a department coordinator in an area or major you are considering (we recommend this for juniors and/or seniors only).

Getting to Know Yourself

Deciding which school is right for you also entails getting to know yourself better and then determining the criteria that are most important to you in choosing a school. Do you prefer a strongly conservative campus, a more liberal one, or something in between? Do you want to be in a

"My first choice college should have lots of closet space."

secluded rural location or a bustling urban environment—or do you prefer the 'burbs? Try to think beyond today and allow for possible changes
in your personality and interests. Sometimes this means not sweating
the small stuff. We remember working with a girl who had gotten into
her dream school—perfect size, region, reputation—and came into our
office after her first visit saying, "I don't want to go there." Taken aback,
we asked why not. She said, "It's a Pepsi campus."

We gave her the benefit of the doubt: had "Pepsi" become a figure of
speech, in the same way that "granola" can mean "hippie"? Nope—the
vending machines on campus were stocked with Pepsi, and she pre-
ferred Diet Coke. With a seventeen-year-old girl's entire future at stake,
we thought fast. "Maybe you could bring a minifridge and a case of Diet
Coke with you when you move into the dorm."

WHY DO ADMISSIONS OFFICERS CARE IF YOU VISIT?

For better or worse, many admissions officers today place great
importance on prospective students' visits to their school. Assuming
you have the financial means to visit, they want to be sure that
you're applying not just because it was easy to fill out their Common
Application. We've even heard that some colleges *count* the number
of times you visit. And admissions officers *may* view not visiting as
a sign that you lack significant interest in their school—that you're
hoping to get accepted but not really planning to attend. No school
wants to admit applicants who aren't serious about attending the
college, because doing so would lower their yield rates (see page 112
for more on this topic). Colleges want informed consumers. Even
so-called safety schools may think twice about admitting candidates
who they suspect aren't serious prospects and will admit less qualified students who they feel are serious about attending.

"Oh, yeah…"

The point of the story is that your priorities as a seventeen-year-old are different from what they will be four years down the road. You'll be spending four years at college and you'll change a great deal during that time. Ideally, you'll want a school that can change *with* you. For example, many of our students plan to spend the majority of their time on campus, but by junior or senior year some of them may find that they want to venture off campus. Sometimes, a cohesive campus located near a city or college town can provide the best of both worlds. No matter what, keep an open mind and seek out schools that will allow you to become everything you want to become, not stay exactly the way you are now.

Which Colleges to Visit?

We know that you may not have time to visit all the schools on your list. Your college list will be made up of 3–4 each of safeties, probables, and reaches. Visiting between 9 and 12 schools may be impossible. We recommend that students determine their top one or two choices in each category and visit those schools. Most important, don't visit only your probables and reaches. That's a mistake. If you ignore safeties, they may cease to be such. Safeties will often reject students who they believe aren't serious about attending (see "Why Do Admissions Officers Care If You Visit?" on page 120). Finally, smaller colleges almost always accord greater importance to visits than larger universities. Smaller schools want to be sure that you understand and embrace their specific culture and values. For example, at a small liberal arts college with a class size of 300 the impact of each student is large. In contrast, a large public university with a class size of 10,000 may be less concerned about whether each individual student fully understands its culture.

POPULAR COLLEGE CLUSTERS

Below is a list of areas with a high concentration of colleges and a sampling of schools to visit in those areas. The colleges span a wide spectrum (few students may be interested in both Emerson and MIT!), and the selection is by no means exhaustive, yet it may be helpful in planning your college visits.

Washington, D.C., area: Johns Hopkins University, University of Maryland, American University, George Washington University, George Mason University, Georgetown University.

Pennsylvania: Carnegie Mellon University, University of Pittsburgh, Pennsylvania State University, Bucknell University, Lehigh University, Lafayette College, Dickinson University, Muhlenberg University, University of Pennsylvania, Princeton University, Temple University, Bryn Mawr College, Haverford College, Swarthmore College, Drexel University, Villanova University.

Boston area: Harvard University, MIT, Emerson College, Boston College, Boston University, Brandeis University, Tufts University, Northeastern University, Babson College, Simmons College, University of Massachusetts Boston, Suffolk University.

New England: Yale University, Wesleyan University, Trinity College, Connecticut College, Fairfield University, Middlebury College, Colby College, Bates College, Bowdoin College, University of Vermont, Amherst College, Williams College, Dartmouth University.

Ten Tips on Planning a Visit

There may be many schools that you can visit during a quick day trip from home, but trips to other schools will require more planning. Whether you're traveling near or far, here are ten tips to consider before you even leave home:

1. If you're traveling far, make sure to visit more than one college. For example, if you're going to Maine to see Bowdoin, look at Bates and

California: Chapman University, California State University at Fullerton, Claremont Colleges (Pomona College, Claremont McKenna College, Harvey Mudd College, Pitzer College, Scripps College), University of Southern California, Occidental College, California Institute of Technology, University of California at Los Angeles, Pepperdine University, Loyola Marymount University, Santa Clara University, Menlo College, Stanford University, University of California at Berkeley, University of San Francisco.

Southeast: University of Richmond, Randolph-Macon College, Duke University, University of North Carolina at Chapel Hill, Elon University, Guilford College, Wake Forest University, Salem College, North Carolina School of the Arts, Davidson College, University of North Carolina at Charlotte, University of Georgia, Emory University, Oglethorpe University, Vanderbilt University, Belmont University, Savannah College of Art & Design, Clemson University, University of South Carolina, Furman University, Washington & Lee University, University of Virginia, College of William & Mary.

New York City area: Columbia University, Fordham University, Barnard College, Yeshiva University, New York University, Parsons School of Design, Fashion Institute of Technology, The Cooper Union, The New School, Sarah Lawrence College, Pace University, Hunter College, Pratt Institute.

Colby at the same time. If you're planning to see Duke, check out the University of North Carolina at Chapel Hill. You may not have the chance to go back.

2. Call the admissions office in advance. Make sure that the admissions office will be open and that an information session/tour will be taking place. Make an appointment for an interview if on-campus interviews are permitted (see Chapter 11, "The College Interview").

3. Try to avoid finals week, move-in week, and spring/summer break. You want your impression of the schools to be as accurate as possible.

4. Ask the admissions office for recommendations on local hotels, motels, and restaurants. Reserve everything in advance. You could be visiting during a reunion weekend and don't want to be surprised by sold-out hotels or exorbitant rates.

5. If you can, plan an overnight stay with a student at the college. The staff in the admissions office can usually help arrange this. The inside perspective of spending the night may be invaluable in helping you get a true impression of the school. Your parents can sleep at the motel down the street.

6. Don't plan on visiting more than two schools per day. If possible, it's preferable to limit yourself to one campus a day. Leave yourself enough time to experience the college: take a tour, attend an information session, audit a class, and speak to students. Try to imagine yourself on the college campus.

7. Get the best possible directions from Google Maps, MapQuest, or another online service. If possible, rent a car with a GPS system. Check the Princeton Review's *Visiting College Campuses* (see Selected Bibliography). There's nothing like bad directions to spoil a trip. Don't let that happen.

8. If you're visiting during a week when classes are in session, try to audit a class in an area that interests you. There are two ways to do this. You can call the admissions office in advance—they should have a list of classes that prospective students can audit. Or you can call a specific department. The coordinator or administrative assistant of that department may be helpful in determining whether there is an introductory class in your field of interest that you can audit. Note: Don't feel intimidated if you can't follow the material; you're not expected to.

9. If you do audit a class, try to approach the professor after the class and thank him/her for letting you "sit in" on the lecture. Be as natural and sincere as possible. Mention something from the lecture that made an impression on you. Do this alone (no parents standing

nearby). It's possible that this meeting will generate a short note that is sent to the admissions office in support of your candidacy.

10. Even if you can't sit in on a class, it may still be worthwhile to meet the department coordinator of your anticipated major, especially if it's in a smaller department that may be actively seeking new students (Classics, Russian, and Art History often fall into this category, whereas History, Economics, and Business are usually fully "booked"). Even a brief meeting can generate a good impression. The coordinator might note this visit with a short letter to the admissions office. These letters can be invaluable and tip the scale in your favor. If you're planning to study the visual or performing arts, meeting the department coordinator and leaving a portfolio or CD/DVD with him or her could prove especially helpful.

11. It's always a good idea to get as much information as you can about a college before you visit. Talk to people who have attended, read what the guidebooks have to say, talk to guidance counselors. The more background information you have, the more meaningful your visit will be.

Thinking Beyond College

As you plan and make your visits, keep in mind that college may be the first step in determining your future direction. Deciding on a college is not unlike choosing a career or accepting a job. The ability to evaluate an environment and interpret the culture is a skill you will use long after your college days are over. In the postgraduate and working worlds, as at universities, there are many, many different cultures A pre-professional school will set you off in a different direction from a small liberal arts college. Don't shy away from this reality: it's an important step in figuring out what makes you happiest.

Many students find their first jobs in communities near the college they attended. They may have interned for a local company during college and accepted a full-time position after graduation. Or perhaps the company came to the campus to recruit job candidates. It is also common for students to seek job opportunities through the local alumni network, which is usually strongest close to campus. Or they seek jobs in the area because they want to stay close to college friends and their own personal network. With this in mind, think carefully about the location of your college. It may have a far greater impact on your life than the four years you spend there as a student.

Staying Impartial

Try to remain impartial during your visits. Distinguish between what is permanent and what is a product of chance. Try to ignore a rainy day (unless the school is in a region known for its rain) or a spectacularly sunny day (it may be the only one for months!). Realize that the timing of your visit may determine how outgoing and friendly people are—students are often more curt and sullen during finals than at other times of the year. The relative attractiveness of a tour guide is not a sound basis of evaluation. Try not to judge a school based on a dorm host, professor, interviewer, or admissions officer at the information session. Determine and prioritize the list of criteria with which you are evaluating schools. Then try to assess each school based only on those criteria and take strange dorm hosts (see below) and cute tour guides out of the equation. This is an area in which parents can have helpful input, if they are in basic agreement with your criteria.

Recently, one of our students visited a small college that occupies two sides of a single street—and was assigned a dorm host who was terrified of crossing that street. The girl refused to attend classes on the other side, let alone show her young charge around any of the buildings there. When the visit ended, the student leaped into her parents' car shouting, "Get me *out* of here!" Of course, in retrospect the student realized that most people at the college were probably not that strange.

It is up to you to determine what is representative of the school and what is not. And if the worst should happen and you find yourself a Coke drinker on a Pepsi campus...just remember, they might change the vending machines next year.

STAYING OUT OF THE WAY

Although you will want to get to know the college too (a good deal of your money will be going to this school), it's important for your child to experience the school on his or her own. Plan to take the tour and information session together, but allow the student to stay on campus overnight, or at least check out the library and student center without you. Interviews (see Chapter 11) are definitely a student-only experience, as are any meetings with professors and coaches. Admissions officers and professors are all too familiar with "helicopter parents," and you don't want to be labeled as such.

Observation List for College Visits

Photocopy the following list of questions or download them from our Web site, www.entrywayinc.com, for each college you visit. Don't wait to record your impressions. You'll forget. Do it during and immediately after your visit. The main question to ask yourself: Do I feel like I fit in here?

Although this list is not exhaustive, learn as much as you can about all of the criteria on it and be prepared to disregard some of these criteria when you find the school of your dreams.

Note: Be sure to sign in—legibly—at the admissions office to let the college know you visited. If you don't sign in, they won't have a record of your visit. Once you contact the school, they will create a file for you and all your future correspondence will be kept there.

1. Academic

- How big are classes? Who teaches the courses (professors or teaching assistants)?
- Do students generally get into the courses they'd like (or have) to take?
- Do most students graduate in four years?
- What are the most popular majors? When do you have to declare?

- Was this school your tour guide's first choice? Where else did he/she apply? Where else did he/she get in?
- Do students generally use the library? Do they find it conducive to studying?
- Do you need math or a foreign language to graduate? Is there a core curriculum?

2. Social

- When students go out at night, where do they go? Is driving involved?
- How big are the fraternities/sororities? How popular? Are there other social options?
- Are the parties generally open to anyone or limited to guest lists?
- If the campus is near a city, do students go to clubs and restaurants there?
- Do students live on campus? If so, do you have some choice about where you live?
- Is the student population homogeneous or does there appear to be a diverse mix of people?
- Do students appear happy or stressed out?
- Do a percentage of students leave on the weekend (that is, is it a suitcase school)?

3. Extracurricular

- Are students active outside of classes? Do you see evidence of clubs and activities that interest you?
- Do students appear to have a lot of school spirit? Is attendance at school sports events high?
- Is there a student center? Is the campus in good repair? Do the classroom buildings and dorms look comfortable?
- What do the gym/health club facilities look like? Are there running routes and courts you can use?
- What is the general feel of the campus? Energetic or mellow? Liberal or conservative?

4. Technological

- How available is the wireless network? Are students expected to arrive with computers? Are you required to purchase a certain type of computer or are there minimum requirements for student-owned computers? Is free printing available?
- Is there a tech help desk with daily support for students? 24-hour support?
- Can you search the library online?
- Do computer clusters appear to be filled with the latest equipment? Are there a lot of available computers?

5. Dining, Dorms, and Off-Campus Housing

- Are there many dining and living options? Do most dining halls and dorms appear clean and convenient?
- Are the dining halls open during convenient hours?
- Is there a supermarket nearby?
- Do most students dine on or off campus?
- Are there healthy/vegetarian/gluten-free/kosher/etc. options to meet your needs? If you have special nutritional needs (for example, celiac disease/diabetes diet), can they be met?
- Is on-campus housing offered for one year? What about years two through four?
- What is the cost and availability of off-campus housing?
- Are there co-ed bathrooms? Are there private bathrooms?
- Are there single rooms? If not, how many students are expected to share bedrooms? Does this number lessen each year? Can you request a quiet room?
- Are the dorms wired?

6. Career

- Is there an office of career services that helps with summer and post-college recruiting?
- What companies recruit on campus?
- Where are current students interning over the summer?
- What percentage of students seeking employment find it?

- How strong is the alumni network? Is it stronger in certain geographical areas or professions?

Don't Forget to...

- Talk to as many students as possible, including those who are not guides.
- Talk to the admissions office and ask them what they look for in applicants.
- Take the student tour. Don't miss the dorms, library, and cafeteria.
- Take pictures of buildings so you remember the campus.
- Read the bulletin boards throughout the campus and in dorms to see what's going on.
- Stop by the career office. How successful have they been in helping students get internships and graduates get jobs?

THANK EVERYONE

Send thank-you notes to everyone you interact with on your visits—especially those you meet on an individual basis (interviewers, professors, financial-aid officers, and so on). A single note is sufficient; there is no reason to send additional notes or gifts. The mother of one of our students once found herself in an admissions office while her daughter was being interviewed. She noticed that the bowl of chocolates she was eating from had beautiful wrappers featuring the school's logo and colors. When she asked the receptionist about them, she was told that an applicant's mother had had them specially made and sent them to an admissions officer. Now here they were, in the corner of a waiting room, being eaten by the mother of a competing student! The chocolates were sweet but the irony was bitter. Blatant attempts to "score points" with admissions personnel are likely either to be ignored or to backfire. A courteous thank-you note, on the other hand, goes a long way. (For a sample thank-you note, see page 217).

Preparing the Activity Chart and Completing the Written Application

8

Overview

In this chapter you'll learn:

- How to complete the activity chart to best convey your accomplishments
- How to prepare an activity chart that highlights—rather than hides—your spike on a college application
- How to avoid the most common activity chart mistakes
- Answers to students' most common questions about completing the written application thoroughly and accurately

The Activity Chart Template

The first section of your college application that we will cover is the activity chart (AC). Think of the AC as your first résumé, a document you will begin creating early in high school and continue to update until you graduate. Your AC is also a "cheat sheet" for the admissions officer reviewing your application—and it has a specific job to do. It needs to briefly summarize everything you've been involved in for four years outside of classes. Most important, it needs to highlight your impressive accomplishments.

Our AC template consists of four main tables and a supplementary section (see page 138 for a sample of the table format):

1. In-School Extracurriculars
   - This category encompasses everything you do in school outside of your classes. French club, tennis team, school newspaper, even your role as a student aide for your Latin teacher: all should be included. Remember, to make your AC truly exceptional, focus on depth, not breadth. Joining high school clubs is easy; becoming a leader and making a concrete contribution to that club, while reinforcing a larger interest, is much more difficult.
     - Sometimes students are incredibly involved outside of school. Does that buy them a free pass to avoid all in-school extracurriculars? Nope. We believe that every student should have at least *some* in-school extracurricular participation (see Chapter 3, "In-School Leadership Activities"), and we feel that it's a red flag to admissions offices if you don't have any at all. Ideally, your participation will involve some leadership positions (but don't worry if it doesn't—colleges need team players as well as leaders).
     - Note our exception: If you are responsible for taking care of a younger sibling, parent, or grandparent, if you or your family is dependent on your employment wages, or if you have some other situation that prevents you from doing extracurriculars, colleges will not expect you to have significant in-school extracurriculars. Just be sure that colleges know about these commitments.

2. Out-of-School Extracurriculars
   - This category includes all extracurriculars in which you participate that do not take place at your high school. Are you involved in a religious or community service organization? Have you participated in a community college course? This is the place to note these activities.
   - This category often includes community service. We believe that community service is important, especially for the most privileged applicants. Many high schools now require community service

"We want you to have fun, as long as it's fun that enhances a college-admission application."

hours. Colleges know that. We recommend that you go above and beyond the minimum community service hours that your high school recommends. Avoid doing community service for the sole purpose of "checking off a box," as that will appear artificial and insincere. Ideally, your community service will reinforce an area of genuine interest. Think of how you can further explore your spike through community service.

3. Summer Experience

- Here's the bad news: admissions officers expect you to do something during your summers besides hanging out and watching TV. In fact, they often look as critically at your

"Summer's coming. How does pre-med camp sound?"

summers as they do at your school year. This doesn't mean
you can simply sign up for a "Teen Tour of Europe" or "Luxury
Vacation with Parents." In general, programs that your parents
purchase for you are likely not very meaningful to college
admissions officers. On the other hand, if they are prestigious
summer programs that strongly reinforce your spike, then they
can be very valuable. (Examples include the RISD Pre-College
Summer Program in Art, the Iowa Writers' Workshop for
creative writing, and the Math Camps at Hampshire College and
Stanford University.) The point is that, if possible, you should
use your summers to expand and deepen your spike. Do research
well in advance to discover programs focused on your area of

interest—or take the entrepreneurial reins and create a program all on your own.

- See Resources (pages 276–88) for a list of highly regarded summer and extracurricular programs in a wide range of areas and topics. It's important to note that admittance to the top programs is very competitive.

4. Employment

- We believe that all work experience—paid or unpaid—is valuable both for college applications and for post-college life. Being part of a team, having responsibilities, and working with people of different backgrounds and levels of education all contribute to a well-rounded student and individual. Employment can also be effective in helping you further explore and add depth to your spike. Get creative in employment; you can launch your own company around your area of interest (for example, Pampered Pooch and PC Senior from Part II of this book) or volunteer at a nonprofit organization or institution (for example, docent at an art museum). There are many real-world ways to explore your passion.

- Recently a Yale admissions officer was asked during an information session what he liked to see students do over the summer. Underscoring the value Yale places on employment, he answered that he likes to see students "pump gas." This quote doesn't necessarily have to be taken literally; nevertheless, colleges do place a high premium on the work ethic and sense of responsibility that holding down a job requires.

5. Supplementary Section: Honors and Awards

- College applications usually include a section for honors and awards. When that is the case, list your honors and awards there. But if an application doesn't have an awards section, list your honors and awards in this section of the activity chart.

Don't be discouraged if, as a freshman, you have few honors and awards. These are typically given during your junior and senior years, and they can encompass everything from a spot on the dean's list to a captain's position on a sports team to a National Merit Scholarship. Some high schools bestow special prizes or awards (for example, Harvard Book Award) on juniors and seniors to commemorate outstanding records. See Resources (pages 275–76) for a list of Web sites of awards and scholarships that you can apply for in the sciences, math, and humanities. These sites will notify you via e-mail of award opportunities based on your grade, interests, background, and so on.

Some points to remember when filling out the activity chart:

- Include one activity per line per table, and don't repeat information. If activities do overlap—as typically happens when you have a job ("Employment") over the summer ("Summer Experience")—choose the category that you feel is the best fit, and/ or in which you have the fewest activities. (For example, if you have nothing listed under Employment, add information to that table first by categorizing the work you did last July as a job rather than as a summer experience.)
- You can, of course, add as many lines to the table as you like.
- List activities in order of importance to you, beginning with the one th*at is most* important and ending with the one that is *least* important. Consider time commitment in your rankings (your most important activity will typically, though not always, be the one in which you invest the most time).

  Note: The AC is an easy and effective way not only to highlight your spike but also to convey the different activities that you participated in to create your area of distinctiveness (see "Burying a Spike" and "Excessive Modesty" below).
- When you are estimating weeks per year, remember that the school year is typically forty weeks long, summer is usually twelve weeks long, and a sports season is usually fifteen weeks long.

- Grammar, punctuation, and spelling matter here as much as in any other part of your application. Have a trusted proofreader review your AC before you submit it.
- For the last column, "Positions Held/Honors Achieved," remember to use words that reflect your commitment, leadership, and responsibility: *elected by, selected for, created, achieved, managed, earned, developed, led, promoted,* and so on. (See "Action Verbs" list on pages 146–47.) Remember to include any and all awards or special designations.
- We recommend starting to fill out your AC early. Freshman year is not too soon (see the appendix "The College Preparation Timeline," pages 252–62). The process of filling out the activity chart is helpful because it:
  - Shows you the areas in which you're lacking in experience (yes, colleges often do expect you to have had a job—paid or unpaid—at some point in high school and to have done something besides "hang out" over the summer).
  - Ensures that you've accurately captured your roles and responsibilities for each activity, each year. Trust us, you won't remember all the details of your sophomore year activities as a senior.
- Your AC must communicate information clearly. The last thing an admissions officer wants is an application she has to work at to interpret or understand.
  - Use concise, easy-to-understand language.
  - Type your AC.
  - Include explanations for any information that is not self-evident (such as what the Amadeus Organization is or what your responsibilities were as an intern at the Wilshire Zoo).
- Most important, don't be afraid to show off, toot your own horn, sing your own praises! Don't lie, but this isn't the place to be subtle or modest. This is your chance to make a case for your candidacy. Make sure your activity chart accurately reflects all that you've accomplished.

Sample Activity Chart*

Name: SS#

IN-SCHOOL EXTRACURRICULARS				
Activity	Years Involved	Hours per Week	Weeks per Year	Positions Held/ Honors Achieved

OUT-OF-SCHOOL EXTRACURRICULARS				
Activity	Years Involved	Hours per Week	Weeks per Year	Positions Held/ Honors Achieved

SUMMER EXPERIENCE				
Activity	Years Involved	Hours per Week	Weeks per Year	Positions Held/ Honors Achieved

EMPLOYMENT				
Activity	Years Involved	Hours per Week	Weeks per Year	Positions Held/ Honors Achieved

HONORS AND AWARDS	
Distinction	Year

*Download the sample activity chart from our Web site: www.entrywayinc.com.

Common Activity Chart Mistakes

Below are the most common mistakes we see in our work with students. Read through our list to avoid these errors as you create your own activity chart.

BURYING A SPIKE

Often students work extremely hard to create distinctive extracurriculars. For example, Amy spent weeks and weeks creating an art show for her local community. Yet, in the first draft of her activity chart, the art show was buried—lumped together with the volunteer work she did at the same location as the show.

Before

OUT-OF-SCHOOL EXTRACURRICULARS				
Activity	Years Involved	Hours per Week	Weeks per Year	Positions Held/ Honors Achieved
Brooklyn Maritime Museum	9, 10, 11, 12	2–20	40	▪ Volunteer and art teacher to less privileged 1st and 2nd graders. ▪ Created Brooklyn Art Show

By listing it under the Maritime Museum heading (because the event took place at the museum), Amy gave her art show far too little emphasis. We advised her to separate the two activities, providing more detail about each and giving her spike the full exposure it deserved. Separating them also let Amy place her volunteer teaching position under "Employment" and her art show under "Out-of-School Extracurriculars" so that neither area was deficient.

After

EMPLOYMENT				
Activity	Years Involved	Hours per Week	Weeks per Year	Positions Held/ Honors Achieved
Brooklyn Maritime Museum— Outreach Art Teacher	9, 10, 11, 12	2–4	40	Art teacher of socio-economically disadvantaged 1st and 2nd graders.

OUT-OF-SCHOOL EXTRACURRICULARS				
Activity	Years Involved	Hours per Week	Weeks per Year	Positions Held/ Honors Achieved
Brooklyn Art Show—a town-wide art show showcasing high school artwork.	11, 12	2–20	20	Creator and Founder. Organized this now annual event. Worked closely with museum administration on all aspects of planning. Please see press clippings for more detail.

EXCESSIVE MODESTY

Don't describe activities in a less than compelling way. Use active, not passive words (see "Action Verbs" on pages 146–47). In the first draft of his AC, Jake provided minimal information on Pampered Pooch and omitted important details about the company:

Before

EMPLOYMENT				
Activity	Years Involved	Hours per Week	Weeks per Year	Positions Held/ Honors Achieved
Pampered Pooch	9, 10, 11, 12	14–20	40	Walk and groom neighborhood dogs.

With the help of added detail, Jake's entrepreneurial business, Pampered Pooch, received its rightful place in the spotlight. Note: don't be afraid to include dollar revenue for entrepreneurial projects; it helps admissions officers gauge the size of the company. If the money you earn is being used for a specific purpose, include that information too.

After

EMPLOYMENT				
Activity	Years Involved	Hours per Week	Weeks per Year	Positions Held/ Honors Achieved
Pampered Pooch–a company that walks and grooms pets	9, 10, 11, 12	14–20	40	Founder and President. Employ two part-time students and generate revenue of over $600 per month. Savings used to fund summer studies in animal behavior.

TOO MUCH INFORMATION!

There *is* such a thing as providing too much information. The AC is a résumé, not a short-answer essay. Be concise and focused in your wording. Daniel participated in his high school's Senior Senator activity. This was one of his few in-school extracurriculars, so he wanted to highlight it by providing lots of detail. Too much detail, however, can be as frustrating as too little.

Before

IN-SCHOOL EXTRACURRICULARS				
Activity	Years Involved	Hours per Week	Weeks per Year	Positions Held/ Honors Achieved
Senior Senator —a 10-year-old program where 18 seniors are trained in social and academic issues in order to teach freshman students and introduce them to the high school community. Matched up with buddies, their progression is followed throughout the year.	12	5–6	22	Selected based on 300-word essay, teacher recommendation, and individual interview. Awarded a statement of recognition at the end of the year. Required to take a pledge to avoid alcohol throughout the year.

We helped Daniel summarize the key points and eliminate irrelevant information. Note: try never to include descriptions that take up more than half a page.

After

IN-SCHOOL EXTRACURRICULARS				
Activity	Years Involved	Hours per Week	Weeks per Year	Positions Held/ Honors Achieved
Senior Senator— selected by teachers and administrators to introduce 9th graders to the high school and mentor them as they navigate academic and social issues.	12	5–6	22	1 of 18 seniors (out of a class of 200) selected based on essay, interview, teaching demonstration, and commitment to being a positive role model.

LAUNDRY LIST

Below is the initial "In-School Extracurriculars" chart that Julie sent us. There's nothing wrong with the activities on it; however, the way it's organized makes Julie look like she's just a jock and buries her non-athletic in-school extracurriculars. Julie wasn't just a jock, and we wanted to make sure her participation on the Student Council and as an Italian Language Aide would shine. We helped Julie consolidate her chart and reorganize it from most important to least important activity.

Before

IN-SCHOOL EXTRACURRICULARS				
Activity	Years Involved	Hours per Week	Weeks per Year	Positions Held/ Honors Achieved
Varsity Tennis Team	11, 12	14–20	15	All-State, 12
Student Council	10, 11, 12	3–15	40	Vice President, 12 Treasurer, 11
JV Tennis Team	9, 10, 11, 12	14–20	15	
Italian Language Aide	11, 12	2	40	
Varsity Swim Team	11, 12	14–20	15	State Semifinalist
JV Swim Team	9, 10	14–20	15	
JV Track Team	9	10–15	15	

By combining sports and reorganizing activities, we helped make Julie's AC more balanced and less focused on sports. We also added detail to help her Student Council and Italian Language Aide activities get noticed. Finally, we deleted JV Track, in which Julie participated for only one year. Most admissions officers would discount this freshman-year activity; it merely took up space on the AC and distracted from her more important activities. Sometimes removing superfluous activities can make an AC *more* compelling.

After

IN-SCHOOL EXTRACURRICULARS				
Activity	Years Involved	Hours per Week	Weeks per Year	Positions Held / Honors Achieved
Student Council	10, 11, 12	3–15	40	Elected Vice President, 12 Treasurer, 11
Tennis Team	9, 10, 11, 12	14–20	15	All State, 12 Varsity, 11, 12 JV, 9, 10
Italian Language Aide	11, 12	2	40	Chosen from a class of 30 to be Language Aide for 9th and 10th grade classes. Responsibilities include grading papers and tutoring students.
Swim Team	9, 10, 11, 12	14–20	15	State Semifinalist, 11, 12 Varsity, 11, 12 JV, 9, 10

To summarize, a good activity chart clearly places your main passions and accomplishments front and center—and doesn't bury them with modest understatement, exhaustive detail, or less-impressive activities. Your AC should reinforce your spike by showing admissions officers which activities mean the most to you, which ones you've given the most effort to, and in which ones you've achieved the greatest distinction.

ACTIVITY CHART UPDATES

Have you earned additional distinctions after your application has been submitted? If so, don't fear that all is lost. Send the admissions office an update (for a sample, see below) highlighting any recent, significant accomplishments. This letter will be included in your file and will also demonstrate your continued interest in the college.

SAMPLE ACTIVITY CHART UPDATE LETTER

To: Top Choice University
     College of Arts and Sciences
     Admissions Office
     17 Smith Street

Re: Chad Davis
     D.O.B. 1/12/1994
     SS: 123-45-6789
     Early Decision candidate

To the Admissions Office:

I recently submitted my application to Top Choice University and I am writing to let you know about a few updates to my résumé:

- I was recently appointed treasurer by the faculty advisor for my school's Model United Nations Congress.
- I was selected as All-League Honorable Mention for my performance this past soccer season.
- Lastly, I was nominated for a NYS Scholarship for Academic Excellence. Three students, in my class of 300 students, received this nomination.

As you know, I am eagerly awaiting news on my early decision application. If I have the honor of attending Top Choice University, I will work to make the University an even more exciting and dynamic place.

Thank you for your consideration.

Yours,

Chad Davis

Action Verbs*

The following verbs will lend an active, powerful tone to the activity descriptions on your activity chart. Compelling language on an application makes for a compelling candidate!

accelerated	computed	established	instructed
accomplished	conceived	estimated	interpreted
achieved	conducted	evaluated	introduced
adapted	constructed	examined	investigated
administered	contracted	exhibited	involved
advised	controlled	expanded	launched
aided	cooperated	expedited	led
allocated	coordinated	explored	lectured
amplified	counseled	extended	listed
analyzed	created	facilitated	maintained
appointed	delegated	focused	managed
approved	demonstrated	founded	observed
arranged	designed	generated	operated
assessed	determined	guided	ordered
assisted	developed	handled	organized
augmented	devised	headed	originated
awarded	devoted	implemented	participated
began	diagrammed	improved	performed
broadened	directed	incorporated	planned
built	displayed	increased	prepared
calculated	distributed	influenced	presented
catalogued	drafted	initiated	preserved
chaired	edited	innovated	processed
compiled	eliminated	installed	produced
completed	employed	instituted	programmed

* Adapted from the Wharton "Guide to Resumes," University of Pennsylvania Career Services Web site: http://www.vpul.upenn.edu/careerservices/wharton/resguide.html#verbs.

proposed	reorganized	set up	taught
proved	represented	simplified	trained
provided	researched	solved	tutored
received	restored	specialized	unified
recommended	reviewed	substituted	volunteered
recorded	revised	suggested	worked
recruited	scheduled	supervised	wrote
reduced	selected	supported	

Completing the Written Application

Although the activity chart and essays (see Chapter 9) may be the most significant parts of the college application and will probably require the lion's share of your time and effort, the other, more mechanical, sections of it are also important and need to be filled out with care. Some of the questions on the application forms—and even which type of form to use—can be confusing. To help you negotiate the potential pitfalls and ensure that you submit clear, legible, error-free applications, below are our answers to our most frequently asked application questions.

WHICH APPLICATION FORM SHOULD I USE?

There are many types of applications, but the most commonly used are the Common Application, the Universal Application, and school-specific applications. Although colleges assure us that they do not prefer one application over another, we typically recommend using the school-specific application for your top-choice college. Although even the Common Application may have a supplement that is specific to that college, using the school's own application still demonstrates a higher level of interest in most cases.

However, in some specific cases we have recommended using the Common Application rather than the college's specific application to a student's top-choice school. For example, after reading the essay questions on both applications, one of our students chose the Common Application because that set of questions allowed her to showcase her talents most effectively. That's a good reason to choose the Common Application.

Note: We don't typically recommend using the Universal Application (UA) over the Common Application. The major difference between them is that the UA doesn't require essays or letters of recommendation—thus leaving you with fewer ways of distinguishing your application.

SHOULD I SUBMIT MY COLLEGE APPLICATION ELECTRONICALLY OR VIA MAIL?

Today, as most college admissions systems are computerized, online usually wins out; however, there is no "right" answer and there are still benefits to using a paper version. Submitting an application online does save admissions offices the time and hassle of scanning each piece of your application into an electronic file system. In fact, some colleges will defer the application fee for those who submit their application online. It is also easier to fill in online applications (if you use the Common Application for multiple colleges, many fields will even auto-populate), and typed data is always neater and easier to read. (Of course, it's okay to hand-write your application, but please use a blue or black no-smudge pen and make sure your handwriting is extremely legible.) Finally, some colleges now encourage—or require—a paperless application for "green" reasons.

Having said that, there are advantages to sending a hard copy. First, you know what you're turning in. Online versions occasionally cause unattractive formatting changes after you press "send." Also, some fields cut off text after a certain character or word count has been reached; if you're not careful, a word or two may be deleted as a result. Finally, with a hard-copy application, it's easy to enclose additional pages—for example, an optional essay, letter of recommendation, or other supplemental materials. Many online applications don't offer an easy way to attach these.

DOES IT MATTER WHAT I WRITE DOWN AS MY PARENTS' JOB?

Sometimes, even the apparently simple process of filling in the data fields (for example, name, address, parents' occupation, parents' education) raises questions for students. We always tell families that their

*"You're moving into a place where all the parents
live well and all the kids test well."*

application may be viewed differently based on their "data fill-ins."
Should you fill in your mother's occupation as "CEO of Large Investment
Bank" or simply as "finance?" Your application will be read differently
if admissions officers believe—based on your parents' professions, your
address, even your high school—that you benefited from significant support during the college application process. (For example, you may have
had SAT tutors, college admissions advisors, or private sport, art, and
music coaches.) That said, if you come from a privileged background,
don't try too hard to camouflage this fact. Your address and high school
alone are revealing. And of course, colleges often target wealthy applicants as a major source of development funds.

WHAT SHOULD I FILL IN FOR "ANTICIPATED MAJOR"?

Don't sweat too much over this question. In most cases, you will not be
held to your answer. If you wish to change your choice once you arrive,
you will be free to do so. At the same time, this question can be a chance

LEARNING TO USE YOUR PARENTS

"I never appreciated nap time when I had it."

The college-application process involves a lot of work, which often peaks just when you're studying for SATs, Subject Tests, and midterms, and busy with your extracurricular activities. For the sake of your sleep—not to mention your sanity—consider enlisting the help of your parents to make the process go more smoothly and ease your workload. Of course, parents are busy too, but in our experience, they are usually happy to devote any time they can spare to helping you.

Some students feel that their parents interfere too much in the admissions process, imposing their frustrated college dreams on their kids. This may be true in a handful of cases, but more often than not, parents genuinely want to help their kids, and their participation does make the process less stressful. This is your chance to guide your parents for a change. Give your parents specific tasks that will help you and save you time while you're studying for finals, pursuing extracurriculars, and prepping for your standardized tests.

Here are some examples of how your parents can help out:

- Registering you for the SATs. Testing registration information is available online (see Resources) and through your high school guidance office.
- Collecting the applications and supplements from each college and putting them in different folders.
- Conducting mock interviews.
- Helping you prep for standardized tests (testing you on vocabulary words, for instance).
- Typing the relevant factual information (employment, address, social security number, and so on) on each application.
- Researching the application requirements for each of the colleges you are considering (such as required or recommended high school classes, Subject Tests, and the like).
- Proofreading essays and applications (if a parent is very detail oriented).
- Sharing feedback on campus visits. Remember that parents have your interests at heart, and they know you really well. Take their views on each college into consideration—but realize that it's ultimately your opinion that counts.
- Scheduling college visits: calling college-admissions offices to inquire about information-session schedules, tours, interview dates, availability of class auditing and overnight stays, directions to campus, and information on where to stay.
- Confirming that your high school has sent all key information to each college on your list (high school transcript, high school profile, letters of recommendation, and so on.) and that your transcript is correct in all details.

(continued on following page)

- Confirming that your colleges received all necessary information and that your file is "complete."

When should you call a college, and when should a parent call? You can have a parent call with questions about scheduling and other factual information. However, the college wants and expects to hear from the student when you are calling about anything else (for example, a specific question for someone in the admissions office).

Of course, the manner in which parents can help will be different for each family. Parents who work full time (and don't, for example, run their own business) may be less able to help. They simply have less flexibility and less time. We've seen significant differences in approach among families. In some families, Mom brought in a spread-sheet with a detailed analysis of at least twenty colleges using at least fifteen variables. In other families, Mom decided that applying to college was the student's sole responsibility and wanted nothing to do with it. Although we hope that parents will offer some help with the college-application process, the relationship between parent and student is different in every family. Establish what works for you—and don't forget to thank your unpaid interns, oops, parents, for everything that they do.

to differentiate your application and support your spike. A few points to consider:

- Some universities (Cornell, Syracuse, and the University of Michigan, for example) require you to apply to a specific school or college within the larger university. At Michigan, for instance, you can apply to the School of Literature, Science and the Arts, the School of Engineering, the School of Architecture, and so on. In this case, you will be held to that decision (although, with some exceptions, you will be able to change anticipated majors within that school once you arrive).

- Don't check off a major just because it is underrepresented at that college. For example, even though Harvard has traditionally had a hard time attracting students to the Classics major, don't declare an interest in it if nothing else in your application supports that choice. Never studied Latin or Greek? No interest in ancient texts? Your choice will appear ill informed.

- Don't choose a prospective major that your grades and standardized test scores can't support. Say you want to be a chemistry major: if your chemistry grades hover around C's and B's and your Subject Test scores are in the low 500s, you may not be able to thrive in college-level chemistry even if you loved the course in high school. Moreover, colleges may question your self-awareness in picking a subject at which you clearly don't excel. (Conversely, if you've taught kindergarteners at a community center for three years and express interest in education, that choice makes sense. Colleges want to see validation for your choice in terms of academics, test scores, and extracurriculars.)

- Finally, a college's standing in different subject areas may differ. Perhaps a university is known for its business courses but is still trying to build up its communications program. In this case, applicants to the business major may be held to a more rigorous standard than applicants to the communications major. Research each college to understand its different strengths and weaknesses.

Finally, we always recommend making one final, holistic review of your application. Read it from cover to cover. Do you feel it truly represents who you are? Is your spike—which you worked so hard on—appropriately showcased? Is any important fact or activity missing? If so, can you provide an optional essay, supplemental item, or letter of recommendation to fill in the gap? Once all of these questions are answered to your satisfaction, you are ready to submit your application.

Essays

Overview

In this chapter you'll learn:

- How to develop an outstanding personal essay
- How to craft winning short-answer essays
- How to use the essays to reinforce your spike
- When to include an optional essay and how to make it effective

Much has been determined by the time you sit down to write your college essays in the summer before your senior year. At that point, there's little you can do to improve your GPA, extracurricular activities, SAT scores, or Subject Test scores significantly. Yet, your college essays give you a chance to demonstrate that you are more than the sum of impersonal grade rankings and test scores. They are your opportunity to show who you are as a person, what your view on life is, what makes you tick.

Most college applications require one or two personal essays and one or two shorter essays. We recommend approaching each type of essay differently.

"Is this the story you want to tell on your college application?"

The Personal Essay

To start, read through the personal essay below.

Question: Please write an essay (250 words minimum) on a topic of your choice. This personal essay helps us become acquainted with you as a person and student, apart from courses, grades, test scores, and other objective data. It will also demonstrate your ability to organize your thoughts and express yourself.

I had been playing the piano ever since my hands were large enough to play a major chord. It was a decision I naturally had no input in whatsoever; I played at the behest of my mother, a classical pianist who had rekindled her love for the piano shortly after I, her fourth and final child, had been born.

Practicing in between lessons was a chore more than anything else. When I was younger, my mother would bribe me with extra dessert or more TV time in order to get me to practice for a measly thirty minutes. As I got older, the pieces I played became more complicated and my practicing more focused; my mother would sit with me to ensure I was playing the right notes and keeping the correct time.

I tried not to let my mother know how much I disliked playing the piano. I wasn't sure what would happen if I told her I wanted to stop, whether the reaction would be anger, disappointment, or resignation. Moments before my mother would pick me up from my lesson, I would say to myself that this would be the day I would tell her I wanted to quit. I would glower as I walked to the car, open the door violently, and look her right in the eye. She, of course, would have a loving look in her eyes and nothing but praise for my diligence.

"It was OK," I would mumble, as I stuffed my face with the Drake's pound cake she put in my lap. The rest of the drive home would be silent. Since I couldn't tell my mother how I felt, my father became my soft shoulder. I would complain endlessly about how I wanted to quit and how I'd rather have time to do more important things, like watch TV or take naps. But he also knew how much the piano meant to my mother and how much she loved that we shared a similar interest. He told me something that as a young child I merely brushed aside but now truly understand. He told me that there would be times when I'd have to do something I didn't particularly like, not just because it was the right thing to do but because it was important to someone who was important to me. Often there are times when we have to make sacrifices, but the personal pain we are forced to endure is small compared to the joy we give to others.

As a young adult, I now better understand what my father was trying to tell me. Sometimes the decisions he spoke of are small, like letting my sister pick what's on television, and sometimes they are big, like switching high schools because my parents felt it would be a better environment for me. And often the things we think are sacrifices turn out to be in our best interest: I'm now a "Laguna Beach" addict, I couldn't be happier at the high school I presently attend, and, all things considered, I'm glad I know how to play Mozart.

After my last piano recital, I went back to sit between my mother and father. My mother told me how proud she was of me and how watching me up there was a true gift I had given her. I smiled. My father put his arm around me. He didn't have to say anything. I knew he was proud of me, but for an entirely different reason.

What makes this a good essay? Is it the student's admission that he hates practicing piano—or that he loves Drake's pound cake? As with any compelling piece of writing, there's something intangible about it that gives you insight into who the writer really is. It doesn't rattle off a résumé of his leadership roles or extracurricular and academic achievements. Rather, it shows you this student *as a person*—a humble, fallible, nap- and dessert-loving teenager who has a close, albeit distinct, relationship with each of his parents. It reveals a person who is capable of self-reflection and understands that sometimes he may not know all the answers.

TOPICS FOR THE PERSONAL ESSAY

Should you write about your spike in this essay? We recommend, quite simply, that you do not. Instead, use the short-answer essays to elaborate on your spike (see "Short-Answer Essays" below). In your longer, personal essay, focus on revealing something about *you*, rather than about your accomplishments. Although there are no hard-and-fast rules for creating a great personal essay, we've tried to outline some simple steps that have worked for many of our students.

STEP 1. SELECT A TOPIC BY BRAINSTORMING A FEW POTENTIAL ESSAY SUBJECTS

Note: In this step, we are assuming that you are completing the Common Application (see pages 147–48) and don't have to answer a specific essay question. If you have to answer a specific question, keep that question in mind as you review Step 1. Even specific questions are often quite open ended.

Most good essay topics have the following in common:

- Whether or not it appears earth shattering to outsiders, the topic is something that has genuinely mattered to the writer.
- The topic and content are unique to the applicant; could a similar essay be submitted by many other applicants?
- The topic is something that has contributed to the writer's growth, maturation, confidence, optimism, hope, and so on.
- The writer is able to focus the topic through at least one very specific incident or anecdote.

Brainstorming Questions:
- How have you changed in the past three or four years?
- Can you identify a particular incident or a funny/terrible day that illustrates the change?
- Who have been the most influential people in your life? The most memorable?

*"Your essay was grammatically correct
but politically incorrect, Arnold."*

"'What I Did on My Summer Vacation,' by special arrangement with the New Jersey State Police."

- What makes you unusual or unique?
- What are you proud of that wasn't covered in any other section of the application?
- When were you able to connect two disparate areas of your life (for instance, school with an outside interest, one class with another, an experience that you read about with something in your own life)?
- Think about a life lesson that rings true to you. What incidents helped you to come to this realization?

There *are* some topics that generally don't make good essays (yes, there are exceptions):

- A topic that's already been clearly explained elsewhere in your application, including anything on your activity chart or award summary, or in your letters of recommendation, and so on.
- Sheer bragging of any kind.
- Political/social/controversial public issues, including world hunger, homelessness, and the environment.

- Trips/events that cost a lot of money (such as summer travel, a luxury vacation, camp).
- A topic that causes the admissions committee to question your judgment, integrity, or ethics.
- A crime, misdemeanor, drunken or sexual experience, or other inappropriate behavior.

PARENTS AND ESSAYS

Parents often love to suggest essay topics—and sometimes even offer to write the first draft (we're not kidding). Not only is this unethical, but this strategy will almost always result in an essay representative of what a forty-five-year-old, not a seventeen-year-old, would want to write about, in both style and substance. Be sure that your essay represents you and your own feelings.

B. Smaller

"My parents didn't write it—they just tweaked it."

- Any kind of cliché (for example, "Practice makes perfect," "Winning isn't everything," "Don't cry over spilled milk," "All's well that ends well," and the like).

STEP 2. DEVELOP YOUR TOPIC INTO A STRONG ESSAY

In general, you want to write about an event that made you see the world, or someone in your world, in a different light. It could be something as simple as listening to a poet recite his or her work, or a conversation with someone whose opinions and beliefs are antithetical to your own. Don't be afraid to write about a low point in your life, but show how it made you stronger. Be specific and use details. Be honest. Write from the heart.

Now that you have a few topics or anecdotes to start with, here's one example of an essay outline that may help you begin. You don't have to use this outline, of course, but following these steps is often a good idea:

1. Open with an intriguing first sentence that draws in the reader.
2. Relate your story or anecdote. Keep it simple and direct, using perfect grammar while maintaining some informality. Don't use words that wouldn't show up in your conversations. Write the story from your perspective, using the first-person "I."
3. Show the reader what you've learned from the anecdote you've chosen. This is the most important part of your essay. Sum up a life lesson in a few sentences.
4. Once you've mentioned what you learned, it's often effective to return to your anecdote, ending the essay with the end of your story.

TIP: Life is confusing. Don't pretend that there is a simple, all-encompassing explanation for—or moral to be drawn from—every situation. Acknowledging that life is complicated is as important as learning from life's experiences.

TIP: Be optimistic in expressing what you've learned. Remember that while sarcasm can contribute to humor, a good roommate (which you want to show you would be) would have a positive outlook on life.

Additional Writing Tips

- "Show, don't tell." Use only a bare minimum of adjectives and adverbs. Employ metaphors and similes whenever possible.
- Use examples and anecdotes to illustrate your ideas.
- Eliminate ALL extraneous words and phrases. Be picky.
- Avoid "life history"–style writing, that is, "First I did this, then I did this…"
- Don't use trite phrases. For example: "I want to help people"; "I learned a lot"; "It was a difficult decision"; "I never give up." *Show* these things through your anecdote.
- Limit quotes from other, more famous people (e.g. Gandhi, Mother Teresa).
- Better to be self-mocking and modest than self-congratulatory or condescending to others.
- Follow directions. If the essay is supposed to be under 250 words, make sure it is!
- Remember that your reader has just sifted through hundreds of other essays. It's important to keep his or her interest.
- Answer the essay question!

See pages 168–79 for a broad range of personal essays gathered from students with whom we've worked.

Short-Answer Essays

In addition to a longer personal essay, most applications (including the Common Application) will also ask you to answer a few short-answer essay questions. Don't assume that just because these essays are short (sometimes as few as 150 words), they don't count. Approach them with as much thoughtfulness as you would your personal essay. Two of the most common short-answer essay questions are:

- The Extracurricular Essay
- Why Do You Want to Attend This College?

SHORT ESSAY #1: THE EXTRACURRICULAR ESSAY (A.K.A. THE SPIKE ESSAY)

This essay question may be worded as follows: "Please briefly elaborate on one of your extracurricular activities or work experiences in the space below, or on an attached sheet" (from the Common Application). This is the ideal space in which to elaborate on your passion, your area of distinction, your spike.

COMMON MISTAKE: REGURGITATING YOUR ACTIVITY CHART

Many students make the mistake of using this essay as an extended version of their activity chart. They will write something like this: "I love playing tennis and was lucky enough to participate in the tennis team throughout high school. I began by playing doubles as a freshman...I became captain senior year." This is a waste of application space. Rather, think of this essay as an opportunity to accomplish three things:

1, **Tell a story, even though it has to be short.** As with any good essay, this one should begin with (or at least include) an anecdote, a point of reference. How did you first become interested in this activity? What led you to create/pursue the extracurricular you want to write about?

2. **Elaborate on your spike.** Although you've undoubtedly engaged in many activities in your area of differentiation, one usually stands out. When did you get the idea to pursue this project? What generated the idea? What steps were required to organize it? What obstacles did you have to overcome in order to bring it to fruition? What plans do you have in place to make sure it continues after you graduate? What do you hope you've accomplished as a result of the project?

3. **Show admissions officers how you would continue to explore your spike in college.** Admissions officers are trying to build a well-rounded freshman class, full of students who bring different passions to campus. They're impressed that you have a serious interest, but what they really care about is how that interest can make their

campus a more vibrant and diverse place. Try to answer these questions: How will you bring your passion to campus? Will it be through an existing organization or a brand-new club? Can your passion best be expressed on campus or through an off-campus organization (one that strengthens ties between the school and community)? There are no right or wrong answers here, but admissions officers do look favorably on students who have done research and thought through these questions.

The final challenge of this essay is that it's extremely short. It's difficult to explain anything in 150–250 words. Be brief and to the point! Although it's hard to get there, most students ultimately realize that their edited, pared-down version is far superior to the wordier first draft.

Obviously, the more space (that is, the greater the word count) you're given, the more you will be able to explore your spike in this essay. If you have the space, you may choose to elaborate on both how your past activities led up to this project and how you hope to continue pursuing this project in college. Providing this context will make it easy for admissions officers to understand the genesis of your passion, the way your activities have built one on the other, and the true depth of your experience in your chosen area.

Note: Even if applications do not ask this short-answer question specifically, you can always include it as an optional essay.

SHORT ESSAY #2: "WHY DO YOU WANT TO ATTEND THIS COLLEGE?"

This type of essay question is often worded in a general way, as follows:

- Tell us what makes Stanford a good school for you.
- Why do you want to attend the University of Chicago?

Common Mistake #1: Not customizing this essay to a specific college and not having specific enough reasons for wanting to attend that college. For example, do you want to attend the University of Miami because of "the amazing weather" or Amherst because you've "always dreamed of attending a small liberal arts college"? Many, many schools fit both of those descriptions; the reasons aren't unique, and the essays won't seem like they've been written specifically for that college.

If you think you can make your life easy by writing one generality-filled essay for all of the colleges on your list, think again. Admissions officers can see right through this generic kind of essay. In fact, more and more colleges are asking this type of short-answer question precisely because they believe that through this essay they can separate the serious applicants from the not-so-serious ones. They are trying to weed out students who submit applications without thinking through why they really want to attend that college.

Common Mistake #2: Reading the question too narrowly. We advise our students that there are two ways of reading this question. The first is literal: Why do you want to come to our college? It's a valid interpretation, but the second is often the more intended reading: Do you understand what makes our campus unique? What will you do to build on and enhance that uniqueness? It's the difference between "What you would get out of our school?" and "What would our school get out of you?" Giving serious thought and answers to each of these questions will help the college determine whether you're a good match for them.

The best way to answer this question is to follow these steps:

1. **Think through the answer from three different perspectives: academic, extracurricular, and social.** No college wants to think of itself merely as an academic experience. Or merely as an extracurricular or social experience, for that matter! Colleges are a combination of the three—and it's this combination that makes them unique and rewarding institutions.

   ■ **Academic questions to brainstorm**: What is academically unique about the school and interesting to you? How do you envision yourself taking advantage of the programs it offers? Which departments and majors are of interest to you? Which professors do you hope to work with? In what internships, study-abroad programs, work-study programs, university "centers," or sponsored summits would you be interested in participating? Are there any courses outside of your specific area of interest in which you would be interested, and how would this cross-disciplinary education enhance your area of academic focus?

Sometimes short essay #2 (Why do you want to attend this college) takes a strictly academic focus. For example, the University of Pennsylvania and the University of Michigan ask the following questions:

- ☐ UPenn offers its undergraduates an eminent faculty and a wealth of research opportunities. Use the space below to name a Penn professor with whom you would like to study or conduct research and explain why.
- ☐ What led you to choose the area(s) of academic interest that you have listed in your application to the University of Michigan? If you are undecided, what areas are you most interested in, and why?

Follow the advice for short essay #2, but focus your answer on academics.

- ■ **Extracurricular questions to brainstorm:** What is unique about the school's extracurriculars? What clubs, organizations, and programs would you like to be part of? How could you continue to pursue your area of interest in college? Would you join existing organizations or found new ones?
- ■ **Social questions to brainstorm:** What is unique about this campus's social life? Meeting people from a wide range of countries, backgrounds, and interests is a privilege and will undoubtedly be an important part of your education. What is unique about this student body? Is there an especially diverse or international population of students? How would you learn from them? What kinds of conversations do you envision having with your roommates? With friends in the dining hall?

2. **Do your research.** The only way to truly answer these questions is to learn about the college. Visit if you can afford to. Stay overnight with a student. Audit a class. If you aren't able to visit, go online. Download the campus paper, check out club sites, and visit online sites to read what the students say about their own school. Admissions offices often provide downloadable videos online or send DVDs about their schools upon request.

3. **Isolate specific and unique reasons for wanting to attend.** Don't fall into the trap of Common Mistake #1. Duke will not be impressed that you want to attend so you can cheer on their basketball team. There are many other Division 1 schools with excellent basketball teams. However, wanting to attend Duke so that you can take classes and work with their nationally ranked economist who specializes in your particular area of interest in economics, is a specific and valid reason.

4. **Show passion.** Colleges want students who are passionate about learning, meeting new people, and creating and building extracurricular programs. Are you excited about learning for learning's sake—or just looking to snag another A on a paper? There's a big difference. Are you excited about long, passionate dining hall debates with roommates and friends from all over the world? Convey your passion and excitement in this essay.

See pages 179–85 for sample short-answer essays.

Optional Essays

If your application reveals a weakness or an inconsistency in your performance, such as an unimpressive "2" on an AP test or low grades vs. high SAT scores, you may be tempted to use your personal essay to address the issue. Although we think it is important for students to provide an explanation for any weakness in their academic record, rather than leaving it up to admissions officers to guess at the reasons, we recommend using the optional essay instead of the personal essay for this purpose. Here are a few tips for writing a convincing optional essay:

1. **Stay positive.** This is not the place to whine and complain. An effective optional essay presents the issue in a mature, constructive, and optimistic tone.

2. **Be thorough.** Were there three compelling reasons why your grades dipped? Spell them out.

3. **Be concise.** Remember, you are asking an admissions officer to read an additional essay. Make sure it is straightforward and succinct.

See sample optional essay on page 186.

Sample Personal Essays

QUESTION: Please write an essay (250 words minimum) on a topic of your choice and attach it to your application before submission. This personal essay helps us become acquainted with you as a person and student, apart from courses, grades, test scores, and other objective data. It will also demonstrate your ability to organize your thoughts and express yourself.

EXAMPLE #1: YESTERDAY'S WINE

My father is wearing his favorite, faded, blue t-shirt. George Jones is singing "Yesterday's Wine" on our old record player. We are all at home together—my dad, my mom, my brother, my sisters and I. Excitedly, I wake up early to the comforting sound of that familiar, thick-voiced southerner rolling from the speakers. I run down the spiral staircase in anticipation of the reassuring good-morning hugs that I know await me. Sure enough, there he is—reading the Saturday *New York Times*, sipping his decaf coffee, and humming along to George. I remember clearly…

"Hmmm, look who it is! Good mornin', darlin'. How's my big girl?" Despite years on the east coast, the curled tone from his Louisiana upbringing is still evident in the greeting that I know so well.

"Good morning, Daddy," I whisper as we hug.

"Are you ready to make breakfast?"

"You bet. I'm hungry."

The blurred vision continues as I see myself propped gingerly on a stool using all my kindergarten strength to whip eggs that would be used for both omelets and banana pancakes. I then cautiously sprinkle grated cheese into the omelet pan like a soft drizzle of rain on an already wet earth. I am Daddy's little helper, being taught perfection through food. The sweet smell of bananas and butter cooking eventually drifts through the bedroom door cracks. Mom, Shannon, Rob, Ashley, and any teenage friends who found their way to our house the night before, hurriedly descend the staircase, ready to feast. The vision ends with a crowded kitchen filled with family, friends, food and love. It is the warmest and richest of places. What we said and who joined us might have changed weekly. But, there was always George, there was always that t-shirt, and there was always that feeling, the one that only being together with my entire family gives me.

Those childhood breakfasts aren't possible anymore. One by one they left home—first Shannon, then Rob, then Ashley—each leaving in impassioned pursuit of his or her dreams. Selfishly, part of me always wanted them to stay. In the last decade I have cheered at college football and soccer games and graduations, been a flower girl and a maid of honor in weddings, become an aunt three times, and helped my brother open his new restaurant. Remodeling has replaced the warm, wood butcher's block, where I once beat eggs like a pro, with a cold marble slab. It's a perfect spot to throw my bookbag. Breakfast now is grabbed on the run. Mom travels. Dad travels. I travel. Sometimes, we travel together. Our old record player was thrown out and has been replaced by the latest CD equipment. Dad did keep his promise to replace all our albums with discs, but he seldom plays George anymore. Life is different.

Untimely birth. There was no warning of the emotional solitude I would feel being ten, twelve, and sixteen years younger than my brother and sisters, and left to be an only child at seven years of age. Nothing prepared me for how quiet our house would become. In some ways, I feel that time has changed everyone but me. At sixteen, I am still that little girl on Saturday mornings, intensely whipping eggs and anxiously waiting for the first bite of my banana pancakes. I wonder: can I still taste the sweetness of the banana and butter?

Perhaps tonight I will pop George into my CD player. Perhaps I will dream of snuggling up to my Dad in that soft, faded t-shirt. Perhaps tonight I will accept that I too am "aging with time, like yesterday's wine."

COMMENTS: In this accomplished student's beautifully written essay, we learn about her family background. There is wistfulness for earlier times, but also a maturity and an acceptance of how time changes situations. The strength of the essay is in its evocative descriptions. We can see her in the kitchen as a younger girl whipping eggs, we can smell the bananas and butter sizzling in the pan, we can feel the softness of her dad's shirt and we can hear her father's Louisiana accent and the twang of the music playing in the background. Through these descriptions we get a better sense of the person she is.

EXAMPLE #2: CONSTRUCTION

"Solamente una mujer, no cerveza, y necesita una educación." It means "a man can only have one woman, no beer, and an education is necessary." This is just one of Walter's many philosophies. This summer, Walter was not only my partner for work, but my teacher.

He picks me up at 5:30 AM in a red pick-up truck. One of his worn, torn, dirt encrusted hands is on the wheel, and the other is holding his large island-decorated coffee mug. He is muscular and tan from all the years working outside. This morning is Walter's anniversary of leaving Costa Rica, and coming to America. At one point on his journey to the United States, he was packed into a mini-van with thirty other people for a six hour drive. When I ask him which place he likes better, he immediately responds "Los Estados Unidos." He says it's "mas limpia," more clean, and has "mas dinero," more money. Back in Costa Rica he would work the same twelve and a half hour day to earn what he makes here in an hour. "Most guys come here to make money, and go home quick," Walter adds. "But I like it here. I like the money, and I like the country. It was easier by myself, but now I need to work all the time, because of my family, but they are more than worth it." I think of my family too. I believe that working for my family will always be worth it.

Once at the construction site, I immediately see a deep trench. Our job is to put the pipe in it and fill the trench back up evenly with stone. Walter hands me the shovel and says, "OK, Brad, este dia, esto es su computadora," meaning "today this is your computer." Walter digs in rhythmically. It is eighty-five degrees today, and humid. I keep up for a good hour, thinking that I am in pretty good shape, but eventually my lower back begins to ache, but Walter keeps moving rapidly. The wet mud from the trench oozes into and all over my boots. I develop bad blisters, but remember Walter's callused hands.

"Whoa, I'm tired" I finally say to Walter who casually wipes the sweat from his brow, but shows no sign of fatigue.

"Brad, but you're young, I am old and not that tired."

"Walter, you're only about thirty and you're una maquina (a machine)."

When the day ends at seven-thirty, I look back at the house, feeling satisfied. Walter and I are drenched in sweat, but our job is complete. We jump in the truck and drive off, listening to Spanish radio. At the final light before my house, Walter tells me in half Spanish and broken English, "Brad, when you have the chance to work, take it, because we will never know what will happen in the future." Our eye contact lasts for an extra ten seconds. That's how it is with Walter. There's no need for words, just action and understanding. He pulls up to my driveway; I jump out of the car, look back at the diligent worker's gentle, worn face, and say "adios mi amigo." Taking off the dirty construction boots, I fall into bed, savoring the feeling of my hard day's work and knowing that Walter's lessons of work ethic, opportunity, and family will last a lifetime.

COMMENTS: This essay shows us that the student understands the value of hard work and has great respect for the people with whom he has worked. We learn about his understanding of, and admiration for, Walter's philosophy and even his desire to emulate some of Walter's values when he has a family of his own. These lessons are sensitively told against the backdrop of one day in the student's job as a construction worker. The essay flows beautifully and his use of Spanish dialogue is sensitive and insightful. We sense that the rest of this student's life must be frenetic, which makes the contrast even more effective. At the end of this essay, we feel as if we know him.

EXAMPLE #3: SAMANTHA

On Wednesdays I volunteer at the Springfield Day Care Center and, like a magnet, Samantha always searches me out. She sits on my lap through snack and story time, holds my hand when we go outside and asks me to lie beside her during nap. I've heard the teachers whisper about her parents' terrible divorce, the boyfriend who lives at her house, her mother who is always late for pickup. Even though I always try to encourage Samantha to be more independent and form friendships with the other children, I do love my ability to comfort and soothe her.

It didn't take me too long to figure out why Samantha and I connected. Although many aspects of my life seem perfectly normal from the outside, a brief peek will reveal that my life is far from normal. Samantha's fear of the unknown and struggle to understand the exact reason things happen in her life was familiar to me. Last week I came home to find all the contents of my desk—my chemistry notes, my college folders, my computer—thrown across my bedroom floor. When I was younger, the attacks were more physical. I'll never forget how he once cornered me at home—when my mom's back was turned, when my dad was out of the room—whispering awful things in my ear and punching my face. The next morning I woke up with the bruises and the pain, horrified at the black and blue marks. What would I say to friends and teachers? I was so ashamed that my older brother had done something like this to me.

My older brother has been diagnosed with so many disorders I've completely lost count: ADHD, Bipolar Disorder, Defiance Disorder, Manic Episodes, Clinical Depression. The list rolls off my tongue. Yet there is still no way to categorize the feeling of living life on a rollercoaster: climbing slowly up, everything seeming to be progressing fine, when all of a sudden, the floor drops out and everything comes crashing down.

And yet through it all, I've tried to be there for my brother. Comfort him. Defend him. Justify and rationalize his actions to my parents. Fight for him to stay in our home. Try to heal him, although I've long since learned that's far from possible.

It's almost time for pickup at the Springfield Day Care Center and Samantha has once again found my lap. For once, I stop encouraging her to be more independent. She rubs her hair into my neck and I fold my arms around her. We'll try again next week.

COMMENTS: A powerful and deeply personal essay about a student's troubled relationship with her brother. The images from the essay stay with the reader—the scenes from the day-care center, the black-and-blue marks the next morning, the precipitous drop of the rollercoaster. The essay also demonstrates the student's maturity, as most family problems do not have clear-cut solutions. Finally, the essay reveals that the student loves working with children, which reinforces the fact that she hopes to study early childhood psychology and development in college.

EXAMPLE # 4: NOTHING GOLD CAN STAY

"Nothing gold can stay," says Robert Frost in his famous poem of the same name. On a Wednesday after school, I was teaching it to a group of students at the East Harlem School. "Nothing Gold Can Stay" is one of my favorite poems; it's bleak, it's dark, it's pithy…it's perfect. I'm not a pessimist, but cynicism comes easily to me; I'm from New York City, after all. However, that day, one of my students raised his hand and forever changed my perspective. Jamal called out, "Miss Anna! If nothing *gold* can stay, then nothing *bad* can stay either." I was floored, not only because Jamal's interpretation of this poem was one I had never even considered, but also because of his unwavering optimism, his fearlessness in connecting to the poem on a personal level. "That's a really great point, Jamal," I responded calmly, "I have never thought of it that way." Jamal heard the encouragement in my voice. I concealed the awe.

As an avid reader and an eager student of both Spanish and Italian, I have always been fascinated by language and words. I tear through and delve into poems, marveling at the technique. On more than one occasion I've run to my Spanish teacher asking for English translations of "por eso" and "puesto que"; sometimes, the Spanish phrase just works better. I love the subtlety of grammar, the nuance of verb choice. Reading poetry now, I see how easily I get lost in the symbolism, the alliteration, the allusion. I realize now that focusing on the poetic devices is easier than internalizing the poems, assuming that "nothing gold can stay"—that all happiness is fleeting—is easier than having my expectations crushed.

In his innocence, Jamal wasn't bogged down by technicalities or self-consciousness. Unlike me, he took the words and immediately absorbed them, applied them to his own life. Though Jamal understood the metaphor "nothing gold can stay," he saw beyond it. While I distracted myself with Frost's usage of nature metaphors and paradoxes, Jamal took the risk. While I planned to point out Frost's biblical reference, Jamal connected with the poem on a personal level. I planned to explain how Frost expressed his gloom. Jamal found optimism in the gloom.

Though I remain a staunch cynic—or as I like to say, a committed realist—Jamal has stuck with me. Sometimes when I find myself complaining that there is no way the movie will be as good as the book, that reality television is ruining my generation, that the airline will definitely lose my luggage, I think of Jamal and a sliver of optimism sneaks through. When I read a poem and go directly to Yeats' rhyme scheme or to Ferlinghetti's word order, I pause and think of Jamal. What does the poem mean to *me?*

COMMENTS: This student writes a poignant story about teaching poetry to a group of socio-economically disadvantaged children. Although she is able to be quite analytical about what she loves—words, poetry, literature—what's so insightful is her understanding that, despite all her studying, learning, reading, analyzing, and so forth, she has much to learn from the students she teaches. As she was applying to the most competitive colleges, it's particularly important that she shows the way her mind works—how she analyzes Frost's metaphors and paradoxes, how she is able to relate one part of her life to another, and how she is able to value what one middle school student sees, and apply it to her own views.

EXAMPLE #5: FRANK O'HARA

There's nothing worse than feeling bad and not being able to tell you. Not because you'd kill me or it would kill you, or we don't love each other. It's space.

I put the book down, blood rushing through the chambers of my heart at an incalculable rate. My breath came in hiccups and gasps. After taking a second, I picked up the book by its glossy spine, found my page again—page 224—and continued to read. It was only when I finished that I realized I hadn't been breathing while I read, but instead had been chewing on my lip, almost in fear of the sublime text on the page. Each phrase had felt like it had been chosen specifically for me. At that moment, I fell in love with a dead poet.

My English teacher had mentioned Frank O'Hara in passing while discussing what she had done that weekend.

"Oh, nothing special. Graded your papers, saw my mom, read some Frank O'Hara."

I will never know exactly why the name caught my attention. True, I was a closet fan of poetry, but my range only encompassed the traditional and generic: Shakespeare, Dickinson, Whitman, and so on. I was helplessly intrigued and asked her about him after class. Pointing to her volume of his collected works on her bookshelf, she offered to lend it to me. But after all, people were watching, and borrowing poetry books from your teacher is not a way to look like an aloof and cool freshman. So I silently decided to come back later. Within a week I had read the book cover to cover. I became a boy possessed; everywhere I went I saw O'Hara's words. Of course this storm of obsession subsided into a gentle wind after a month or two.

By reading his words more carefully, I was able to examine myself as a person, as a poet, as a gay male, as a teenager, as everything he had been and more. Soon, not only what he said fascinated me, but also what he didn't say—the spaces between stanzas, the arrangement of phrases into staggered lines, even the titles held my attention in a vise-like grip.

I began to see connections between the themes O'Hara explicated and other aspects of my life. The spaces that I had found so enthralling in his poems manifested themselves not only in my own writing, but through other lenses. In my photography classes, I began to try and take pictures of what wasn't there, focusing on the more subtle aspects of the art. Frank's hands guided me as I manipulated shadow, light; sharp contrast and ominous blurs waged war on my prints.

Today, as I pick up my camera, I can feel Frank O'Hara's lines of verse pulling my lens, guiding me through the superfluous and to my target—

I observe a heart tangled in the lines of my verse, as in those surrealist paintings where an object wails of intended magnificence

—Click.

COMMENTS: In this essay, we are exposed to the thoughts of a student who is obviously a very deep thinker. His essay explains the significant impact the poet Frank O'Hara has had on him. In the process, he reveals himself—as a person, student, poet, and budding intellectual—to the reader. He also shows us how this impact has spread to other parts of his life—to his photography, for example. One cannot doubt the significant contribution this student will make in his college classes.

EXAMPLE #6: SAM AND CYCLOPS

The dog was beautiful, a Golden Retriever, but with a reddish sheen that's rarely found in the popular breed. Unlike some of the other animals that entered the ward, this dog, Sam, didn't pull away from me, whine or claw at the speckled yellow linoleum. He looked right at my face and licked my hand. He appeared so sure of himself that I was inclined to believe him—of course he would be fine! I looked forward to leading him out to the waiting room the same way he had entered; with his tail wagging, tongue lolling out of the side of his mouth. I even imagined a quizzical yet calm curiosity in his eyes—it was as if he was asking me what was going to happen and trusting that I would keep him safe.

An hour later when I saw him, legs splayed, on the steel operating table, I couldn't help but remember how he had looked while trotting by my side. Even though I had witnessed the operation from anesthesia to conclusion, I still wasn't sure that somehow, someone hadn't played a trick on me. There was no way that this prone form belonged to the same russet dog that I had caressed. I even managed to remain detached when the vet called Sam's owner. I only heard snatches of the conversation, but it was enough to realize what was going on. "Cancer"…"metastasis"…"I'm sorry"… Somehow, I kept calm as I placed the vial of barbiturates into the surgeon's gloved hand. As he injected the fluid into Sam's IV, I struggled to maintain the fantasy that the scene in front of me was not real. There was no way this dog was going to die.

Despite attempts at deluding myself, I soon realized that what had happened was real, that there was nothing I could do. As soon as the black plastic garbage bag closed, the floodgates opened. I choked back my tears as I wiped the operating room table clean.

When I decided to intern at an animal hospital for the summer, I knew that eventually I would have to deal with a situation like this. I had even anticipated my emotional reaction to it.

So I was prepared, at least mentally, for what happened on that day. I was not surprised by my sadness or even by its intensity, but I wasn't ready for the anger, frustration, and feeling of sheer helplessness and uselessness that followed. Initially, my tears were purely a response to the unexpected euthanasia of an animal, but I realized that I was also mourning the loss of an illusion.

No matter what anyone did, Sam died. Looking back, I suppose that my expectations were naïve, but on some level I had expected the diploma on the wall that read "DMV" to magically cure Sam's cancer. It was painful to realize that no matter how many diplomas you have or how many years you spend studying, there are some things that will always be beyond your control.

After I had cleaned the table, I went to check on the gray kitten in the corner cage. I called him Cyclops. He had been found lying half-dead in a construction site, and the sun and sand had caused an ulcer that cost him the sight in his right eye. He was also found to be FIV positive, infected with a feline variant of the HIV virus. In spite of his condition, a few weeks under the care of the vets had turned him into a sleek, energetic, naughty cat. When he jumped onto my shoulder and batted his paws at my ponytail, I was heartened. For every Sam, there's a Cyclops.

COMMENTS: What we notice first in this essay is the writer's optimistic yet maturely realistic view of life: "For every Sam, there's a Cyclops." Against the backdrop of her summer internship at an animal hospital, we learn how she becomes emotionally involved with the animals, and yet is able to stand back and view the larger picture. Her descriptive abilities are beautifully displayed in this essay. This student went on to Yale and is presently in veterinary school, fulfilling her ambitious dream.

Sample Short-Answer Essays: "Most Important Extracurricular"

QUESTION: Please briefly elaborate on one of your extracurricular activities or work experiences in the space below or on an attached sheet (150-word limit).

EXAMPLE #1

I have always loved fashion. I've also loved teaching young children. Since freshman year, I've worked with kindergarteners at the local Jewish Community Center in an after-school program. During my junior year, I observed the way the children loved to dress up. I decided that I wanted to see if they also behaved differently when they dressed up. After getting permission from the JCC and parents, I began collecting items such as scarves, glasses, boas, and blow-up guitars. I brought in these items and observed each of the children as they dressed up; many danced, sang, or impersonated their favorite rock star or superhero. After taking pictures and writing anecdotes, I created a booklet titled "Dress Up and Discover" (please see enclosed). I hope to repeat this project in early December at the JCC with a new group of children and continue to study early childhood behavior in college.

COMMENTS: This student describes a unique program she developed, based on her own interests and strengths. An admissions officer reading this essay would see the student's focus and leadership qualities. He would be impressed by the fact that she started with a small step (observing children dressing up), found a way to combine her love of fashion and teaching young children, and developed an unusual project based on her intended college major (early childhood behavior).

EXAMPLE #2

I have always been interested in cooking. Today, I'm a Food Network addict, chef to my family, and have even taken cooking classes (a fact I don't often reveal, as it sets expectations too high). As a varsity athlete I understand the importance of eating right. That's why I created Sam's Smart Snacks, workshops to help kids learn that healthy cooking is fun and delicious. In addition to educating kids about the benefits of healthy food, my cooking workshops also incorporate age appropriate math concepts, such as halving and doubling ingredients. Today, these workshops take place at the Indian Hill Children's Center in Cincinnati, Ohio. I recently won a grant to expand my workshops, am teaching other teens at my high school the Smart Snack curriculum, and in college, plan to bring Smart Snacks to a local day care program, all to ensure that Smart Snacks continues once I graduate.

COMMENTS: In a mere 150 words, this short essay communicates a tremendous amount about the student. Sam's dual interest in food and athletics inspired him to create an entrepreneurial community service program (with a catchy name). These activities, layered upon each other, create an application that clearly spikes. Sam points out the primary and secondary benefits of the program: it not only teaches disadvantaged kids how to cook healthy snacks but also reinforces basic math skills. In addition, he's figured out a way to expand the program and make sure that it will continue after he graduates. Finally, the student's lightly humorous writing style conveys that he will probably make a great roommate and be a welcome addition to a college campus.

Sample Short-Answer Essays: "Why Do You Want to Attend This College?"

EXAMPLE #1

QUESTION: Describe your intellectual interests, their evolution, and what makes them exciting to you. Tell us how you will utilize the academic programs in the College of Arts and Sciences to further explore your interests, intended major, or field of study (Cornell).

As a sophomore I read the book "The World Is Flat," by Thomas Friedman, and it changed the way I viewed the world. I began to understand that our continents have become increasingly interconnected due to globalization and technological advancements, resulting in practices such as outsourcing. Today's global financial crisis makes our underlying connectivity even more clear. Consequently, I learned it is not enough to understand our own country, language, and culture; we must also understand the history, cultures, and customs of others. At the same time, I have seen nationalistic barriers continually being erected and ongoing conflict in various regions of the world. This dichotomy has led me to realize that historical understanding and appreciation are vital.

Because of this realization, I hope to major in History at Cornell. I don't yet know my specific focus, but I am excited by the vast array of classes offered. I would love the opportunity to study with eminent Professors such as Duane Corpis and to take his course discussing Western Civilization and its developments in technology, economy, politics, and social ideals. Additionally, I would like to study the history of Asia with Professor Sherman Cochran, whom I had the opportunity to hear lecturing during one of my many visits to Cornell. I was fascinated by his interpretation of imperialism and of modernization as a political ideology. After class, I approached Professor Cochran. We discussed not only his course and the History department, but also the vast academic resources offered to Cornell students. While this conversation reaffirmed how much there is to take advantage of at Cornell, what most impressed me was the way Professor Cochran made himself accessible to me, a prospective student.

I also hope to take advantage of the Mario Einaudi Center for International Studies. I am fascinated with Western Europe and want to understand the region from an interdisciplinary perspective, appreciating its language, culture, and customs. Through the Institute for European Studies I would love to research and learn with both Cornell faculty and distinguished visiting scholars. I am excited at the prospect of participating in the programs the Institute sponsors, including lectures, seminars, and study abroad opportunities.

Finally, I hope to take full advantage of the College of Arts and Sciences and take cross-disciplinary courses. I would love to take International Relations and American Foreign Policy in the Government department as well as International Economics and China's and India's Growth Miracles in the Economics department. I know I will be able to apply historical insights to these courses and likewise allow these courses to influence my understanding of history.

After college, I hope to continue my quest to understand countries and customs, perhaps as a member of the Foreign Service, continuing to live in, appreciate, and negotiate cultures in a world that seems to be increasingly connected, yet fragmented. Ultimately, I hope to use my education to create ties between disparate cultures and foster understanding.

COMMENTS: In this essay, the student has made it abundantly clear why he wants to study not just history, but history at Cornell. We learn why he is interested in history, how his interest has evolved, and the extensive research he has done into Cornell and its specific courses and professors.

The admissions office will recognize that this student understands exactly why and how Cornell is a great fit for him and how he will contribute to the college.

EXAMPLE #2

QUESTION: What led you to choose the area(s) of academic interest that you have listed in your application to the University of Michigan?

I always hated movie previews. I saw them as tedious messages, delaying the start of the movie that I was dying to see. However, as I got older, I started to pay more attention to these advertisements. I was intrigued by the methods a company used in order to promote their product. Was it through racing a split second car chase or an ominous voice over a quiet, serene backdrop? I then realized that everywhere I looked—the insides of shipping boxes, dry cleaning bags, sidewalks, taxicabs, the actual content of movies—there were advertisements. These advertisements tried to influence me to buy certain products in increasingly subtle and persuasive ways. In order to simply remain impartial, I had to become a skeptical consumer.

I can't think of a better place to study this exchange between brands and individuals than as a Communication Studies major in the College of Literature, Science and the Arts. The Communication Studies program will enable me to gain a thorough understanding of mass communication—its creation, dissemination, and reception—while still receiving a strong liberal arts education. Although I want to pursue communications over the long term, I feel that a liberal arts education is extremely important. It will allow me to think, analyze, and explore fields outside of communications, permitting me to bring greater understanding back into my major.

The University of Michigan's Communication major is also distinctive in that it does not have specific public relations or advertising courses. I love that the teaching is more theoretical, focused on how to think rather than how to execute a specific skill set. This combines perfectly with the department's emphasis on real-world internships for practical experience. In particular, I would love to work with Professor Brad Bushman. His research on the causes and consequences of human aggression challenges many societal myths. One of his papers, entitled "The Effects of Media Violence on Society," was fascinating; it proves that media violence does in fact lead to greater societal violence. I would also love to take Bushman's class, Media Process & Effects, which introduces research on mass communication processes and effects from the perspective of the social sciences. The University of Michigan's Communication Studies major will help me better understand mass communications and reach my goal of becoming a professional in the communications industry.

COMMENTS: This student has thoroughly researched her desired major, Communications, at the University of Michigan. She shows the Admissions Committee that she understands how the University of Michigan's Communications major differs from that of other schools. She also points out that this major is found within Michigan's College of Literature, Science and the Arts, affording her a broader area of study than just communications. She has also thoroughly researched professors and courses and shows how she is clearly a good fit for the school.

EXAMPLE #3

QUESTION: What led you to choose the area(s) of academic interest that you have listed in your application to the University of Michigan?

A career in science had never crossed my mind. Even with seven physicians in my immediate family, medicine was never a consideration. As a young child, "What do you want to be when you grow up?" would be fielded with ever-changing answers: an artist, an illustrator of children's books, a ballerina, a lawyer, a writer. "A scientist" or "a doctor" never made the list.

But in my freshman year of high school, everything changed. Science was no longer just another subject in school. It became my life. Every aspect of biology—the molecular basis of inheritance, the function and physiology of the human body, evolution—all seemed to be inextricably linked to our lives, and so biology became indelibly ingrained in my thought processes. Biology was suddenly a constantly growing, evolving entity; headlines such as "A new enzyme is discovered," "A DNA sequence is linked to a sleep disorder," "Successful exchange between artificial and natural amino acids" began to catch my attention.

Every summer since I took that first biology course, I have conducted medical research to further my exploration of science. Not only has my research expanded my knowledge, it has exposed me to the realm of clinical research and medicine. Knowing that my work could have a profound effect on others, that my discoveries could impact the course of a treatment or influence someone's understanding, made my work seem all the more invaluable.

I'm excited to continue my research at the University of Michigan's school of Literature Science and the Arts. Having the chance to study with Professor Landor and learn more about her research into fruit flies would be an unparalleled experience. Working on Professor Ambran's research study on diabetes as well as taking his class titled Biotechnology and Society would also teach me so much.

Science is not just another subject in school. It is not just a subject that fascinates me. It is a field that affects our world, and I can think of no better place to study biology than the University of Michigan. So the next time anybody asks what I want to be when I grow up, you bet I will have my answer ready.

COMMENTS: In this essay we get a sense not only of this student's very impressive intellectual capacity, but also of her passion for science. We understand why she loves scientific research and why she wants to continue to study it at Michigan. We also see how hard she has has worked in different labs, even using her summers to deepen her knowledge.

Sample Optional Essay: When GPA Is Significantly Lower than SAT Scores

I believe that my application presents an engaged and dedicated student, but there is one element I feel needs clarification. There is a large gap between my cumulative GPA and my SAT scores.

From kindergarten through eighth grade I attended a small, private, all-boys school. As a result, I became used to a certain type of system and was able to do well in my classes without a lot of effort. When I arrived at American High School, I was not mentally prepared for the differences between middle school and high school; I became over-involved in extracurriculars and mistakenly thought that I could do well in classes without putting in much effort. As a result, my grades were lower than they should have been.

Another contributing factor to my relatively low GPA is the fact that American High School does not have grade inflation. As you can see from our High School Profile, our grades are curved around a "C" rather than a "B," as at many other high schools. I worked hard for the more recent grades that I received, even if they do not initially appear as such on paper.

For these reasons, I hope you will consider my GPA in light of American High School's grading system and my SAT scores, as well as my extracurricular and employment experience. I truly hope I have the chance to attend Top Choice University.

Letters of Recommendation

Overview

In this chapter you'll learn:

- Whom to ask for letters of recommendation
- How and when to ask your teachers for recommendations
- How to approach non-teacher recommendations (that is, from employers, alumni, guidance counselors, peers, and others)
- How letters of recommendation can reinforce your "be alike but spike" strategy

Recommendations: Myths and Truths

The most common question we get about letters of recommendation is, "Does it help to have more than the required number?" This question is asked primarily by parents, and the answer is invariably no. Unless there is a good reason to include additional letters of recommendation, straying from the application guidelines will hurt, not help. Besides, there's an old maxim in college admissions: "The thicker the kid, the thicker the application file." Piling on the recommendations looks like overcompensation, and usually is. We once worked with a father who wanted *all* of his daughter's teachers to write recommendations for her, as he had no doubt that she was the most brilliant student in the history of the school.

We assured him that a standard-sized sampling of their glowing testimonials would do just fine.

Recommendations: Things to Keep in Mind

- **Letters of recommendation should show that you are as qualified as other applicants who have applied to that college.** The parameters here may vary, depending on the college and its degree of competitiveness. At the very top schools, admissions officers may actually *expect* to read phrases such as "In my 25 years of teaching English, John is one of only 3 or 4 students who belong in this esteemed category of students," whereas at less competitive schools, being in the top third or half of all graduating students is considered an esteemed category.

- **Letters of recommendation should reinforce and verify your spike.** How can your teacher reinforce your spike? Choose one who knows you well and can include stories or anecdotes that illustrate how you are special and distinctive. Has your teacher worked with you on extracurricular activities—coached you in ice hockey, directed you in school plays? Can she back up your claim that you independently created and organized a charity orchestra recital while leading study sessions to help fellow students with the Chemistry Subject Test? Approach that teacher for a recommendation and politely ask that she mention your extracurriculars as well as your in-class work. Although you should proudly present your accomplishments on your applications (for example, on your activity chart and in your short-answer essay questions, as well as through supplemental materials), having a teacher gush about your accomplishments is even better.

- **Don't take recommendations lightly.** Many admissions officers feel that the recommendation is among the most important aspects of the college application. In most instances it is immodest to boast about yourself, but a recommendation provides a perfect opportunity for others to boast about you. Colleges also use recommendations to compare you to other applicants. Not every student can be "outstanding" (top 10 percent) or "one of the best I have taught in my career." The recommendation also allows them to assess characteristics they cannot determine simply by looking at transcripts. Is the student creative and intellectually engaged or just a grinder or grade grubber? Does the student help other students learn? How does the student contribute in class? These questions are all vitally important to admissions officers and can only really be addressed through the recommendation.

- **A bland recommendation can hurt you.** In our culture of not saying bad things about other people, a neutral recommendation can be interpreted as unfavorable (otherwise known as "damning with faint praise"). These recommendations are far more common than poor recommendations. A bland recommendation calls into question many aspects of a student's application, as well as how accurately the student assesses herself and her relationships with her teachers. Evidence has shown us that a bland or bad recommendation will often get a student rejected at the most competitive colleges.

Guidelines: Whom Should I Ask?

- Choose teachers who know you very well. In other words, teachers you've had for multiple classes, worked with on extracurricular activities as well as classes, or sought out for extra discussion after class. Make sure these teachers know you both as a student and as a person.
- Choose teachers whom you like and who like you, too.
- Choose teachers who write well. One tip is to ask graduating seniors which recommenders have helped students gain admission to the schools they hope to attend.
- Don't choose teachers who worked with you only in freshman or sophomore year. This suggests that you didn't have anyone to ask

from your junior or senior year. An exception would be asking a teacher you had in your sophomore year and will have again in senior year.

- Try to create variety in your choices (unless you're applying to a school with a specific focus, such as engineering, in which case you'll ideally want recommendations from a math teacher and a chemistry teacher). For a liberal arts college, you should ideally have one recommender from math or science and one from the humanities. Your math/science recommender can address your quantitative and analytic abilities, while your English or history teacher can evaluate your writing ability. Also, if you are planning to major in the humanities, make sure you have a recommender to support your strengths in that area. Don't choose a teacher from an elective subject, unless that elective is your anticipated college major.

VIEWING YOUR LETTERS OF RECOMMENDATION

Officially (that is, on the recommendation portion of your college application), students should always "waive" their right to view their letters of recommendation. If you don't, colleges will not view your recommendations as honest assessments of your abilities. *Unofficially,* however, many candidates are shown their letters of recommendation. (Some students even share their letters of recommendation with us. See three examples on pages 197–202.) If you are not shown your letters of recommendation, however, don't despair. In fact, some high schools have strict policies against students viewing their recommendations, whereas other high schools encourage teachers to share recommendations with their students. You should not ask to see them. If you feel you need to see the recommendation, you've probably asked the wrong person.

- Consider where the recommender went to college. Teachers who graduated from a school comparable in quality to the one you're hoping to attend may be best situated to write you a recommendation.
- Has a teacher asked you about writing a letter of recommendation? The best recommendations will come from teachers who volunteer for the task!

How to Ask Teachers for a Recommendation

- **Lay the groundwork.** The "wooing process" for recommenders should begin months before you need the letter of recommendation. We don't mean that you have to bring your potential recommenders shiny apples every day, but we do mean that you need to get to know these teachers, approach them for help whenever necessary, and make an effort to be a dynamic presence in their classrooms. It's not enough to be a charming, personable student who doesn't engage with the class material, or a brilliant student who never interacts with the teacher. You want recommenders to know you, and like you, as both a student and a person.
- **Approach them early.** Let teachers know in the spring of your junior year that you hope you can ask for a recommendation in the fall.
- **Give them a chance to say no.** They may seem hesitant. Or ask you if you've considered other teachers. Or tell you that they are busy now, but if you come back in the fall … all of these are subtle (and not so subtle) ways of letting you know you should look elsewhere.
- **Most important, come prepared.** First, schedule a short meeting. Bring your activity chart (see Chapter 8) to the discussion. Be sure to let the teacher know what you have done both in and out of class, as you hope that both will be addressed in the recommendation. If appropriate, you might come with a few past papers or an exam on which you did really well. You might even share specific stories and anecdotes you hope the teacher will address. Show what you learned

in each instance. Be sure to know (and communicate) why you liked the teacher's class so much. Although preparing for a short meeting with your teacher may require a little extra work, we think it's worth it, for three reasons:

1. It shows that you don't take the request for a college recommendation lightly. You've thought carefully about which teacher you should ask, and you understand how much work writing a good recommendation entails (see below for more on this topic).

2. The simple act of scheduling and preparing for a meeting reflects positively on your maturity and diligence.

3. Coming prepared with specific papers, examples, and anecdotes from your teacher's class increases your chance of getting a recommendation that shows—rather than tells—how accomplished and distinctive you are.

What Does a Good Recommendation Look Like?

A good recommendation:

- Is single-spaced, 1–2 pages.

- Shows rather than tells by using anecdotes. These anecdotes might refer, for example, to how much you have improved over the course of the year as a result of hard work, persistence, and willingness to approach the teacher for help. They might talk about how you always contribute to the discussion and introduce outside information, such as mentioning an op-ed article you read in the paper and showing how it pertains to a particular topic in U.S. History class. Examples like these make a recommendation come alive.

- Doesn't unnecessarily repeat facts such as grades, SAT scores, or class standing that are mentioned in other sections of your application.

- Shows the less quantifiable aspects of how you learn. How do you interact with other students? How do you share knowledge and communicate in class? How do you react to criticism? Do you have a passion for knowledge? Do you help other students learn?

- Includes observations about you, both in and out of the classroom.
- Shows your development over the course of several years.
- Compares you with other students in your teacher's class or past experience ("the best I've seen in the past 30 years of teaching," for example), and thus places you and your work in a context.
- Addresses some of the following character traits: curiosity, initiative, organization, independence, perseverance, maturity, work ethic, intelligence.

Non-Teacher Recommendations: Guidance Counselor, Employer, Alumni, Celebrity, Peer, and Parent

- **Guidance counselor recommendations.** Get to know your guidance counselor. Stop in and introduce yourself. Your guidance counselor is responsible for assembling input from many teachers and then adding his or her own evaluation. With many students applying to a college from the same high school, guidance counselors need to rank the students, so their opinion counts. Colleges pay attention to this recommendation because it reflects your *overall* experience as opposed to your experience in just one subject. How do you stand out from the other three hundred students in your grade?
- **Employer recommendations.** It is almost always a good idea to include an employer recommendation if you have had a part-time job. Long-standing employment—especially during the school year—demonstrates dedication, responsibility, and maturity, not to mention time management. If your family was ultimately dependent on the income, be sure your recommender notes that fact. Note: Some employers may need guidance in writing these recommendations as they may not be familiar with college recommendations (see "Ghostwriting Recommendations" on page 196).
- **Alumni recommendations.** These are most helpful when the alumnus is a major donor or very well known within the college.

*"So, What are we aiming for, Timmy—
the Nobel Prize or 'Inspected by No. 7'?"*

In such cases, even if the alumnus doesn't know the candidate well, the recommendation may be influential. As you'd expect, the most valuable recommendations are from alumni who both know the candidate well and are important to the college. Ask the recommender to include specific examples of why you want to attend that school and why you are a good fit for the school. If he/she does not know you well, offer to provide this information.

■ **Celebrity recommendations.** As impressed as *we* may be that Matt Damon's uncle's barber went to school with your father's boss, the college won't be. Unless the celebrity truly knows you on a personal basis, these recommendations are a waste of time. Worse, they could hurt your chances. However, if you studied with a well-known scientist or performed alongside a noted musician, by all means ask that person to write a persuasive recommendation. As always, offer to supply a few paragraphs with specific examples you hope the writer will include.

- **Parent recommendations:** Some schools (though very few) offer parents the chance to write about their child. Our advice to parents is to embrace this opportunity and to write from the heart. Try to begin with a story and be specific. Think of an anecdote that conveys your child's intellect, creativity, and passion. Don't feel that you need to reveal his positive *and* negative characteristics. You don't. Stick to the good stuff. You don't need to be college educated to write effective letters. Admissions officers will view a heartfelt letter from someone who obviously does not have a college degree with as much—if not more—admiration as a letter from someone who is college educated. In fact, parents for whom English is not their first language or are not highly educated reveal obstacles that the student will have had to overcome. Also, if there were family circumstances that may have hindered a student, be sure to include those.

  Note: Parents, write this recommendation only if the college specifically requests it.
- **Peer recommendations.** Some colleges require a peer recommendation. As with teachers, you want to pick someone who knows you well, someone you trust (this part is important), and someone who can effectively articulate your best qualities on paper. For obvious reasons, don't choose anyone who is also applying to the school that requires the peer recommendation. If possible, choose a friend who is willing to let someone you trust review the recommendation before it's sent.

Final Tips

- **Say thank you.** Your recommenders aren't paid to write your recommendations. Make sure to thank them in a thoughtful note after the process is completed. You can even send a small, inexpensive gift.

  Note: When you hear from colleges, let your recommenders know which colleges you got into and which one you will be attending, and thank them again.

GHOSTWRITING RECOMMENDATIONS

Recommenders less familiar with the process of writing letters of recommendation may ask your son or daughter to supply a few paragraphs or an outline of what should be included in the recommendation. If this is the case, you may want to step in and help. Self-assured and extremely confident kids suddenly get very shy and modest when faced with the prospect of writing even parts of their own recommendation. Parents are often much more able to write effective and supportive recommendations that reflect what the admissions officers want to learn from a recommendation. Of course the recommender should edit, delete, add, or subtract as needed. By doing so, they make the letter their own. Encourage that process. But don't be afraid to make sure the outline or draft you give them is strong, filled with specific, compelling anecdotes. That way, even if they edit it down, the editing begins at a high level. Also, be sure your recommender understands the intense nature of college admissions, where sterling recommendations are in many cases the norm.

- **Make sure your recommendations arrive on time.** Check with the college admissions office to make sure your recommendations have arrived. An incomplete file can ruin your chances of ever being reviewed, much less of gaining admission. Don't wait until the last minute to check on your recommendation status. If your letters have not arrived, call your recommenders and gently inquire about their status. Ask if you can help in any way. Politely remind your recommender of the deadline and then continue to follow up. If time is very tight, you might even ask them to e-mail you once they have sent the letters. This usually does the trick. Remember, don't wait until the last minute to follow up on recommendations. Applicants have been denied because their letters of recommendation arrived past the application deadline.

Sample Letters of Recommendation

The following selection of letters of recommendation should give you a sense of what superlative—and not so superlative—letters of recommendation look like.

EXAMPLE #1

Guidance Counselor Recommendation: Elise

In describing Elise to me one of her past teachers said of her that she "represents the best in youth today." At that time I felt that a most apt comment. Today that feeling is even stronger. Elise was most impressive when I first met her at the start of her sophomore year, but in the last two years I have come to cherish her as a person and as a student.

Elise's transcript attests to her intellectual strength. She applies herself fully and has done extremely well in her college preparatory program of all A level, Honors and Advanced Placement courses at our competitive suburban high school. Elise's brilliance showed early when, in ninth grade, she decided to complete an Algebra II Honors course, starting it in January while enrolled concurrently in Geometry Honors. She received an A+ in both courses. Elise studied Advanced French last year on an independent study basis with one of our instructors at our school. Her performance in Subject Tests/ Scholastic Aptitude Testing and in the American College Testing Program has been superior.

In addition to Elise's academic achievements, she stands out due to her gracious, warm demeanor and her supportive, sensitive nature. A leader in student government at our school, Elise has worked hard to make American High School a better place for all. Staff and her peers admire her and her work as a committee and board member. Elise is chairperson of the Academic Life Committee. Elise is also a member of the United Nations Club and competes in varsity tennis. Elise has also developed an art therapy program funded by the United Way, through which she works with geriatric patients each week. She has been involved with this program at two facilities for the last four years. Recently she has met with our state's Congressman regarding implementing her program throughout the state. Elise has developed a manual for this program, leaving one of many legacies to American High School. She has competed in the Physics Bowl, is editor and a contributor to our school's literary magazine, tutored other students in our school Learning Support Center and received numerous departmental awards and college book awards.

Not one to let time waste, Elise has always planned and used her summers well. She attended the summer pre-college session at Rhode Island School of Design and developed her art therapy program at the end of sophomore year. Last summer she opted to attend the Telluride Association's summer program in "Citizen Participation" at Cornell University, being one of sixty students selected from one thousand applicants world-wide. In order to do this she had to forsake selection to represent our state in Japan with the Sony Corporation's Student Project Abroad program and an invitation to represent our state at the High School Honors Program at the Fermi National Accelerator Laboratory in Batavia, Illinois. Elise is a Board of Directors member with the United Way. She serves on the Board of Directors of the YMCA and is a member of our town's Junior Fine Arts League.

Students don't come more academically talented, conscientious, intellectually curious; possessing more balance in the arts, science or mathematics; more gracious, warm, personable and sincere than Elise. She is a school counselor's "dream come true." In twenty-four years of working with young adults it has been rare for me to work with a young person so talented and so distinguished.

Sincerely,
Guidance Counselor
American High School

COMMENTS: This letter is truly exceptional. The counselor's genuine admiration and respect for the student shines through as he highlights not only her academic brilliance but also her leadership, community involvement, and high moral character. Phrases such as "in twenty-four years of working with young adults" and "a counselor's dream come true" leave no doubt about how strongly this counselor is recommending Elise. It's hard to imagine any college turning her down—and in fact, she was accepted at Harvard Early Action.

EXAMPLE #2
Physics Teacher Letter of Recommendation: Chloe

I've taught Chloe in both Physics and AP Physics. Since she entered Jefferson we have both been elected representatives on the Jefferson Governing Board. I have also watched her play on the Jefferson field hockey team. I am very confident saying that Chloe is an outstanding talent in Physics, a delightfully responsible young adult and a committed contributor. Add the outstanding writing skills, the number of leadership positions accepted, her interest in photography and her ability to work with people of all ages and you complete the credentials of an outstanding applicant.

Last year in Physics Chloe was scheduled for English during the first half of lab each week. By working after school or learning more quickly than others, she easily completed the missed work. Missing this instruction did not keep her from obtaining an exceptionally high subject test score last June—even though we were still studying electromagnetism in class and she missed several school days for state field hockey tournaments. That result is consistent with her test achievement throughout the year. Equally impressive was her laboratory work and homework problem solving. Qualitative and quantitative aspects of her work were superlative. For a final project, she learned about chaos theory—no easy assignment. Clearly she belongs in that top 1%, the one a teacher encounters once or twice in a lifetime.

Her solid math achievement is a matter of record, and she is now entering her second year of Calculus. She represented Jefferson on the Math Team, which finished third in the state. Based upon her high scholastic achievement, she won the Society of Women Engineers Award and is the best student in this year's graduating class. This year in Electronics she is trying and enjoying the practical aspects of science. Experiences like the Junior Science and Humanities Symposium fill her with excitement and ideas.

Whether as a group leader, part of a lab team or seeking an answer to a question after class, I'm impressed by her ability to comprehend and listen. Her words are carefully chosen, often soft spoken, yet with a power and conviction that one might miss at first. When I ask the class a question, I hear her answer with the rest. If she says she will do something—consider it done. If she desires some assistance, she is willing to ask.

Chloe is both contributor to and editor of the Jefferson literary magazine. Her ability to write is a trait often missing in mathematicians or scientists. Add a genuine love of people with her ability to communicate through photography and you have an unusual array of strongly developed talents. And she makes the adjustment necessary to withstand the strain of competition in field hockey. The end of the field hockey season and the following tournaments tested the persistence of the team. They rose to the occasion.

Chloe genuinely enjoys all aspects of her diversified commitments. I see a smile when she enters class, eyes that never close, a curious voice that instinctively asks the right questions and a mind that seems to sense where I am going before I get there. Chloe gives so much so easily. The class or group is always better with her being there. Respectfully, based on some twenty years of teaching Physics, some may equal but none surpass her credentials. Chloe has earned a key place in my student hall of fame. I recommend her highly and without reservation both academically and personally. They don't come any better.

Science Division Coordinator

COMMENTS: In this letter, the Physics teacher sets out to show the reader just how special this student is by giving concrete examples—her mastery of chaos theory, her athletic ability, her way of relating to her peers, and so on—that set her apart from other strong physics students. This student was accepted at Princeton.

EXAMPLE #3
History Teacher Recommendation: John

Dear Admissions Committee members:

This letter of recommendation is submitted in behalf of John Doe, who is applying for admission to your college for the fall of 2010. I have known John since the beginning of his sophomore year at Yourtown High School, when he enrolled in my World Literature class. He subsequently took two courses with me his senior year of high school ("American Literature" and "Latin American Writers"). During those three years, John and I had a number of conversations about a wide range of topics and I probably know John as well as did any Yourtown faculty member, and I'm pleased to write on his behalf.

My first meeting with John occurred in World Literature. John was writing good essays and was a verbal participant in class discussion, and curious in the best sense of the word. In fact, he was one of the top 4 students in my class. Unfortunately, his work in "Latin American Writers" was not as strong. Perhaps he wasn't as engaged with the material or just distracted with social and extracurricular pursuits. While there is no doubt in my mind that John is a very bright student, it has been a constant process for him to respect his intellect and produce appropriate work. As expected, his overall GPA is low—2.91, with a class rank of approximately 301/525. I was not in the least bit surprised when he announced that his SAT scores are both low 700s. Because of John's many social activities, it has been difficult for him to truly live up to his potential.

What are the best parts about John? First, John is deeply engaged with his family's southern roots. This is clear in his personal essay. Second, John is effusive and enthusiastic. Never lacking for energy, he spearheads new club ideas, organizes student groups, and led two athletic teams to state semi-finals last year. John is a presence in whatever group he finds himself.

What are John's areas of improvement? Not surprisingly, John is often in a rush—both physically and thoughtfully. His academic work would benefit tremendously from time spent refining his output. He also needs to stop and think a bit more before speaking. In conclusion, I recommend John to you. His SAT score is a good measure of his potential and intelligence. His energy and likeability are clearly major assets.

I recommend John with reserved enthusiasm. Please give me a call if you would like more detail on my recommendation.

Best regards,
Literature Instructor

COMMENTS: Although this teacher has some positive things to say about John, they are not without reservation. Even when he compliments John's writing in his World Literature class, he says it is "good," not "excellent." He addresses the student's immaturity. A telling sentence is "I recommend John with reserved enthusiasm." Even more damaging is, "Please give me a call if you would like more detail on my recommendation." This is a coded way of saying: "I have more negative things to say about this student but didn't want to put them in writing." Any admissions officer would be very wary of admitting a student whose teacher (whom the student himself chose to write the letter of recommendation) makes these comments.

The College Interview

Overview

In this chapter you'll learn:

- How to be alike and spike in your college interview
- How to prepare and practice for interviews
- How to ace your interview on the big day

Interviewing: Important Today and Tomorrow

Not long ago we got a call from a mother who was particularly stressed out about her son's interviewing skills. It seems he was overly shy and couldn't relate well to interviewers, a problem that she blamed for his having been waitlisted at his top-choice school. When we asked which college had put him on the waitlist, there was a short silence. "College?" she repeated. It turned out that her son had been vying for enrollment in one of Manhattan's most exclusive preschools.

Although no one should ever worry this much about an interview—particularly during the first three years of life—interviewing is a skill that it pays to learn. The ability to make a great first impression in a thirty-minute conversation will help you not only in the college-admissions process, but also in life after college. In fact, unlike calculus or multiple-choice exams, interviewing is one of the key aspects of college admissions

B. Smaller

*"He doesn't have to worry about his preschool
placement—he interviews well."*

that you will use decades after college is over. Multiple interviews are
necessary for most professional jobs and graduate schools. We've heard
that people stay in jobs they don't enjoy because they are too scared to
interview for new positions. That's silly. The more you interview, the better you'll get at it, and you may even learn to enjoy the process (there are
worse things than talking about yourself for half an hour). Most important, you'll reap the dividends throughout your life.

Don't despair if you feel that your interview skills are average—or
even below average. Even the most natural interviewees still require
focused preparation before that big day. And shy or reserved candidates
can improve their skills immensely with a little prep work. While we
work with many students who have already interviewed for jobs, schools,
scholarships, and/or internships before their college interviews, most
students encounter their first serious interviews during the college-
admissions process.

"Be Alike but Spike" Interviewing Strategy

Interviewing in and of itself will rarely "get you into" the school of your dreams. However, remember that you're seeking admission into a dynamic intellectual community. Having a meaningful conversation with an adult about academic and extracurricular activities is something admissions officers expect you to be able to accomplish as part of that community. In this regard, a good interview shows the admissions staff that you are mature and poised enough to make a valuable contribution to their college.

How do interviewers determine whether you will be a good fit? They will likely want to know that you have favorite classes, beloved authors, and challenging teachers. That is, in your answers to their questions, they'll want to detect a love of learning—a necessary quality for any successful college student. They will also want to know that you can conceive and communicate original ideas—crucial skills in any classroom discussion. Finally, they'll want to make sure that you're interesting, respectful, and friendly—important qualities in any good roommate. None of these traits will distinguish you from other qualified applicants. Rather, through your answers to these questions, admissions officers will be able to determine whether you are like other students at their school in your ability to handle college life.

However, the interview can *also* be used to show admissions officers and alumni how you are different from the rest of the applicants. What makes your character and achievements stand out? How have you personally contributed to your high school and your community? As we have said before, admissions interviewers (in college and beyond) will assume that past performance is indicative of future performance and that a leader in high school will continue to be a leader in college. Colleges are looking for candidates who will make a difference and leave their campuses better than they found them. It's your job to articulate your spike clearly during any interviewing session (see "'Spike' Answers" on page 211). Also, if you have the opportunity to interview on campus, your interviewer will most likely be a representative of the admissions office. This affords you the added bonus of making your case directly to a person with a seat at the admissions table, where real decisions are made.

Interviewing 101

The key to any successful interview is thorough preparation, and the college admissions interview is no exception. Like job recruiters, admissions officers or college representatives expect candidates to have done prep work prior to their meeting. Failing to do so is disrespectful:

FACEBOOK FIASCO: SOCIAL NETWORKING AND COLLEGE ADMISSIONS

Recently, one of our students interviewed with an admissions officer at her top-choice college. At the end of the meeting, she was practically guaranteed admission. When she found out she had been waitlisted, she and her family were shocked and disappointed. What had happened? Further investigation revealed a Facebook entry that was controversial, to say the least. The moral of this story? Don't post anything online that you wouldn't want published on the front page of the *New York Times*.

As social networking sites like Facebook and Twitter become more ubiquitous, students should keep in mind that everything posted online is available to anyone who takes the time to look at it, admissions officers included. Especially at smaller colleges, where the impact of each individual student is significant, admissions officers can be expected to examine social-networking Web sites very carefully. Make sure yours is "grandparent-ready" (that is, it doesn't include anything that you wouldn't want your grandparents to read).

admissions officers may feel that you're wasting their time and aren't really interested in their school. Never make the careless mistake of asking your interviewer a question that is answered on the first page of the college brochure or requesting information about a major that doesn't exist. For example, asking about Harvard's business major would be a bad idea (not only does Harvard not offer business courses to undergraduates, but it doesn't even have "majors"—Harvard calls majors "concentrations").

DO YOUR HOMEWORK

What can you do to prepare yourself for college interviews? First, research the schools at which you're interviewing. From your point of view, what about each school is unique in terms of academics, extracurriculars, and social life? Although you won't be expected to know everything about the school, you should know something about the areas in which you're interested. Second, and most important, be prepared to explain why you've chosen to apply, and make sure the reasons are compelling. (Compelling to *them*, not just you—the school's amazing Greek life and proximity to great surfing don't count.) Last but not least, prepare answers to a list of anticipated questions (see "Top Fifteen Interviewing Questions" 210–11).

AN OPTIONAL INTERVIEW ISN'T OPTIONAL

We believe that an interview is never "optional." If the college offers it, take them up on it. If they suggest an on-campus interview and you have the financial resources to travel to the school, by all means, schedule an interview with the staff of the admissions office. Assuming that your interview goes well, you will have just gained an inside supporter in the admissions office. If colleges offer both on-campus and alumni interviews, don't hesitate to do both.

Not doing an interview suggests to a college that you are not truly interested in the school and/or have problems with interpersonal communication. Neither is a favorable signal to send to admissions officers.

The relative importance of the interview can differ from school to school. Off-campus alumni interviews do not necessarily bear heavily on the student's application. Small liberal arts colleges tend to attach considerable importance to the on-campus interview, as these colleges want to ensure that a given student will be a good fit for their small, tight-knit communities. Whatever the case, the best rule of thumb is the one already mentioned: if a school offers the interview, schedule it—and prepare for it as thoroughly as possible.

Types of Interviews

- **Off-campus with alumni.** Many colleges have created a network of alumni throughout the world who have agreed to interview prospective candidates who are unable to travel to the college to interview on campus. These interviewers are former students who have fond memories of the school, but may not be up to date on the most recent changes. Alumni interviews generally take place at the interviewer's office or home or a local restaurant and last between thirty and sixty minutes. While important, most alumni interviews do not have as much impact as an on-campus interview conducted by an admissions officer.

  Note: Alumni interviewers may be more "unpredictable" than on-campus interviewers. Why? Keep in mind that your alumni interviewer may be a twenty-three-year-old "Wall Streeter," a sixty-five-year-old retired teacher, or a forty-year-old stay-at-home dad (and the only connection between these individuals may be that they share the same alma mater!). Be aware that you will need to adjust your manner slightly, according to their age, point of view, profession, outlook, and so forth.

- **On-campus with an admissions officer.** Many colleges offer on-campus interviews conducted by admissions officers. These interviews generally take place in their office and last approximately thirty minutes. Admissions officers are representatives of the college, so they are the most informed about the school and its most recent changes. This type of interview tends to carry the most weight because the interviewer has a seat at the admissions table and can speak directly and personally on your behalf when your application is reviewed.

- **On-campus with an upperclassman.** Some colleges offer you the opportunity to interview with an upperclassman on campus. Don't be fooled into thinking you can treat student interviews lightly because they will be the easiest. Upperclassmen can be critical, and they're not easily fooled. They remember how difficult the admissions process was and may even see a tough interview as a rite of passage. Approach a student interview as you would any other: prepare thoroughly and remember that the interviewer, although a student, is still a representative of the admissions office.

- **Two-on-one or three-on-one interview.** Most often set up to interview candidates for scholarships and selective programs (and rarely for college admissions), this type of interview can be the most intimidating. Often three or four representatives from the scholarship or school administration, past award recipients, and/or professors involved with the program will interview you at once. Some tips for these interviews:

  - Never assume that one person at the table is more important than the others. Try to divide your attention equally among all the interviewers. Remember to smile, shake hands, and make eye contact (a little, not too much) with each interviewer.

  - As with college interviews, be concise in your answers. There are many interviewers and each will have questions.

  - Try to link different questions together (for example, "In answering your question, I'm going to draw on my response to Paul's…") and as much as you can, engage the interviewers in a conversation.

How to Ace Your College Interviews

TOP FIFTEEN INTERVIEWING QUESTIONS

The first step in preparing for your college interviews is to write (yes, actually write) answers to the fifteen questions we've provided. Writing down your answers accomplishes three things. First, it forces you to think through your answers. Are there *three* reasons you enjoy your favorite class most? List them. Are there *two* accomplishments of which you are most proud? Jot them down. Second, writing your answers helps you formulate compelling responses that present you in the most favorable light. Colleges don't want to know your *real* weaknesses, like procrastination or cookie dough (or that one time in the gym...see "Practice Makes Perfect" below). Rather, they want an example of a substantial setback that you've overcome—a story that demonstrates the building of character, not the lack of it. Finally, writing down each answer will help you *remember* your answers. As you probably already know, you recall things better after having written them down. Write, revise, rewrite. Before you know it, your answers will be committed to memory and you'll have the benefit of prepared answers during those first tense admissions interviews.

Below are our top fifteen, most commonly asked questions. Note that this is not intended to be an exhaustive list. Although there are endless variations on each one, preparing answers to these is a great way to start gaining the confidence you'll need to sail through that interview.

1. Tell me about yourself.
2. Tell me about your family/community.
3. What are the strengths and weaknesses of your high school? What would you change about it if you could?
4. Why are you interested in this college specifically?
5. What subjects interest you most? Why?
6. What classes are you taking this year?
7. What extracurriculars are most important to you?
8. What has been your greatest failure or disappointment in high school?

9. Of what accomplishment are you most proud?

10. What are you going to do this summer (or what did you do last summer)?

11. How would your close friends describe you? How would they describe your strengths and weaknesses?

12. What do you think about [a current event that occurred in the past week]? What recent current events have sparked your interest?

13. What is your favorite book and who is your favorite author?

14. If you could meet any important figure, past or present, who would it be and why?

15. What questions do you have for me? (See pages 216–17 for guidance on this question.)

"SPIKE" ANSWERS

As you prepare your answers, pay special attention to your "spike" areas—the subjects you love most and excel in, the extracurriculars you're most passionate about, your special talents and interests, and so on. Inevitably, you'll find that these topics dominate the interview. Why? Put yourself in the interviewer's place: her job is to listen to hundreds of kids who have similar, if not identical, grades, test scores, school subjects, sometimes even extracurricular activities and job histories. She'll be looking for something to remember you by—something that really stands out as representative of your personality—and of course, you'll want to be remembered, too. Think carefully about what defines you best and be prepared to talk about it at length. An interviewer will always be more interested in the art exhibition you created for your town or the pet care company you run than about the good grade you (and a thousand other students) got in AP English (for more on this, see Part II, "Spike").

PRACTICE MAKES PERFECT

The second step in preparing for interviews is practice, and the best way to practice is through mock interviews. Mock interviews will help get some of the interview anxiety out of your system and will also help

WHAT ARE MOCK INTERVIEWS?

Very simply, mock interviews are pretend interviews that allow the interviewee a chance to practice interviewing before the actual interview. The best mock interviewer is a parent or other trusted adult. If they've interviewed in this capacity before and know what questions to ask, great. If not, provide a list of sample questions. (If you like, you can use the list of questions in this chapter as a general guide.) You shouldn't try to repeat the answers to those questions verbatim. Rather, you should attempt to answer each question just as you would in the admissions office: smoothly, with poise and confidence, and as if it were the first time someone had ever asked you that question. Most important, treat the mock interview as you would a real interview (that means no giggling, jokes, or responses ending with "How did that sound, Mom?").

flush out some of the answers you *don't* want to give during real interviews. In the mock sessions we conduct with students, we hear plenty of answers we're glad the student tried out on us first. Our favorites are the Shocking Confessions—statements that begin with, "You probably don't want to hear about..." or "It wasn't my fault that..." One student bared his soul about the time he and a girl sneaked into the school gym at night and tripped a silent alarm that alerted the police. The interview isn't a confessional: set aside your guilty conscience, feelings of insecurity, or self-doubt, and present yourself in the best possible light.

INTERVIEWING AND CULTURAL DIFFERENCES

When interviewing, it's important to consider not just what you're saying, but how you're saying it. Recently, we met with a brilliant and self-confident Japanese student for a mock interview workshop. As he approached us, his posture became stooped; his handshake, limp.

As we spoke, his gaze was directed downward. Although his body language and lack of eye contact would have been entirely appropriate had he been interviewing in parts of Asia, at an American university his bearing would have been misinterpreted as timid and insecure. Be aware that there are often dramatic cultural differences in interviewing norms. Understand the messages you are sending through your body language and be prepared to practice through mock interviews until you're sure you're sending the messages you intend.

GIVE AND TAKE

When preparing for your interviews, remember that a great interview is akin to a really great conversation. It has give and take—not just questions and answers. A good conversation moves to common ground. Focus on areas that the interviewer seems to find interesting. Feel free to ask the interviewer questions: Where is she from? Why did she choose this position? What does she like most about the university? A little small talk is okay too, especially if an obvious subject presents itself. A student we worked with once entered an interviewer's office and found it filled with grandfather clocks, cuckoo clocks, and every other imaginable kind of clock. It was only natural for her to comment on such a distinctive collection. Most important of all, listen to, and show interest in, the interviewer's answers.

Scheduling the Interview

Always schedule your interviews in reverse order of preference. Is your top choice College X? Schedule that interview *last*. After mock interviews, the best form of interview preparation is actual interviewing. By the time you interview at your top-choice school you want to be a seasoned interviewee. Interviewing is something that everyone gets better at with practice. Each answer will get smoother and crisper after your tenth time delivering it. Finally, we recommend that you schedule all of your interviews by June of your junior year. Although that may sound early, interview spots for the summer and fall get booked up early!

Stay Current

Although you may feel like every second of your day is spent studying for school exams, AP Tests, and SATs, as well as participating in extracurriculars, college interviewers will still expect you to be up to date on current events. What's the best way to keep abreast of the news before your interviews? Read the top stories in a major newspaper such as the *New York Times, Washington Post, Wall Street Journal,* or your city's leading paper each day. You might even choose to follow a few of their columnists. Read a weekly magazine such as *Time* or *The Economist.* (Political blogs and talk shows can help round out these other sources, but don't rely on them too heavily—most are strongly biased.) You may find that you've begun to enjoy being up on world affairs and that you've formed opinions on the issues of the day. Perhaps you'll even develop a taste for your favorite commentators and op-ed writers. Before you know it, this will become a life-long habit.

Countdown to the Big Day

The interview day has finally come. You've done all your practice and prep work. Here is a list of dos and don'ts to help you perform your best:

DOS

- Dress simply, neatly, and just a little more nicely than you might ordinarily. We advise students to feel comfortable in what they are wearing; *this is not the time to break out the suit you have worn only once.* Make sure your clothes are clean (of course) and avoid extremely casual items (open-toe shoes, shorts, jeans, T-shirts, and the like).
- Bring a pad of paper and pen so that you can write down interesting aspects of the conversation and the interviewer's name and e-mail address.
- Be sure you know your interview location. If it's on campus, check the location of the office you'll be meeting in. If it's in your neighborhood, make a practice run to the house, office, or restaurant a day early. Check

the parking and confirm the address and directions. These steps will make you extra confident on the big day; you won't have any logistical worries to frazzle you. Arrive five minutes early to an office location and right on time to someone's home. Never arrive more than five minutes early: we feel it's just as rude and disruptive to arrive too early as too late. This means you may need to wait a few minutes before you ring the doorbell or check in. That's okay. Bring a newspaper or a cheat sheet of answers to your fifteen interview questions to review while you try to relax. (If reading answers to the questions is going to cause you more stress, by all means leave the cheat sheet at home!)

- During the interview, make casual eye contact (no eye contact and excessive eye contact are equally disturbing—try for something in between). Listen carefully to what the interviewer is saying; try not to fidget, pull your ear, touch your hair. We always advise taking occasional notes on interesting points the interviewer makes. It's something to do with your hands (you're less likely to fidget!) and you'll be able to refer to these notes when you write your thank-you note to the interviewer. See page 217 for a sample interview thank-you note.

- Remember, the best interviews are actually conversations. While the interviewer will ask you most of the questions, try to make the interview a dialogue. Look at their walls, bookshelves, and pictures. If they have a lot of basketball memorabilia, ask them about it; if you see a bunch of pictures of their newborn, ask them about the baby. These observations demonstrate perceptiveness and set a positive tone for the entire interview.

DON'TS

- Don't rush into answering any question or answer it in a rote, memorized way. It's okay to take a few minutes to collect your thoughts. Even if you've heard the questions many times before during practice interviews, try to deliver your answers in a fresh way.
- Don't guess if you don't know the answer to a question. This may happen if an interviewer asks about a political event or a test score you

WHAT ABOUT US? INTERVIEW TIPS
FOR PARENTS

Parents have an important role to play *before interviews*. You are often in charge of scheduling college visits and interviews. Moms and dads can make excellent mock interviewers and can even be good clipping services, cutting out interesting articles about current events. During the interview, however, parents should be invisible. That may mean waiting outside the admissions office—or in the car if the interview is at an alumni's house—until your son or daughter is finished. We even recommend refraining from introducing yourself to the interviewer. They're interested in your son or daughter, not you!

just don't remember. Tell the interviewer that you'd like to think about the answer or check your records and will e-mail her a response.

- Most important, unless specifically asked, don't offer opinions on controversial issues (religion, gun control, political candidates, the relative attractiveness of their newborn baby, and so on), and be open to alternative views and perspectives.

EXIT QUESTION: WHAT QUESTIONS DO YOU HAVE FOR ME?

Interviewers will almost always save a few minutes at the end of the interview for your questions. Don't make the mistake of thinking that their last question (otherwise known as "What questions do you have for me?") is optional. Be sure to have a response. Not asking a question is a clear indication that you're either not interested in the school or not prepared for the interview. Neither leaves a good final impression.

Prepare a few questions that aren't covered on the first page of the college Web site. If you have a specific question, wonderful. If you're stumped, you can always ask a question that requires the interviewer's perspective.

For example, what, in the interviewer's opinion, are the best and worst aspects of the university? What does she like best about the school? Listen to her answers, and when possible, ask follow-up questions. Everyone likes to offer his or her own point of view—even interviewers.

FINISHING THE INTERVIEW

Finish every interview with a solid handshake and say, "Thank you so much for taking the time to meet with me. I really appreciate it." Request a business card or confirm the correct spelling of the interviewer's name and e-mail address. Immediately after the interview, jot down a few specific notes about your discussion. Trust us, you will not remember the details of your discussion as well the next day. In your thank-you note, you can reiterate something unusual you learned about the school, and you may *briefly* mention why you think you would be a great fit for the school. We recommend mentioning at least one topic covered during your discussion—refer to any notes you took in the course of the interview. E-mail or hand-write a proofread note within twenty-four hours. See "Sample Thank-You Note below.

Sample Thank-You Note

Dear Ms. Smith,

Thank you so much for meeting with me last Tuesday. I really enjoyed our conversation on Philip Roth's *American Pastoral*, and your recommendation on which classes to audit was perfect. Professor Hightower's American History class was amazing. My visit only confirmed that College X is my first choice for college.

Thank you again for all your help, and I hope to see you next fall!

Best regards,
Amy Simons

Supplemental Application Materials

Overview

In this chapter, you'll learn:

- What kinds of supplemental application materials are appropriate to send, and where to send them
- How to prepare and edit supplemental application materials (performance videos, art portfolios, and the like)
- How to prepare a supplemental explanation of infractions such as a grade dip or academic misdemeanor

Sending supplemental materials along with your application is an important and valuable way to highlight your passion, skill, and expertise in a given area. Discussing these accomplishments in your essays is important, but in some areas words can go only so far. Colleges will want to see concrete evidence of your passion—be it sports, art, dance, or music—through supplemental materials.

An important note: We're not talking about gimmicks. Unless your passion is baking confections, sending chocolates in the shape of a college crest won't do much to enhance your candidacy. Think of supplemental materials as the tangible proof of the passion or spike you've cultivated in other parts of your application.

What Supplemental Materials Should You Send?

As a rule, if your talent is…

- **Music:** A CD or DVD of your music; an additional letter of recommendation from your music teacher; a listing of awards.
- **Theater/Dance:** A DVD of your performance; an additional letter of recommendation from your drama teacher, dance teacher, and so forth; a listing of awards.
- **Art:** Slides of your work on DVD; an additional letter of recommendation from your art teacher; a listing of awards.
- **Sports:** A DVD of performance; an additional letter of recommendation from your coach; a listing of awards.

In addition:

- **Newspaper clippings.** Any spike can benefit from a newspaper endorsement. Even a mention or an article in a small, local newspaper carries weight. Note: If for whatever reason you've had hundreds of newspaper articles written about you, don't send the whole album; just pick the best.
- **A letter from you.** This should accompany any submission of supplementary materials. In it you should express a passion for your skill, a very short summary of your accomplishments (not a résumé), and a description of how you would hope to continue your passion at *that* particular college. Be specific. Close with a sincere desire to attend the school (see "Sample Letter to Accompany Supplemental Materials" on page 220).

To ensure that your submitted materials don't get lost in the shuffle, make sure your name, date of birth, and the name of your high school are included somewhere on all materials that you submit. And be sure to check each college's Web site carefully to determine what supplemental materials are accepted.

SAMPLE LETTER TO ACCOMPANY
SUPPLEMENTAL MATERIALS

Prof. Dean Phillips
Visual Arts Department
Top Choice University
Main Campus, 123 Jefferson Street
Smithfield, MA 02100

April 9, 2012

Dear Professor Phillips,

Thank you for taking the time to speak with me last Wednesday. Hearing your perspective on the Visual Arts Department only confirmed my desire to attend Top Choice University. I plan to apply under your early decision program this fall. During my visit next month, I'm looking forward to auditing the class you recommended, Mr. Byron's survey course on Drawing, as well as visiting the studio department.

Please find a selection of my slides included on DVD. As you can see, they encompass a range of materials: charcoal, oil and watercolor. Also note the enclosed list of awards and prizes my artwork has won.

Again, I look forward to meeting in person next month. Thank you so much for your time and attention. If you have any questions, feel free to contact me at 555 555-5555 or anybody@email.com.

Best regards,
Jane Doe

Who Should Receive Your Supplementary Materials?

The answer to this question often depends on the college to which you are applying. At some colleges, admissions officers want to evaluate the work. At others, they prefer that you contact the admissions office to determine which department it should be sent to for evaluation. In other cases, the admissions office will send the material to the appropriate faculty member for review. Ask beforehand where you should send your supplementary materials and follow the advice you receive. Also, note the following:

- Faculty members are often strong advocates for students with special talents. If the college is a top choice, offer to meet personally with the person evaluating your work. At this meeting, express your desire to attend that college and explain why. Remember to send a thank-you note after this meeting. Doing this will offer you the best chance of gaining a written endorsement to the admissions office from that faculty member.

- Although it may seem obvious, be sure to send your submission to a particular person or department (ideally, the admissions office can provide this information), not a general address. Double-check all spelling and address information.

- Whenever supplementary materials are sent to a faculty member, you want to make sure that the recipient is aware of all of your accomplishments in your specialty, including your awards in that area. Because the faculty member won't necessarily see your activity chart or the rest of your application, we advise listing your awards and honors in the cover letter that accompanies the materials.

The Well-Edited Submission

- **Opt for quality over quantity and avoid redundancy.** On the one hand, sending the kitchen sink (in other words, every piece of art or music you've completed since freshman year) can hurt your application. On the other hand, sending too little can make your supplemental materials seem irrelevant. A small, well-selected display of your skill is best. Don't make admissions officers or faculty evaluators weed through poor work to find the good stuff (they may not!). Send only what is exemplary and if possible, make it a diverse sample (artwork in various media, music in various genres). Get a second opinion if necessary.

- **Send materials that are yours alone** (not a group mural or a recording of your entire youth philharmonic). Admissions officers want to assess *your* talent, not the talent of your team.

- **Don't submit academic work.** Thinking about sending that fifty-page research paper that earned you your school's first-ever A plus plus? We wouldn't recommend it. Generally speaking, schoolwork doesn't belong in your application file (although any awards it wins do belong in your list of honors and awards). However, you can ask the admissions office for a contact in the relevant academic

NOTE FOR ATHLETES

As you may already know, there are rules governing how a coach can get in touch with a student. Students must first register with the NCAA, and coaches are not allowed to contact students before July 1 prior to the student's senior year. Even during the recruitment process, contact is governed by NCAA rules.

However, *there are no rules preventing a student from getting in touch with a coach.* Contacting coaches at your top-choice schools during junior year can be very beneficial, as it will increase the chances that you will then be sought out during the actual recruitment process. Expect the coaches you contact to ask for grades, DVDs of your athletic performances, and the like. If they ask for any of these materials, feel free to send them directly to the coach rather than through the admissions office.

department. Send that paper to an appropriate professor and have her evaluate the work; ideally she will send a note to the admissions office in support of your candidacy. See "Who Should Receive Supplementary Materials" above for guidelines on sending work to departments.

- **Follow the rules.** Most schools have specific guidelines for the submission of supplemental materials. For example, Stanford requires applications to be submitted earlier if they contain supplemental materials. Other colleges still prefer receiving slides of your artwork instead of a DVD. Look on the application and/or the admissions Web site to find these guidelines. When in doubt, call the admissions office. Don't wait until the last minute! You don't want to miss these deadlines.

- **Different schools evaluate talent differently.** Obviously, a Division III school will evaluate your athletic prowess differently from a Division I school. Similarly, the music department at a small college may evaluate your musical ability differently from Juilliard. Even within the same college, a pianist or violinist (of which there are typically many applicants) may be held to higher standards than a harpist or tuba player (of which there are few). Know your audience.

Note: Don't worry if your passion is uncommon or even outlandish— Hindi traditional dance, circus trapeze—colleges love niche activities. In general, they are prone to admit students with strong, varied, and specialized interests.

Supplemental Information: Offering Explanations

In our twenty years of providing advice to students and families, we've encountered a wide range of negative issues that students have had to address directly in their applications to schools. Some students have had a year of terrible grades, or dismal grades in a certain subject. We've had students with disciplinary issues ranging from misdemeanors to ethical crimes. Whenever we're faced with these problems, we try to stress the following points:

- Address the issue head-on. Don't pretend that the admissions office won't notice a grade dip or that your guidance counselor or teacher won't mention your misdemeanor. You have to assume they will—either in their letter of recommendation or in conversation about you. Never try to bury, avoid, or ignore the situation; always be completely forthright.

- Consider the nature of the infraction. For a disciplinary issue, much depends on what exactly you did wrong. The worst types of infractions are usually academic: cheating, plagiarizing, and so on. These are viewed seriously and require serious analysis and consideration. Getting caught smoking, on the other hand, may not be a positive credential, but it certainly won't be viewed in the same way.

- Consider the timing of the infraction. If you committed it in senior year, you will have more work to do in explaining and compensating for the error. Ninth-grade blunders provide you with more time to a) develop a clean post-infraction record and b) demonstrate that you've gained maturity and learned from your mistakes.

- In certain cases, it may be best to have a guidance counselor discuss a grade dip with colleges. For example, as a third party, a guidance counselor can objectively discuss how a death, divorce, illness, or other hardship may have impacted you and caused a temporary dip in your performance. Your honest perspective on this issue can supplement a guidance counselor's professional perspective.

No matter what the problem or infraction, be sure to discuss it with your guidance counselor. Ideally, the two of you can work as a team to address it in an objective, mature, and truthful manner, giving you the best chance that admissions officers will understand it for what it is: a blemish on an otherwise strong record. Remember, no one—not even an admissions officer—is perfect.

Financial Aid

Overview

In this chapter you'll learn:

- How to reduce tuition costs
- The three types of financial-aid policies that colleges adopt
- How to apply for financial aid
- How to use the "be alike but spike" strategy to maximize the aid you receive

The Hard Facts about Financial Aid Today

It is hardly news that it costs a lot to attend university. At the time of this writing, the top private colleges cost more than $50,000 per year for tuition, room, and board, and prices are only rising. However, colleges don't want to be affordable only to the privileged and wealthy, and they do recognize the huge financial burden that tuition places on most families. Thus, while tuition increases have occurred at almost every university, many of the most elite schools have taken steps to make college more accessible to Americans of average income. In 2007, for example, Harvard issued a sweeping change to its financial-aid policy, declaring that students whose families earn less than $60,000 per year no longer have to pay for undergraduate tuition. They also expanded financial-aid eligibility more generally, offering it to all families earning less than $180,000 per year.[*]

In this chapter we will help clarify the often complex world of financial aid and provide strategies for cutting tuition costs and maximizing the aid you receive via your application. Strategies for presenting your financial need as persuasively as possible on the FAFSA (Free Application for Federal Student Aid) or PROFILE forms are beyond the scope of this book; for more information, we recommend visiting FinAid.org or contacting a financial-aid advisor in your area.

What Does College Cost?

TUITION

In the past decade, total costs at private colleges have increased dramatically. Even parents who started saving for college in a 529 College Savings Plan on the day their child was born often have to supplement their savings (for more information on this and other college savings plans, see pages 268–72). As a result, families are more likely than they once were to "shop around" and make cost comparisons among colleges.

Different types of schools charge different tuition amounts:[**]

Type of College	Average Tuition/Year
Public two-year	$2,402
Public four-year (in-state)	$6,585
Public four-year (out-of-state)	$17,452
Private four-year	$25,143

---

[*] Sara Rimer and Alan Finder, "Harvard to Aid Students High in Middle Class," *New York Times*, December 11, 2007, U.S. section, online edition.

[**] "2008–09 College Prices," CollegeBoard, http://www.collegeboard.com/student/pay/add-it-up/4494.html (accessed August 13, 2009).

Remember, however, that "sticker price" isn't everything. Some of the most expensive private colleges have the most extensive financial-aid programs.

OTHER COSTS

In addition to the tuition costs listed above, there are other significant costs that must be taken into account:

- Room (that is, rent or the cost of living quarters on campus)
- Board (that is, food and/or college meal plans)
- Fees (for example, gym fees, health-care co-pays, lab or technology fees, fraternity and sorority dues)
- Textbooks
- Computers and printers
- Health insurance
- Transportation (for example, travel to and from home)

These costs can vary widely depending on the student, the school, and its geographic location. It's much more expensive, for example, to live in cities than in suburban or rural areas. In 2009 students seeking a one-bedroom, off-campus apartment in Manhattan in August faced an average rent of over $3,100 per month! Other major variables include a student's distance from home (travel expenses), choice of major (lab fees, and so on), and consumer tastes (fine wine vs. cheap beer, for instance). No matter what, tuition and non-tuition costs combined add up to a bill that many families are desperate to reduce.

College Made Cheaper: Ways to Reduce Your Tuition Bill

- **Attend a public university as an in-state resident.** Obviously, attending a public university ("state school") will cost less than attending a private college. For true savings, however, you must attend a public university in your state of residence. But what if you fall in love with a public university in a state in which you are not a resident? Is it possible to change your residency to that of the state in question after your first year of college? The answer is a qualified yes. First, some state schools are now conferring automatic in-state residency on desirable out-of-state students. Second, some states have lenient residency laws and will grant you in-state residency after your first year of college. In other states, making the switch is much harder. For a full state-by-state breakdown, consult the Guide to State Residency on the CollegeBoard Web site (http://professionals.collegeboard.com/testing/international/state).

- **Transfer from a community college to a private university.** Some students use the cost-saving strategy of matriculating at a community college and then transferring to a private university (making sure, of course, that all credits earned at the one are transferable to the other). Although this strategy allows you to build up college credits at a much lower cost, transferring successfully is far from a foregone conclusion. Selective colleges accept many more transfer students during some years than others. Moreover, your community college transcript and letters of recommendation will be evaluated with particular care by private universities considering your application. Finally, you may not be eligible for financial aid as a transfer student; you will need to check with the college's financial-aid officer first. That said, selective schools often do like transfer students from community colleges. They bring a more distinctive background and often greater maturity than other transfer candidates, and are less likely to have been rejected from a previous pool of applicants.

- **Consider free schools.** From liberal arts colleges to music conservatories to military academies, a variety of tuition-free schools are available. At some of these schools, the tuition is subsidized by a large endowment. At others, mandatory work-study programs subsidize tuition costs. Admissions selectivity varies from high to moderate; for example, the Curtis Institute of Music, a tuition-free music conservatory, has an acceptance rate of 7 percent compared to approximately 43 percent at Alice Lloyd College in Kentucky. Military academies, meanwhile, will pay not only for students' tuition but also for books, room, board, and medical costs, as well as an average monthly stipend of $800. For these privileges, students must complete five years of active duty and three years of reserve duty in the military.

College Abroad? Pros and Cons

Attending college abroad can also be significantly less expensive than going to college in the U.S. During the 2008–2009 academic year, 1,230 out of 7,200 students at Scotland's University of St Andrews were Americans. Attending college outside the U.S. may not appeal to everybody, but there are clearly some advantages to consider—as well as a few drawbacks to bear in mind. In this section we will focus on universities in the United Kingdom and Canada, as schools in non-English-speaking countries require fluency in another language and are beyond the scope of this book.

UNITED KINGDOM

The U.K. offers many benefits to prospective college students. First, it is less expensive to attend a university in the U.K.; each year costs less than a private U.S. college and an undergraduate degree there is typically completed in three years rather than four. (Note, however, that although tuition at U.K. universities is minimal for European Union residents, it is higher for American students, and no financial aid is available. Also, varying currency exchange rates make tuition and the cost of living in the U.K. fluctuate accordingly.) Second, U.K. universities afford an international, cosmopolitan college experience; for example, you will be virtually guaranteed easy access to the entire continent of Europe via cheap air travel from the U.K. Finally, many U.K. universities offer great prestige, having established rich traditions over hundreds of years.

There are, however, potential downsides as well. U.K. schools typically offer students a more focused education than their U.S. counterparts; many do not emphasize a core curriculum, and at some it is difficult to take courses outside of your department. This means that students are able (and expected) to concentrate on their interests; for example, you will not be "forced" to take a math or science class if you're interested only in studying poetry. However, if you want the ability to change majors and the luxury of exploring a wide range of subjects, this narrow focus may not be for you.

Prospective U.S. students should also be aware of the U.K. application process. Ideally, your high school has offered the International Baccalaureate curriculum, as those courses are recognized by the British system. If not, your application will be evaluated primarily on SAT, Subject Test, and AP test scores (AP test scores in the 4–5 range are viewed especially favorably), as well as your GPA. Extracurriculars are of little importance. No essays or activity charts are required. Unless your differentiating spike is academic, it will be of little concern to U.K. or Canadian universities.

Note: Studying overseas may require a student visa. Begin this process as soon as possible, as delays are common!

MOST PRESTIGIOUS OVERSEAS COLLEGES

UNITED KINGDOM

Cambridge University

LSE (London School of
    Economics)

Oxford University

Trinity College, Dublin

University of Edinburgh

University of St Andrews

CANADA

Dalhousie University, Halifax

McGill University, Montreal

University of British Columbia

University of Toronto

University of Western Ontario

In general, we would recommend applying only to those overseas universities with "brand names" recognizable in the U.S. (see "Most Prestigious Overseas Colleges" below for examples), as this name-recognition factor is an important post-college consideration. Moreover, even the best-known British universities will offer a more limited U.S. alumni network, making it harder to land a job if and when you return to the U.S.

CANADA

Depending on the exchange rate, Canadian universities can be a very attractive option for U.S. families seeking to cut college costs. In fact, in 2008 the average yearly tuition cost for full-time, international undergraduate students at Canadian universities stood at just $14,487—more than $10,000 cheaper than the cost of an equivalent U.S. institution. Not coincidentally, the number of Americans studying at Canadian universities has risen by over 50 percent since 2001. As with U.K. universities, we recommend seeking out institutions with high name-recognition value in the United States (see "Most Prestigious Overseas Colleges")—unless, of course, you plan to start your postgraduate career up north.

The Three Types of Financial-Aid Policies

Once you've decided on the type of college you wish to attend, you'll need to navigate the varying financial-aid policies adopted by different schools. There are three main policy types:

1. **Need-Blind.** Students' financial-aid needs are not factored into admissions decisions, and the full needs of all admitted students are met. (Note: the amount of aid that colleges view as sufficient may differ from the amount your family considers sufficient.) In need-blind admissions, whatever portion of college costs cannot be financed through a family's own savings is covered through a combination of grants, loans, and work-study commitments (see "How to Apply for Financial Aid" on pages 233–37). It's important to remember that many public state schools are need-blind for in-state residents only.

2. Need-Conscious/Need-Sensitive. Admissions officers are aware of the financial situation of each student and consider a student's need when making admissions decisions. With financial-aid budgets decreasing due to lower endowments, fewer alumni donations, and greater student need, many formerly need-blind colleges now admit that they've had to become merely need-conscious or need-sensitive. Under this new policy, the most desirable students will be granted more generous financial-aid packages, while less desirable students may still be admitted but granted less attractive financial-aid packages. Some students may find themselves "gapped," or accepted but not granted the financial aid they need to attend. How can a student be gapped? Many admissions offices will rank admitted students in terms of how encouraging the school's financial-aid offer should be. In some cases, colleges will meet full need *only* for the students they want most.

Is it possible to file for financial aid after being accepted at a college with need-sensitive admissions? It's a sad question, but an important one nowadays, as not seeking financial aid when applying may increase your chances of being admitted. Some schools allow this option; others do not. Ask the college's financial-aid officer to be

"TEST-OPTIONAL" SCHOOLS AND MERIT-BASED AID

Students applying to "test-optional" schools (see page 39) often assume that test scores are as irrelevant to financial-aid distribution as they are to admissions consideration. However, many colleges that question the validity of SAT or ACT scores in college admissions, and therefore don't require them, still use these scores in awarding merit-based scholarships. Examples include Dickinson, Gettysburg, Goucher, Gustavus Adolphus, Hobart and William Smith, Lake Forest, Muhlenberg, and Lawrence University.

sure. If the school allows it, apply for financial aid during the second semester of your freshman year. Be aware, however, that applying for aid does not guarantee that you will get it, or that the aid you're granted will be sufficient.

3. **Merit-Based.** Aid is granted on the basis of achievement (academic, athletic, artistic, etc.), rather than need. Stanford, for example, grants merit-based aid for athletic ability. Many other colleges (University of North Carolina, University of Virginia, Emory, Vanderbilt, Duke, and Wake Forest, for example) award merit-based aid to students they "really want," that is, students with highly desirable athletic, artistic, and academic talents. This aid can be quite substantial: a student we worked with was recently flown to North Carolina to interview for the Angier B. Duke Scholarship, a merit-based full four-year scholarship to Duke University. Notably, the Ivy League and the Little Ivies (Amherst, Williams, and Wesleyan, for example) do not offer merit-based aid, maintaining that all students accepted are equally deserving and desirable.

How to Apply for Financial Aid

FORMS

First and foremost, beware of deadlines! Financial-aid forms are extremely complicated. Leave yourself enough time to gather the necessary information and complete them.

The following instructions are adapted from the federal government's Free Application for Federal Student Aid (FAFSA) Web site (http://www.fafsa.ed.gov) and the CSS/Financial Aid PROFILE section of the CollegeBoard Web site (http://www.collegeboard.com). Further details on the process outlined are available through these two sources.

- FAFSA is the form you must submit to determine how much financial aid you'll need. Access the form at www.fafsa.ed.gov, call 1-800-4-FED-AID, or ask your guidance counselor for a copy. You

"Dad, the dean has gone over your financial statement, and he doesn't think you're working up to your full potential."

can apply to receive a PIN number for your FAFSA in November of your senior year.

- Do not submit your financial-aid application before January 1 of your senior year. In judging your family's eligibility for aid, the Department of Education factors in all income and tax information from the most recent tax year (which ends on December 31). Financial-aid applications submitted before January 1 will be rejected.
- Send in your FAFSA *as soon as possible after January 1*. Don't wait until your taxes are done; you can use estimates of your income in the meantime, and you'll be able to correct any miscalculations later. If you wait too long, you might miss the deadline for state aid (early February for some states). After

submitting a FAFSA, you may apply for a Federal Pell Grant—which considers such factors as the cost of attending a given school—and other types of need-based aid. Note: To learn more about Pell and other federal grants, visit the federal student aid site at http://www.studentaid.ed.gov.

- After you submit the FAFSA, you will receive a Student Aid Report (SAR), typically in March. Your SAR contains all the data submitted through your FAFSA. Review this report for accuracy and confirm that it reflects your most recent tax returns.

- The supplement to FAFSA is called PROFILE and is administered by the College Board. More detailed than FAFSA, it is required by many private universities to determine your eligibility for nonfederal financial aid. Unlike FAFSA, the PROFILE form can be submitted in the fall of your senior year. Note that it may calculate your need differently from FAFSA, and that there is a fee for submitting this form to each school or scholarship you select.

AID PACKAGES

After you've submitted all of the necessary forms—including the FAFSA and the PROFILE supplement required by some schools—those colleges that accept you will send you a letter detailing the specific mix of aid you've been awarded. Called a financial-aid package, it typically comprises:

1. **Grants.** Money given to you that *you do not need to pay back*. Grants are typically based on need and/or merit. Awarded by nonprofits (for example, the government), they are also usually tax-exempt. Try to maximize this component of your overall aid package (see "Maximizing Financial Aid" section below).

2. **Loans.** Money lent to you by the federal or state government, a private company (for example, Sallie Mae), and/or the college itself that *you must repay*. Note: the amount of loans you are expected to pay back may increase from year one through year four of college.

3. **Work-Study.** Aid granted in exchange for work you will be expected to perform, that is, by taking a student job. Note: your work-study hours may also change from year one through year four. Some schools don't require first-year students to participate in work-study programs. Some schools also exempt athletes from work-study, replacing it with other forms of aid due to the extreme time constraints posed by college athletics.

4. **Scholarships.** Money awarded to you by the school, your state, or an outside organization. Scholarships are usually based, at least in part, on merit, tend to have set criteria for selection, and are provided by organizations that are not necessarily nonprofit. After a scholarship is awarded, a student may be expected to maintain a certain level of academic performance. There are also scholarships awarded to athletes, musicians, and minority students, as well as many other kinds of students—there is even a scholarship for left-handed students attending Juniata College in Pennsylvania (see FinAid.org for more information on unusual scholarships). How a scholarship is factored into your overall award amount differs from school to school. Scholarship money may be taxable; check with your college. See the end of this chapter for top scholarship Web sites.

FINANCIAL-AID "LEVERAGING"

The formula used to determine the combination of aid for a given student is usually undisclosed by colleges. In general, those students who are most attractive to a college—by whatever measure—will be offered the most attractive aid packages (that is, grants and scholarships, rather than loans and work-study commitments) as an incentive to attend. This process is known as financial-aid "leveraging." Thus it helps to consider not only which colleges you're most interested in but also which colleges might be most interested in you (see "Seek Colleges That Are Seeking You" on pages 238–39).

APPEALS

If you're dissatisfied with the financial-aid package you've received from your first-choice college, can you appeal? Yes, but the package is unlikely to change unless:

- Your family's financial situation has significantly changed recently (for example, due to job loss or illness).
- You've received a better package from another school, ideally one similar in caliber to your first-choice school. In this case, you may wish to try negotiating with the appropriate financial-aid officer (see "Negotiate" on page 239).

Maximizing Financial Aid: "Be Alike But Spike"

Following the "be alike but spike" strategy we've discussed throughout this book will help distinguish you not only as a college applicant but also as a financial-aid candidate at any college that accepts you. Here are three ways you can use your distinguishing passion to boost the amount of aid you receive:

1. **Spike Through Scholarships.** In terms of financial aid, scholarships serve two purposes. First, winning scholarships helps lessen the tuition burden of college. Second, and more important, any scholarships you receive while still in high school will help distinguish your

application, enhancing your spike and making you more *desirable* to colleges. The $1,000 award you receive for accomplishments in your spike area (be it dancing or volunteering at hospitals) may seem paltry in relation to your overall tuition bill; however, even that small recognition will make you a much more attractive college candidate, earning you not only acceptances but also enhanced financial-aid packages. Accordingly, we encourage you to pursue every scholarship for which you might reasonably be eligible. If you succeed, the benefits may far surpass the dollar amount you're awarded. See Resources (pages 275–76) for a list of top scholarships, and the list of top scholarship Web sites at the end of this chapter.

2. **Seek Colleges That Are Seeking You.** Applying to colleges that really, truly want students like you will improve your chances of receiving the most attractive aid package possible. But how can you determine whether a college fits that description?

- **Safety schools.** Review your college list (see Chapter 6, "Researching and Creating a Working College List") for "safeties" that you'd be happy to attend. Better yet, identify good safeties that offer need-blind admissions; that way, your financial need won't factor into any acceptance decisions. Safeties are safeties because you've outperformed other applicants to these schools in both the "be alike" *and* "spike" areas. For example, your GPA and SAT scores fall within the top 25 percent of candidates admitted, *plus* you have a terrific distinguishing extracurricular interest. Assuming these conditions, all the safeties on your list are schools that would really want you as a student.

- **Schools that like your spike.** First, look to your college list for "probable" colleges, that is, schools in which your GPA and SAT scores fall within the top half of admitted students. Unfortunately, those numbers alone won't be enough to guarantee a favorable aid package. But combine them with a school that's trying to launch a program related to your extracurricular spike, or that needs your specific skill for one of their campus organizations, and you may have a big advantage over other applicants—one that could translate into an enticing financial-aid package. Note: What colleges need often changes from year to year. Luck and timing are always factors in college admissions.

- **Schools offering merit-based aid.** Even if you don't need financial help, your spike may help you receive merit-based aid, which, as described above, is issued to particularly desirable candidates regardless of need. Again, your distinguishing spike is all-important in capturing this type of aid.

3. **Negotiate.** Ideally, once you've applied to colleges that fit the descriptions above—and that you'd be happy to attend—you will receive an aid package from one or more schools. Just as with job offers, we recommend attempting to negotiate financial-aid offers. Although doing so isn't guaranteed to get you more aid from your first-choice school, it never hurts to try. Most financial-aid officers don't haggle, but there are some that do, and a polite request can sometimes elicit a positive response.

We believe that using your spike to maximize your financial aid is an essential part of the process. College is expensive. It's your responsibility as a consumer to reduce that expense by comparing aid packages, negotiating better ones wherever possible, and picking the right school *and* package for you.

Web Resources—Scholarship Search Engines

Below are three of the most popular college scholarship search engines and Web sites, at the time of publication:

- FastWeb's scholarship search engine. (http://www.fastweb.com)
- CollegeBoard Scholarship Search, located on the CollegeBoard Web site (http://www.collegeboard.com).
- FinAid's scholarship listings (www. http://www.finaid.org)

For additional financial-aid and scholarship resources, see the Resources and Selected Bibliography appendixes.

College and Beyond

Overview

In this section you'll learn:

- What steps to take when you get the all-important acceptance letter
- How to apply the skills you've developed as part of our "be alike but spike" strategy throughout college... and beyond

Congratulations, You're In! Now what?

You've opened your mailbox (or more likely, logged onto your college account or read your e-mail) and—wonder of wonders—you've just been accepted to your dream college. Tears form in your eyes. As you reach for that box of tissues, here's some advice on what to do next.

First, make sure you know the response deadline. If you were accepted regular decision, that date is most likely May 1, but check the acceptance letter for exact dates and details. The college will need to receive your deposit and acceptance of their offer of admission by that date. Second, if the acceptance was from your top-choice college and you're not considering any other schools, withdraw your applications from all other prospective colleges and decline acceptances from other schools to which you've been offered admission. Doing this promptly is not only polite but also opens up spots at these schools for other students—for example, those who have been waitlisted and deferred.

Although this may seem obvious, we do not recommend declining any offers of admission until you've also received acceptances from colleges that are clearly preferable. But suppose you've been admitted to two or three colleges and are having trouble choosing between them?

In this case, don't rush to make your decision. First, decline all acceptances from colleges that you are not considering. Next, plan to visit the colleges you are still interested in. (You may have already visited these schools. Try to visit again.) Most colleges have a special weekend devoted to admitted students. As we advise in Chapter 7, "How to Visit Colleges," don't hide out indoors: get as full a sense of the school as possible during your visit. Spend a night on campus with students in a freshman dorm; eat lunch in the dining hall; hang out in the student center; visit the library; attend a student performance or sports event. Also, visit the academic department in which you hope to major, speak to the coordinator about major requirements, and ask to attend a department class. In essence, try to imagine yourself at the college. After these visits, your decision should be clearer.

Note: In some cases, it may pay to respond more quickly to an offer of acceptance. For example, some schools have limited housing for students hoping to live on campus. Know your college's policy: if you want student housing and it's distributed on a first-come-first-served basis, you may want to give your answer sooner rather than later.

College Application Skills, in College and Beyond

You're finally at college, experiencing what many believe to be the best four years of your life. The skills you developed while creating a top college application can fall by the wayside, right? Not so fast. Read on to learn more about how to apply your college-application skills in college and beyond.

Be Alike But Spike, in College and Beyond

In the course of working with hundreds of students and families, we've come to understand that the process of creating a spike is useful for more than just the college-admissions process. In fact, its effects last far beyond college. Identifying a genuine passion and engaging in activities to explore that passion—layering one activity upon another—to build an area of differentiation, certainly leads to short-term success in admissions, but it can also lay the groundwork for a lifetime of fulfilling work. And although these future benefits may seem distant and unimportant now—especially compared to that acceptance letter from Top Choice University—they may prove to be far more rewarding in the end.

The spike process begins with a simple truth: do what you genuinely enjoy. In high school, most students choose their activities without caring how they are remunerated or evaluated by society. Their interests are genuine. However, we've observed that as they age, they often stop listening to themselves and begin listening to outside voices. Accordingly, their standards change: what are the "cool" careers? What are my friends interested in pursuing? What is a respected or prestigious profession? What pays the most? What do my partner/my parents/my in-laws want me to become? Their interior voice gets muffled and they quickly lose track of pursuing what they're truly passionate about.

We encourage college students and postgrads not to give up on their genuine passions too quickly. Remember the case studies we discussed in the earlier chapters? The students we've worked with have continued to pursue and build on their high school interests, achieving great things in college and beyond.

The process these students went through in high school—figuring out what they were interested in and finding creative ways to explore it—has stayed with them. They have continued to explore outlets for their passions both during and after college. Intentionally or unintentionally, they've expanded upon their high school experience again and again.

Pursuing a Passion

What steps did these students take in high school that they expanded upon in college and beyond?

1. They figured out what they were interested in.
   - This is easier said than done. However, our students brainstormed ideas in ninth, tenth, and eleventh grade—before expectations of prestige, wealth, and so forth clouded the picture.
2. They explored their interest from many different angles—that is, they "layered." Through this process, they saw their interest transform into a passion.
3. They took their exploration outside the confines of their high school, gaining practical, real-world entrepreneurial experience.
   - This extracurricular exploration required working with adults who weren't affiliated with their high school—and thus developing and using their interpersonal skills. Our students had to convince others to help them (and unlike their teachers, these adults were not paid to help them succeed).
   - Exploring their interest outside of high school also required the organization, planning, and scheduling skills necessary to see a project through to fruition.
4. They learned how to market themselves and their passion on the college application.
   - They had to use the college application—four pages—to represent seventeen years of their lives!
5. Finally, on a practical level, they learned how to excel at interviewing, create impressive activity charts, and earn outstanding letters of recommendation. These skills become more, not less, important in postgraduate life.

Application Skills, Applied in College and Beyond

Unless you plan to be a writer, you will not be expected to write essays to secure your first summer internship or postgraduate job. However, you *will* need to interview, create a CV or résumé (similar in many ways to a condensed activity chart), and secure recommendations. This section is not meant to be a post-college career guide; rather, it is intended to give you a general sense of how your college-application skills will continue to be important and applicable in the real world.

INTERVIEWING

Get good at interviewing; it is truly a skill that you will use for the rest of your life. Being able to walk into a room, conduct a conversation with a person you've never met, answer their (often difficult) questions, exchange ideas, convey your experience, and (ideally) impress that person matters not only in the job-search process but also in much of real-world business and social life.

In the college-admissions process, few students are accepted on the basis of a great interview alone. The importance of interviews, however, increases dramatically once you've entered the job market. When you apply for summer internships or post-college jobs, you're rarely judged on standardized test scores or answers to essay questions. Instead, the vast majority of job decisions are based upon a thirty-minute interview. Even if you have an outstanding résumé, your job prospects may be very limited if you can't ace those thirty minutes.

However, most companies—like colleges—expect all qualified candidates to have basic interviewing skills—presenting yourself well, speaking articulately, exchanging ideas intelligently. Once you move beyond entry-level positions, these skills will rarely be enough to get you hired. Advancing further will require communicating what makes you stand out from your peers—in other words, displaying a spike. As in college interviews, you'll need to explain specifically how that spike will further the company's mission, making you a valuable asset to the organization.

"Will my office be near an ice machine?"

Here are a few other "musts" that apply to all interviews, not just the college admissions kind.

1. **Do your research.** Before you interview, find out as much as you can about the organization. Know what it's best at and how it's trying to grow. Most important, know why you want to work there and why they should hire you. (Just as there are bad answers to college interview questions, there are bad job interview answers. "Your office is close to my apartment and offers free coffee and breakfast" is not a valid reason for wanting to join a company.) Arriving at an interview uninformed is disrespectful and demonstrates that you're really not that interested in the job.

   The best ways to do this kind of research:

   - Speak to people who already work there or used to work there.
   - Go online. Search for the company Web site and newspaper articles about the company. (Our advice: stay away from gossip-ridden blogs.)

2. **Practice, practice, practice.** Remember the mock interviews we recommended for college interviews? Outside of actual interviews, we believe that mock interviews are the best way to prepare for job interviews. Create a list of likely questions and prepare answers to those questions. Below we list a few, but our advice is to get a job guide or contact your college career service office for a complete list that is customized to your industry or area of interest. Remember to schedule your interviews in reverse order of preference. Schedule the interview for your top-choice job last.

   The following questions frequently come up during job interviews. Note the similarity to college interview questions!

   - Tell me about yourself.
   - What are your primary strengths? Weaknesses?
   - Why did you decide to attend your college/choose your major?
   - What was your favorite/least favorite class?
   - Why do you want to do this (type of work)? Why do you want to work for us?
   - What could you contribute to our company?
   - Tell me about this internship or part-time work experience. What were your responsibilities? What did you learn? What did you contribute?
   - Do you have any questions for me? (Always answer yes, and always prepare a few questions ahead of time.)

3. **Connect past to future.** As we've emphasized throughout this book, employers, like college admissions officers, assume that past performance is indicative of future performance. Though they may not count as "real-world" work, college extracurriculars can generate an impressive record of achievement. Building the reader base for a college newspaper, producing a college play, spearheading fundraisers for a nonprofit student organization... these experiences, and the skills you gain from them, are valuable and transferable to the real world. Employers will assume that having achieved a goal once—even in a college environment—you'll be able to do so again and again in a professional setting.

RÉSUMÉS

Think of your activity chart as your first résumé. Sure, it's in a different format, and it's slightly longer than a typical one-page résumé, but beyond these superficial disparities, there are more similarities than differences. Like your AC, your résumé is a "brag sheet": a one-page document that tells potential employers important details about your academic, professional, and extracurricular background. Like the interview process, it also increases exponentially in importance once you graduate from college. As your grades and test scores become a thing of the past, it's your past experience that counts. And much of that experience is represented by this single sheet of paper.

What lessons carry over from your activity chart to your real-world résumé?

1. Begin creating your résumé early (during your freshman year of college) and keep it up to date. You will need a résumé as long as you are working, and that includes jobs and internships during college.

2. As you write your résumé, continue to use the list of action verbs we provided in Chapter 8 (see pages 146–47). Why? Because your résumé is only one page long. Each word must convey leadership, responsibility, and results. Get used to using concise, action-oriented language to describe what you accomplished within an organization.

3. As on the activity chart, don't be afraid to brag on your résumé. More important, do so in quantifiable terms. How much did you increase readership for your magazine when you were circulation manager? What were the results of your prize-winning direct mail campaign? What was the value of the acquisitions you worked on last year? How much revenue were you responsible for bringing into the company? Your assertions mean much more if you can back them up with hard facts.

4. Show a progression in responsibility. Perhaps you worked at the same campus newspaper for all four years of college. How did your positions change over the years? What new tasks were you given? If you worked at the same summer job for two summers, don't lump those summers together. Rather, show how your job titles changed and your responsibilities grew from the first summer to the second.

5. Accentuate your accomplishments. Just as we help students emphasize their spikes on the activity chart, we encourage them to do so on their résumés. If it's marketing you want to pursue, don't bury that marketing internship—highlight it. How can you accentuate your area of strength?

  - Give it more room on the résumé: include more bullet points and go into greater detail about your accomplishments. Since your résumé is limited to one page, think carefully about how to divide up that real estate. More space signifies greater importance.
  - List it higher on the page. People read from top to bottom. (Of course, résumés are also organized from most to least recent position, so this may mean eliminating more recent but less important experiences where necessary.)
  - Be creative. Even if you're not yet getting exactly the kind of experience you want, you may be able to pursue it tangentially. Look for opportunities to explore your true interest within your existing position, or in your free time through volunteer opportunities.

6. Check and double-check your résumé. Have three, five, or even ten people review it. Check grammar, spelling, punctuation, capitalization… we can't emphasize this enough. This one page represents you and it should be error-free. Often applicants with error-ridden résumés won't even warrant a job interview.

RECOMMENDATIONS

Recommendations are as important for job seeking as they are for college admissions. Out in the real world there are two main types:

1. Written recommendations by a college professor or employer. These are typically needed for graduate school applications and, as with college letters of recommendation, may involve a standardized form.

2. Oral recommendations from one employer to another. Prior to extending a job offer, an employer may contact one of your past employers or colleagues as a reference. The method may be more casual, but this type of recommendation is just as important.

For both types of recommendations:

- Pick someone you trust. If you have questions about what your recommender thinks about you, there's usually a reason. Choose someone else.
- Pick someone who knows you well and likes you.
- Pick someone you worked with recently, either in the academic or professional sphere. A choice from too far in the past will seem suspicious; your recommender should be able to discuss recent and applicable experiences. Generally speaking, if you're employed, one of your recommenders should be the person to whom you report. (There is an exception: you do not need to ask your supervisor in cases where your job would be at risk if your employer knew that you wanted to leave.)
- Pick someone who can confirm the assertions you make on your résumé and can boast on your behalf.
- Remember, a bland or neutral recommendation can hurt you. You want your recommendation to be wholeheartedly enthusiastic.

As with college recommendations, we advise scheduling a meeting at which to ask your professor, supervisor, or colleague to serve as

"Do you have any references besides Batman?"

CAREER SERVICES

Use your college career services office; it's an amazing resource. Its staff should be able to advise you on all aspects of summer and post-graduate planning and exploration: career opportunities, graduate and professional schools, fellowships, internships, interviewing, résumé and cover letters, company research, on- and off-campus recruiting, alumni contact information, and more. Remember that the office serves not only current college students but alumni as well.

recommender. Bring your updated résumé as well as examples of anecdotes or experiences you might like your recommender to stress.

Finally, remember that writing a recommendation or speaking to a potential employer on your behalf takes time—don't forget to say thank you!

A Final Note

The skills we nurture in our students help make them flexible and resilient during the college-admissions process, in college, and beyond. As we hope this book has shown, passions can and should be explored in many ways, and the skills you gain through exploring them are adaptable to many opportunities and circumstances. Because we can never foresee changes in our future, this flexibility is a valuable asset.

Learning how to develop a passion also gives you the ability to *create* opportunities, rather than staying on the sidelines and waiting for them to "spring up." The students we've worked with understand how to influence and take charge of their futures. Just as important, they aren't afraid of becoming leaders. They understand, from personal experience, that all seemingly overwhelming projects begin with very small steps. The entrepreneurial skills they develop in high school become second nature. And they apply them again and again, achieving a lifetime not only of success, but also of fulfillment.

Appendixes

The College Preparation Timeline

This timeline is designed to provide an overview of the steps we advise students to take during the fall, spring, and summer of each of their years in high school in preparation for applying to college. Detailed advice about these steps can be found in the chapters cross-referenced below.

Note: Although our timeline is broken down by season, many students will need to plan the timing of these steps around extracurricular commitments. For example, dedicated lacrosse players may find it more difficult to focus on college preparation during the spring, when their sports schedule is most intense. Take these conflicts into account ahead of time, adjusting to ensure that you complete all of the necessary steps within a given year, even if you can't get all of them done in the season we recommend.

Freshman Year

Freshman year isn't too soon to begin thinking about college. The first step toward college admission is laying the groundwork for success early in high school. Many students tell us that they've heard that colleges don't really "count" freshman year (in calculating GPA, for example). Don't believe this—every year of high school is important. Although there are colleges that don't count your freshman year grades in your overall GPA, many do.

FALL

- Begin exploring a variety of in-school extracurriculars. Start identifying which extracurricular organizations you enjoy most (see Chapter 3, "In-School Leadership Activities," pp. 64–69).
- Review the activity chart (AC) categories. You don't need to begin filling out an AC; just note the different categories: In-School Extracurriculars, Out-of-School Extracurriculars, Summer Activities, and Employment. Ideally, by the end of your senior year, you'll be able to include activities in which you've participated in each of these categories. See Chapter 8, "Preparing the Activity Chart and Completing the Written Application," (pp. 131–47).
- Begin brainstorming your spike, or area of interest. See Chapter 4, "Creating Your Spike" (pp. 73–80).
- Determine whether you will be taking any SAT Subject Tests at the end of freshman year. See Chapter 2, "Standardized Tests" (pp. 37–63).

SPRING

- Meet your guidance counselor and review your course track. In most cases, it's too soon to begin thinking about AP courses, but if you're aiming for the Ivy League, those colleges will want to see that you've explored the most competitive courses that your school offers. Taking these courses may require you to be on the advanced track from freshman year onward, especially in math and science. Some students use the summer to take a catch-up course so they can be on a more advanced track. See Chapter 1, "Academic Achievement" (pp. 21–36).
- Read good books and articles; this is the single most important preparation for the Critical Reading part of the SATs, advanced English/humanities classes, and in many ways for college itself. See Chapter 2, "Standardized Tests" (pp. 37–63).
- Speak up in class and contribute. If you're having trouble in any class, seek out extra help before or after school with your teacher. See Chapter 1, "Academic Achievement" (pp. 21–36).

- Use the upcoming summer for more than just hanging out. Apply for internships and summer jobs. See Resources (pp. 276–90) for summer programs that might reinforce your area of interest. Getting a job, even one that's not tied to your area of interest, such as landscaping, pumping gas, working in construction, or full-time caregiver, can also be an excellent learning experience.

Sophomore Year

For many students, sophomore year may feel like the last year of simply being a high school student without facing an onslaught of applications, standardized tests, interviews, and school visits. Take advantage by doing as well as you can in classes. Seek out teachers for extra help. Brainstorm ways to develop and enhance your spike, or area of differentiation—look for opportunities both within and outside of your high school.

FALL

- Begin filling in your activity chart. This is your ongoing résumé. Get in the habit of updating it and noting if any sections look suspiciously empty. See Chapter 8, "Preparing the Activity Chart and Completing the Written Application" (pp. 131–47).
- Register for the PSAT if your high school encourages this. (There's no downside; colleges never see PSAT scores unless they are exceptionally high.) See Chapter 2, "Standardized Tests" (pp. 37–63).
- Continue pursuing and seeking in-school extracurricular activities that interest you. See Chapter 3, "In-School Leadership Activities" (pp. 64–69).
- Begin speaking to older students and alumni about colleges. See Chapter 6, "Researching and Creating a Working College List" (pp. 96–115).

SPRING

- Begin researching ideas for the summer. Employment, a pre-college summer program in your area of interest, or working closely with a nonprofit organization are all excellent activity choices. Sitting on the couch watching movies is not. See Chapter 4, "Creating Your Spike" (pp. 73–80).

- Evaluate the classes you're taking. How are you doing in them? Are they too easy for you or have you taken on too much? As a very general rule, if you can't maintain a B- in a course even with extra help, regardless of the level of difficulty, the class is probably too tough for you and you should consider moving down to an easier level. See Chapter 1, "Academic Achievement" (pp. 21–36).

- Register for any Subject Tests and AP Exams you plan to take. Note: You may or may not need Subject Tests (typically, the more competitive colleges require one, two, or even, in some cases, three Subject Tests). See Chapter 2, "Standardized Tests" (pp. 37–63).

- If you have any learning issues, and especially if you are already getting extra time for tests at your high school, this is when you will need to apply for extra time on the SAT or ACT. You may need to get tested by an independent psychologist. See Chapter 2, "Standardized Tests" (p. 61).

- At year's end, once you have your two-year GPA and PSAT results, begin to think seriously about colleges and start compiling a working list. See Chapter 6, "Researching and Creating a Working College List" (pp. 96–115). After you have prepared your list, review your colleges' testing requirements (SATs, ACTs, Subject Tests, etc.).

SUMMER

- Do preparatory work for the October PSAT. This is especially important if you believe you have the potential to be a National Merit Scholar Semifinalist or Finalist. See Chapter 2, "Standardized Tests" (p. 44).

- Register for junior-year courses. Be "realistically ambitious" in your choices. Competitive colleges are looking not only for a high GPA but also for a course load that is sensibly challenging.

Junior Year

Many students feel that this is the most difficult year of high school. You are not only working hard to keep up your grades, participating in extracurriculars, and further developing your spike, or area of differentiation, but also preparing for and taking standardized tests. Remember, however, that some down time is important too.

FALL

- Continue developing your spike. If you can, try to incorporate community service into your area of differentiation. This is particularly important for the most privileged candidates. See Chapter 5, "Layering Your Passion" (pp. 81–93).
- Update your Activity Chart and make sure employment is a part of your extracurriculars. (An exception would be if you are the primary caregiver for a sibling, parent, or grandparent.) A job with real-world responsibilities is seen as a crucial building block by many admissions officers. See Chapter 8, "Preparing the Activity Chart and Completing the Written Application (p. 135).
- When you get your PSAT results, analyze them and figure out where you need the most work. This analysis will help you efficiently prepare for the SATs. Begin to explore tutoring options, if necessary. See Chapter 2, "Standardized Tests" (pp. 37–63).
- Focus on your classwork. Junior year grades are important—in some cases, they're the last grades some colleges may see. See Chapter 1, "Academic Achievement" (pp. 21–36).
- Begin to consider which two teachers you will ask for letters of recommendation. Typically, they will be junior-year teachers of academic subjects (math, science, English, history, or language).

Make sure you are doing well in their classes and try to establish a rapport with them. See Chapter 10, "Letters of Recommendation" (pp. 187–202).

- Sign up for ACTs/SATs, SAT Subject Tests, and AP Tests. Remember that most colleges have a score-choice policy, which permits you to decide which scores to allow the schools to see (see p. 50)—but do not take them unless you are fully prepared. Some colleges will want to see *all* of your scores (at the time of this writing, Stanford, University of Pennsylvania, Pomona, USC, Cornell, and Yale are on this growing list). Prepare thoroughly for each test. We typically advise 4–6 months of prep for SATs and ACTs, and 3 months for Subject Tests while you are taking the relevant courses.

   Note: You may also need prep for AP Tests. Check with your teacher to see if you will be tested in any areas that are not covered by your classes. If so, seek out extra help. See Chapter 2, "Standardized Tests" (pp. 56–58).

SPRING

- Based on your GPA and practice standardized test scores, continue to refine your college list, balancing safeties, probables, and reaches. It's easy to find reaches that you would love to attend, but harder to find great safeties; research carefully to find schools that will both accept you and provide an atmosphere that you'll enjoy. It's also a good time to start looking at the colleges' application forms. Their essay questions will give you a good idea of the kind of student they are seeking. This is often a good way to judge if you are a good fit for that college, even at this early stage. See Chapter 6, "Researching and Creating a Working College List" (pp. 96–115).

- Meet with your high school college guidance counselor. Plan to discuss with him/her the kind of college you hope to attend. See Chapter 6, "Researching and Creating a Working College List" (pp. 106–7).

- Visit colleges during your spring break and over long weekends. Speak to friends, older siblings, alumni, etc. Attend college fairs and information sessions at your high school. See Chapter 7, "How to Visit Colleges" (pp. 116–30).

- Register with the NCAA Clearinghouse if you are interested in college athletics. See Chapter 12, "Supplemental Application Materials" (p. 222).

- Take SATs, SAT Subject Tests, and AP tests. See Chapter 2, "Standardized Tests" (pp. 37–63).

- Before summer vacation, ask two teachers if they will write you letters of recommendation in the fall. Ask early to confirm that they are willing and eager; if they are reluctant, there is still time to approach others. See Chapter 10, "Letters of Recommendation" (pp. 187–96).

- Think about this upcoming summer as another opportunity to build upon and expand your spike. Explore internships and local jobs as well as pre-college programs. See Chapter 5, "Layering Your Passion" (pp. 81–93) and Resources (pp. 276–88).

SUMMER

- Begin working on your personal essay for admissions applications. We recommend preparing one general personal essay that can be used or at least "tweaked" for most college applications. Short-answer essays are often more specific and difficult to tweak. Have your parents review your essays and provide feedback. See Chapter 9, "Essays" (pp. 154–86).

Senior Year

The final stretch. Continue to work hard academically while preparing applications that reflect all of your hard work and creativity. Finally, once spring rolls around, don't fall prey to senioritis—colleges do revoke acceptances for precipitous drops in grades.

FALL

- Revisit each teacher you asked for a letter of recommendation. Provide them with self-addressed stamped envelopes (or online equivalent) for each of the colleges on your list. Give them six weeks to prepare their letters. Remember to send thank-you notes to the teachers who write your recommendations. See Chapter 10, "Letters of Recommendation" (pp. 187–202).

- Double-check your transcript to make sure there are no errors. See Chapter 1, "Academic Achievement" (p. 30) and "The Team Approach: Learning to Use Your Parents" (pp. 150–52).

- Finalize your college list. Review it with your guidance counselor to make sure the list is appropriate and contains adequate numbers of safeties, probables, and reaches. See Chapter 6, "Researching and Creating a Working College List" (pp. 96–115). Decide whether you have a clear first choice to which you want to apply Early Decision (ED). Visit overnight and attend classes at the colleges to which you are considering applying ED. See "How to Visit Colleges" (pp. 116–30).

- Update your Activity Chart with your summer and senior year activities. Note any remaining gaps and attempt to fill them in. See Chapter 8, "Preparing the Activity Chart and Completing the Written Application" (pp. 131–47).

- Ask your guidance counselor to review your essays and provide feedback. Continue to refine your essays. See Chapter 6, "Researching and Creating a Working College List" (pp. 106–7), and Chapter 9, "Essays" (pp. 154–86).

- Go to commonapp.org or the Web site for each college on your list and download applications. Pay close attention to application deadline dates, requirements, and rules regarding the submission of any supplemental materials (including supplements to the Common Application). See Chapter 8, "Preparing the Activity Chart and Completing the Written Application" (pp. 147–53).

- Note which of your schools, if any, conduct admissions on a rolling basis. The earlier the application is submitted to these schools, the better, and the earlier you will be notified of their decision. See Chapter 6, "Researching and Creating a Working College List" (pp. 113–15).
- Register for the SATs and/or Subject Tests as necessary. Confirm all test dates, as the schedule varies in different states and for different tests. See Chapter 2, "Standardized Tests" (p. 53).
- Attend any college fairs or presentations offered at your high school or in your community. Meet the admissions officers and collect their business cards. Send follow-up thank-you notes to any universities that you are interested in. See Chapter 6, "Researching and Creating a Working College List" (p. 104).
- Confirm that letters of recommendation (from both teachers and guidance counselor) and transcripts have been sent to the colleges on your list. See Chapter 8, "Preparing the Activity Chart and Completing the Written Application (pp. 147–53) and Chapter 10, "Letters of Recommendation" (p. 196).
- Work hard in class and maintain your grades. Senior year counts. Many colleges will want to see your first-semester grades prior to making their decision. See Chapter 1, "Academic Achievement" (pp. 35–36).
- Take or retake SATs and Subject Tests. Assuming that you prepare fully for these tests, data suggests that students improve their scores by (re)taking them during fall of senior year. See Chapter 2, "Standardized Tests" (pp. 37–63).
- Complete and submit Early Action/Early Decision 1 and Rolling Admission applications. Continue working on Early Decision 2 and Regular Admission applications. See Chapter 6, "Researching and Creating a Working College List" (pp. 110–15).
- Call the admissions offices of the colleges to which you applied Early Action/Early Decision 1 and/or Rolling Admission to confirm that they have received the necessary information from you and your high school and that your application is complete. Your

application cannot be reviewed before it is complete. A missing letter of recommendation can cause an application to be designated incomplete and can mean the difference between an acceptance and a rejection. See Chapter 6, "Researching and Creating a Working College List" (pp. 110–15) and "The Team Approach: Learning to Use Your Parents" (pp. 150–52).

- Before the end of the year, you should hear from your ED1 and EA schools. If accepted to your ED1 school, withdraw all other applications. If deferred from either, write a compelling letter stating your continued desire to attend the school and submit updates on achievements relevant to your candidacy. See "College and Beyond" (pp. 240–41) and appendix "Deferral and Waitlist Strategies" (pp. 263–67).

WINTER

- Finish all outstanding applications (if necessary). Once they have been sent, call the colleges' admissions offices to confirm that they have received all required information (your application as well as high school transcript and letters of recommendation). See Chapter 6, "Researching and Creating a Working College List" (pp. 110–15) and "The Team Approach: Learning to Use Your Parents" (pp. 150–52).

SPRING

- Hear the news and evaluate your options! If you have been deferred or waitlisted, see appendix "Deferral and Waitlist Strategies" (pp. 263–67). If you have received multiple acceptances, try to visit all the schools you are seriously considering. Once you have made up your mind, inform all colleges of your decision to attend or not attend. See "College and Beyond" (pp. 240–41).
- Send in deposit and all housing forms promptly to the school of your choice. Remember, at some schools, housing is limited. The

earlier you send in your forms, the better. See "College and Beyond" (pp. 240–41).

- Beware of senior spring. Colleges do withdraw acceptances if your GPA drops significantly. If you're used to getting A's, don't get anything lower than a B—and definitely don't let your grades fall across the board.

- Register for your remaining AP exams, prepare thoroughly, and take the tests. Remember that successful performance (as determined by each college) can be used for college credit. See Chapter 2, "Standardized Tests" (pp. 48–50).

- Graduate! Send your final transcript to the college you will be attending.

Deferral and Waitlist Strategies

Deferrals

It is possible that, despite your best efforts, you will be deferred from your Early Decision, Early Action, or Rolling Admissions college. If this happens, take heart and keep two things in mind. First, the decision is not personal; the college simply had too many applicants for too few spots. Second, you haven't been rejected. Don't give up!

That said, you need to be realistic and plan accordingly. If you were deferred by your top-choice school, you need to prepare for the worst-case scenario: that you won't be admitted in April. Apply to a full range of reaches, probables, and safeties. You should also take into consideration that you were deferred by your top-choice *reach*—and be sure that you have the appropriate number of safeties and probables on your list.

If you applied Early Decision, a deferral releases you from your contractual obligation to attend that college. Although it may still be your first choice, you no longer *have* to attend if admitted. Therefore, the first question you need to ask yourself is whether you still really want to attend this college. If so, proceed to "Next Steps for Deferral and Waitlist Candidates" below.

"Don't cry, Mom. Lots of parents have children who didn't get into their first-choice college, and they went on to live happy, fulfilled lives."

Waitlist

Again, despite their best efforts, each year many students are waitlisted at their top-choice colleges. And again, the first thing to realize in this situation is that it was not a personal rejection; it merely means that the school had fewer openings than qualified candidates. Waitlist sizes and policies differ from college to college. Some use their waitlist to "gently reject" students who have connections to the school (children of alumni or applicants with ties to a faculty member, for example), preferring not to reject them outright. Other colleges use their waitlist to manage their yield; after determining how many of the students they have accepted will actually attend, they fill any shortfall from the waitlist. As a result, there are years when colleges will take no waitlist candidates, whereas

DEPOSITS

Can you give one school a deposit while remaining on the waitlist for another? Yes, because waitlists are not sure things. If the waitlist school comes through, you can then let the school to which you've sent a deposit know that you are no longer interested. Because it wasn't a school you applied to ED, you aren't bound to attend; you will, however, forfeit your deposit.

in other years, they will take a hundred. It all depends on how many accepted students choose to enroll.

So what should you do if you get a waitlist letter? First, ask yourself whether your heart is still really set on that school. Are there other schools to which you've been accepted that you would rather attend? If that's the case, then all you need to do is notify the school and ask to be removed from their waitlist. If, however, you want to stay "active" on the waitlist and hope for an eventual acceptance, here are the next steps you should take.

Next Steps for Deferral and Waitlist Candidates

1. Write a letter to the admissions officer responsible for your district or high school, restating your desire to attend. If you've been waitlisted, doing this will ensure that you remain "active" on the waitlist. If you've been deferred, this will ensure that the college knows you still really want to attend. The letter should briefly answer the following two questions as specifically as possible: Why do you want to attend? What will you contribute that will make the campus a better place?

   Note: As with any letter you submit to a school, include your name, e-mail address, date of birth, social security number, and high school. Always close with an affirmation that the college is your first choice and that you are committed to attend if admitted.

2. Do well in your classes. This may sound obvious, but many students ignore this point—especially during the second half of senior year. Admissions officers will consider these grades carefully when determining who gets offered admission.

3. Submit any supplementary materials that you believe would improve your chances with the admissions committee. These materials should not duplicate anything you've sent before, but if you've been featured in a newspaper article, received an additional letter of recommendation, or written an additional college essay—one that demonstrates *something new*—since first applying, then by all means, submit it. But be selective. Do not submit, for example, a chemistry exam on which you received an A.

   Note: Don't bombard the admissions office with daily letters or e-mails. Admissions officers do not want stalkers. However, it is wise to keep admissions officers apprised of your progress in different areas with several letters over a period of a few months.

4. Update the admissions office on your extracurricular spike. Have you developed it further since you first applied? If so, describe your progress and reiterate how you would bring your project to their college community, if you were lucky enough to be accepted. Have you been successful in training an underclassman to take over your project after you graduate? This is the time to tell the admissions office. Your spike is what sets you apart from the rest of the applicants and reemphasizing it may tip the balance toward acceptance.

   Note: Sometimes admissions officers are trying to fill specific holes in the class. They may decide they don't have enough artists, for example, or musicians or mathematicians. Having a distinctive focus will set you apart and may be the key to earning you an acceptance letter.

5. If you can afford it, it's always a good idea to visit the school again. Plan the trip carefully. Even if you've already interviewed, schedule a meeting with someone in the admissions office, ideally the admissions officer responsible for your high school. That way, when that officer goes into committee meetings about whom to accept, he or she

will be able to argue for your admission from a more compelling and personal perspective. Audit a class in your area of interest. Thank the professor after class and let him or her know how much you hope to attend the college. You can also write a letter to the admissions office letting them know how much you loved the course and the professor.

Finally, don't give up! We've seen many instances of students who have persevered in this way and have been accepted in the regular applicant pool (in the case of deferral) or taken off the waitlist. Be assertive and positive and give it everything you've got. Your efforts might just result in that precious acceptance letter to the college of your dreams.

College Savings Plans

The following chart presents the key features of the four most popular college savings plans—529 College Savings Plans, Coverdell Education Savings Accounts (ESAs), UGMA/UTMA Custodial Accounts, and Rebate and Loyalty Programs—making it easy to compare and contrast them. Most likely, by the time you read this book and are applying to college, you and/or your parents will already be familiar with one or more of these plans. Obviously, the earlier you start to save for college, the better, but even at this stage there are steps you and/or your parents can take to increase your savings.

The chart is meant to be a general guideline. The specifics of these plans change often and may vary from state to state. For more detailed information, the Web sites listed below are good places to start. As with any financial decision, everyone's situation is different. If possible, you should consult a financial planner or an accountant to determine the savings plans that are the best for you.

College Savings Plan	529 College Savings Plans	Coverdell Education Savings Accounts (formerly Education IRAs)	UGMA/UTMA (Uniform Gifts to Minors/ Uniform Transfers to Minors) Custodial Accounts	Rebate and Loyalty Programs (see affinity programs listed below)
What can the savings plan pay for?	Qualified college educational expenses	Qualified K–12 and college expenses	Any expense for the child, not just educational. Asset distribution must be for the child.	Tuition benefits, credits to a 529 College Savings Plan or Coverdell ESA. Average rebate is 4–5%
How much can I contribute?	Minimum contribution is as low as $15. Maximum contribution is between $100,000 and $350,000, depending on the state.	Minimum varies by firm. Maximum contribution of $2,000 per year.	Minimum contribution is $2,500 per year. Maximum contribution is $13,000 (or $26,000 for a couple) per year.	Unlimited. Register your credit card with companies (see below). They track your purchases at the designated stores and reward you with rebates to your savings plan.
Is my contribution limited by my income?	No	Yes. As of 2009, this type of account cannot be opened if a single filer earns more than $95,000 or a couple earns more than $190,000.	No	No
What is my child's age limit?	No age restriction	Child must be under 18 to receive contributions and must use assets before age 30.	Child must be a minor (under 21)	None

College Savings Plan	529 College Savings Plans	Coverdell Education Savings Accounts (formerly Education IRAs)	UGMA/UTMA (Uniform Gifts to Minors/ Uniform Transfers to Minors) Custodial Accounts	Rebate and Loyalty Programs (see affinity programs listed below)
Who controls the money?	Parent	Parent	Parent or custodian controls the account until it is transferred to the child at age 21.	Parent
Is my gift revocable?	Yes. You can withdraw money at any time.	Yes	No	N/A
What can I invest in?	Assets are professionally managed; parent can select portfolios.	Parent researches and chooses investments (mutual funds, stocks, bonds, and so on) on behalf of the child.	Parent researches and chooses investments.	The following affinity programs currently offer college savings rebates: BabyMint, BabyCenter, MyKids College, SAGE Tuition Rewards Program, UPromise, Ebates, FatWallet, BondRewards. Also consider credit card companies' college rebate programs.
What is the tax advantage?	The savings plans are tax-deferred and qualified distributions are exempt from federal income tax. Some state 529 savings plans have state income-tax credits.	No federal income tax on earnings when distributions are used to pay qualifying educational expenses. There is a penalty if money is used for non-educational purposes.	At least part of the investment earnings may be exempt from federal income tax. Some of the investment may be taxed at the child's rate.	Rebates aren't subject to income tax or sales tax.

College Savings Plan	529 College Savings Plans	Coverdell Education Savings Accounts (formerly Education IRAs)	UGMA/UTMA (Uniform Gifts to Minors/ Uniform Transfers to Minors) Custodial Accounts	Rebate and Loyalty Programs (see affinity programs listed below)
Can the beneficiary be changed?	Yes, to another family member	Yes, to another family member	No	N/A
Whose asset is the account, the parent's or the child's?	Parent's asset	Parent's asset	Child's asset	Parent's asset
Who can open this account?	Can be opened by anyone on behalf of the minor.	Can be opened by anyone on behalf of the minor.	Can be opened by anyone on behalf of the minor.	N/A

COLLEGE SAVINGS PLANS ONLINE REFERENCES

- General information on college savings plans
  http://www.finaid.org/savings/
  http://www.fastweb.com/financial-aid/articles/1481-introduction-
    to-saving-for-college by Mark Kantrowitz, publisher of FinAid.org
  IRS Publication 970: Tax Benefits for Education for use in preparing
    2009 Returns (www.irs.gov)
  Fidelity Investments—Fidelity.com College and Planning (http://
    personal.fidelity.com/planning/college/college_frame.shtml.cvsr)

- 529 College Savings Plans
  529 Plans: Questions and Answers
    (http://www.irs.gov/newsroom/article/0,,id=213043,00.html)
  http://cashmoneylife.com/2009/03/09/college-savings-plans-529-
    plan/

- Coverdell Education Savings Accounts (ESAs)
  http://www.irs.gov/newsroom/article/0,,id=107636,00.html
  http://cashmoneylife.com/2009/03/10/college-savings-plans-
    coverdell-educational-savings-account-esa/

- UGMA/UTMA Custodial Accounts
  http://www.finaid.org/savings/ugma.phtml
  http://www.financialaidfinder.com/ugma-utma-college-savings.
    html

- Rebate and Loyalty Programs
  http://www.finaid.org/savings/loyalty.phtml
  http://www.529rewards.com/529-articles-tim.php
  http://www.familyresource.com/finance/529-college-savings-plans/
    college-savings-reward-plans-making-them-work-for-you

Resources

The following list of general college-admissions Web sites, scholarships, study abroad programs, gap year programs, and summer programs, although extensive, is only a beginning. Parents and students should review each reference carefully, as they often change management, leadership, goals, and even Web addresses from year to year. All of the information comes either from our own research or from students of ours who have participated in the programs. To the best of our knowledge, this list is reliable, accurate, and current.

Note: Web site addresses change over time. If you are unable to access a site with the given address, do a search for the name of the program to determine its updated online address.

Books
For all book resources, please see Selected Bibliography (pp. 289–90).

General College-Admissions Web Sites
American College Testing Program (http://www.actstudent.org)
The official ACT Web site.

The College Board (http://www.collegeboard.com)
*The College Board is the administrator of the SAT, the PSAT, and the Advanced
Placement (AP) tests.*

College Confidential (http://talk.collegeconfidential.com/)
Web site for college-bound students and parents.

Colleges That Change Lives (http://www.ctcl.org/)
Profiles of some forty less-well-known but academically strong regional colleges.

The Common Application for Undergraduate College Admission (http://www.
commonapp.org)
Hundreds of colleges accept this application.

EDU, Inc., Common Black College Application (http://www.eduinconline.com)
*Apply to 33 historically black colleges with one application and one fee of $35
for all 33 member institutions.*

Enrichment Alley
(http://www.enrichmentalley.com/programs/search)
A search engine for summer, gap year, and school year programs.

FastWeb (http://www.fastweb.com/)
Information on scholarships, financial aid, student loans, and colleges.

Free Application for Federal Student Aid (http://www.fafsa.ed.gov)
Contains the FAFSA and other financial-aid information.

Gapwork.com (http://www.gapwork.com)
Online resource for gap year jobs and volunteer work.

International Baccalaureate (http://www.ibo.org/)
Online resource for the IB program

Naviance (http://www.naviance.com)
*Products and services for college research, coursework planning, and career
exploration.*

NCAA Eligibility Center Online (https://web1.ncaa.org/eligibilitycenter/
common/)
*Provides information about initial eligibility at NCAA Division I and II
member colleges and universities.*

Unigo (http://www.unigo.com/)
College reviews by college students.

Prestigious Scholarships

All scholarships listed are offered to college-bound high school students. For official application guidelines, please see the individual programs' Web sites.

Apple Scholars Program (http://www.scholarships4students.com/apple_scholars_program.htm)

Robert C. Byrd Honors Scholarship Program (http://www.ed.gov/programs/iduesbyrd/index.html)

Coca-Cola Scholars Program Scholarship (https://www.coca-colascholars.org/cokeWeb/jsp/scholars/Index.jsp)

The Concord Review (http://www.tcr.org/)

Davidson Fellows Scholarships (http://www.davidsongifted.org/Fellows/)

Elks National Foundation Most Valuable Student Competition (http://www.elks.org/enf/scholars/ourscholarships.cfm)

Gates Millennium Scholars (http://www.gmsp.org/)

Intel Science Talent Search (http://www.intel.com/education/sts/). See also Science Training Program Directory for Intel Talent Search (http://sciserv.org/sts/students/stp_directory.asp)

Intel International Science and Engineering Fair (http://www.societyforscience.org/ISEF/)

International Biology Olympiad (http://www.ibo-info.org/)

International Chemistry Olympiad (http://www.icho.sk/)

International Mathematical Olympiad (http://www.imo-official.org/)

International Physics Olympiads (http://www.jyu.fi/tdk/kastdk/olympiads/)

National Foundation for Advancement in the Arts, youngARTS Program (http://www.youngarts.org/home.html)

National Institutes of Health Undergraduate Scholarship Program (https://ugsp.nih.gov/home.asp?m=00)

National Merit and National Achievement Scholarship Programs (NMSC) (http://www.nationalmerit.org/)

NCTE Achievement Awards in Writing (http://www.ncte.org/awards/student/aa)

Rotary Foundation Ambassadorial Scholarships (http://www.rotary.org/en/StudentsAndYouth/EducationalPrograms/AmbassadorialScholarships/Pages/Howtoapply.aspx)

Siemens Awards for Advanced Placement (http://www.siemens-foundation.org/en/advanced_placement.htm)

Siemens Competition in Math, Science & Technology (http://www.siemens-foundation.org/en/competition.htm)

USA Today All-USA High School Academic Team (http://www.enotes.com/scholarships-loans/usa-today#All-U.S.A._High_School_Academic_Team)

U. S. Presidential Scholars Program (http://www.ed.gov/programs/psp/index.html)
Wendy's High School Heisman Award (http://www.wendyshighschoolheisman.com/)

Study Abroad Programs/International Travel

AIFS: American Institute for Foreign Study (http://www.aifs.com/)
American Intercultural Student Exchange (nonprofit foundation; http://www.aise.com)
ASA Academic Study Associates (http://www.asaprograms.com/)
Oxbridge Academic Programs, (Oxford, Cambridge, England, or Paris; http://www.oxbridgeprograms.com/index.php)
Putney Student Travel (http://www.goputney.com)
Sojourns Abroad (includes Siena and Paris programs; http://www.sojournsabroad.org)
TASIS: American Study in Switzerland (http://www.tasis.com/page.cfm?p=540)

Gap Year Programs

Amigos de las Americas (http://www.amigoslink.org)
Center for Interim Programs (http://www.interimprograms.com)
Cross Cultural Solutions (http://www.crossculturalsolutions.org)
Global Routes (http://www.globalroutes.org)
Oxford Advanced Studies Program (http://www.oasp.ac.uk)
Where There Be Dragons (http://www.wheretherebedragons.com)
Where You Headed (http://www.whereyouheaded.com)
World Wide Opportunities on Organic Farms (http://www.wwoof.org)

Summer Programs

ARCHAEOLOGY

Crow Canyon Archaeological Center Summer Camps (http://www.crowcanyon.org/archaeology_adventures/summer_camps.asp)

ARCHITECTURE/URBAN DESIGN

Cornell University's Architecture Art Planning (AAP) Summer Programs for High School Students (http://aap.cornell.edu/ddp/summerprograms.cfm)
Pratt Institute Program for High School Students (http://www.pratt.edu/academics/continuing_education_and_professional/pro_credit_programs/precollege/hs_programs/)
Summer Academy in Architecture, Roger Williams University (http://www.rwu.edu/academics/schools/oldsaahp/summer_academy/)
Washington University in St. Louis, Architecture Discovery Program (http://www.arch.wustl.edu/summer-programs/architecture-discovery)

ASTRONOMY / AEROSPACE
Northwestern University Center for Interdisciplinary Exploration and Research
   in Astrophysics (http://ciera.northwestern.edu/Education/edu_summer_
   programs.php)
Summer Science Program in Astronomy/ Celestial Mechanics (http://www.
   summerscience.org/home/index.php)

BIOLOGY / GENETIC BIOMEDICAL RESEARCH
Cornell University Plant Genome Research Project High School Summer
   Internship (http://www.bti.cornell.edu/educationInternships.php)
Duke University's Howard Hughes Precollege Program in the Biological Sciences
   (http://howardhughes.trinity.duke.edu/outreach/pre-college)
The Harvard School of Public Health Summer Research Apprenticeship
   Program (http://www.hsph.harvard.edu/administrative-offices/human-
   resources/employment/rap-program/)
Human BioMolecular Research Institute High School Research Internships
   (http://www.hbri.org/ScienceEducation.htm)
Iowa State University, George Washington Carver Internship Program, College of
   Agriculture and Life Sciences (http://www.ag.iastate.edu/diversity/gwc/HS.html)
The J. Craig Venter Institute Discover Genomics! Internship Program
   (http://www.jcvi.org/cms/education/internship-program/)
The Jackson Laboratory Summer Student Program (http://education.jax.org/
   summerstudent/index.html)
National Cancer Institute, Werner H. Kirsten Student Intern Program, (http://
   web.ncifcrf.gov/careers/student_programs/internships/SIP/)
National Heart, Lung and Blood Institute, Summer Internship Program
   in Biomedical Research, (http://dir.nhlbi.nih.gov/oe/summerprogs.
   asp#content)
National Human Genome Research Institute, Summer Internship in Biomedical
   Research (http://www.genome.gov/page.cfm?pageID=10000218)
Pittsburgh Tissue Engineering Initiative Summer Internship Program (see also
   Engineering/Science) (http://www.ptei.org/interior.php?pageID=53)
Summer Internship in Biomedical Research at the National Institutes of Health
   (http://www.training.nih.gov/student/sip/)
University of California-San Francisco, School of Medicine, Department of
   Pediatrics, Biomedical and Health Sciences Internship for High School
   Students (http://www.pediatrics.medschool.ucsf.edu/youth/training/
   intern.aspx)
Vanderbilt University, Research Internship Program (http://www.
   scienceoutreach.org/research.php)

BUSINESS/INTERNATIONAL RELATIONS

Columbia University Introduction to Business Finance and Economics (http://
ce.columbia.edu/Summer-Program-High-School-Students/Introduction-
Business-Finance-and-Economics)

Georgetown University Summer Programs for High School Students:
Fundamentals of Business—Leadership in a Global Economy, International
Relations (http://scs.georgetown.edu/summer-programs-for-high-school-
students)

The Jerome Fisher Program in Management and Technology/Summer Institute
at the University of Pennsylvania (see also Engineering/Science) (http://
www.upenn.edu/fisher/summer/)

Julian Krinsky Senior Academic Enrichment: 2- to 3-week sessions with instruction
in business at Haverford College (http://www.jkcp.com/enrichment/)

Julian Krinsky Summer Internships in Philadelphia (http://www.jkcp.com/
internships/)

LEAD: Leadership, Education And Development Program in Business; for
minority students (http://www.leadbusinesssite.org/)

Notre Dame Pre-College Programs: Entrepreneurship (http://precollege.
nd.edu/summer-scholars/programs-of-study/investments-and-
entrepreneurship)

University of Southern California Exploring Entrepreneurship (http://cesp.usc.
edu/2010/summer/summer_seminars_entrepreneurship.shtml)

CHESS

USA Chess National Summer Chess Camp Tour (http://www.usachess.
com/?p=services_camps_summer)

COMPUTERS

Adventures in Computing Computer Camps (http://www.computercamps.ca/
index.htm)

Camp CAEN (Computer Aided Engineering Network) (http://www.engin.
umich.edu/caen/campcaen/index.html)

Digital Media Academy (http://www.digitalmediaacademy.org/teens-kids/
teen/)

Game Camp USA (http://gamecamp.com/Game-Camp-USA/Home/Better-
Than-Computer-Camp.html)

Java Passport Summer Workshop at University of Maryland (http://www.
cs.umd.edu/projects/passport/webPage/)

Johns Hopkins University Engineering Innovation (http://engineering-
innovation.jhu.edu/)

HISTORY (SEE ALSO PROGRAMS FOR GIFTED STUDENTS AND SUMMER PROGRAMS FOR ACADEMIC CREDIT)

Pre-Collegiate Summer Program in Early American History at the College of William & Mary (http://www.wm.edu/as/niahd/precollegiatesummer/index.php)

JOURNALISM

Asian American Journalists Association (AAJA) J Camp (http://www.aaja.org/programs/for_students/journalism_trainings/j_camp)

Ball State University Journalism Workshops (http://bsujournalismworkshops.com/pages/2009/12/09/2010-summer-student-workshops/)

Indiana University High School Journalism Institute (http://journalism.indiana.edu/programs/hsji/)

Northwestern Summer Journalism School (http://www.northwestern.edu/nhsi/)

JUDAIC STUDIES

Bronfman Youth Fellowship in Israel (http://www.bronfman.org/)

Genesis at Brandeis University (http://www.brandeis.edu/genesis/)

JCC Maccabi Israel Summer Team Tours (http://www.jccmaccabiisrael.org/)

LANGUAGES (SEE ALSO STUDY ABROAD PROGRAMS/ INTERNATIONAL TRAVEL)

Abbey Road Programs, High School Study Abroad & College Prep in the U.S., France, Italy, Spain, and Greece (http://www.goabbeyroad.com/)

ASA (Academic Study Associates) pre-college and cultural immersion programs in Spain, France, Italy (http://www.asaprograms.com/)

Oxbridge Academic Programs, La Academia de España (http://www.oxbridgeprograms.com/barcelona_acad/index.php)

Rassias Summer Language Programs at Dartmouth College and in France, Spain, and China (http://www.rassias.com/)

Summer Language Institute at the University of Virginia (http://www.virginia.edu/summer/SLI/index.html)

University of Chicago Summer Program for High School Students: Intensive Language Study (https://summer.uchicago.edu/minisite/index.html)

DEBATE/ FORENSICS

Northwestern Debate Institute at Northwestern University (http://www.northwestern.edu/nhsi/debate/index.html)

Stanford National Forensic Institute at Stanford University (http://www.snfi.org/)

Summer Debate Programs at Dartmouth (http://debate.dartmouth.edu/workshops.php)

University of Iowa, National Summer Institute in Forensics (http://www.continuetolearn.uiowa.edu/debate/)

University of Michigan Debate Institutes (http://www.michigandebate.com/#)

ENGINEERING/SCIENCE

Baylor University High School Summer Science Research Program (http://www.baylor.edu/summerscience/)

Boston University Summer Programs: Research Internship in Science and Engineering Program (http://www.bu.edu/summer/high-school-programs/research-internship/)

Columbia University, Summer Program for High School Students: Engineering Design Via Community Service Projects (http://ce.columbia.edu/Summer-Program-High-School-Students/Engineering-Design-Community-Service-Projects)

Cooper Union Summer Research Internship Program (http://www.cooper.edu/classes/summer/new.html)

Cornell University College of Engineering, The Curie Academy for Girls Interested in Engineering (http://www.engineering.cornell.edu/diversity/office-diversity-programs/summer-programs/highschool-programs/curie-academy/index.cfm)

The Forsyth Institute Educational Outreach Program/Scientific Scholars Program, Boston; focus on minority and disadvantaged candidates (http://www.forsyth.org/community/eossp.html)

Introduction to Engineering at Notre Dame University (http://www.nd.edu/~iep/)

The Jerome Fisher Program in Management and Technology/Summer Institute at the University of Pennsylvania (see also Business) (http://www.upenn.edu/fisher/summer/)

Johns Hopkins University Engineering Innovation (http://engineering-innovation.jhu.edu/)

Junior Engineering Math and Science Summer Workshops at University of Idaho College of Engineering (http://www.engr.uidaho.edu/jems2009/)

MIT MITES (Minority Introduction to Engineering and Science) (http://web.mit.edu/mites/)

Pittsburgh Tissue Engineering Initiative Summer Internship Program (see also Biology/Genetic Biomedical Research) (http://www.ptei.org/interior.php?pageID=53)

Research Science Institute at MIT (http://www.cee.org/programs/rsi)

Science and Engineering Apprenticeship Program (SEAP) at George Washington University (http://www.gwseap.net/default.asp)

Smith College Summer Science and Engineering Program for High School Girls (http://www.smith.edu/summerprograms/ssep/index.php)

Summer Science Camps at Lawrence Hall of Science, University of California, Berkeley (http://www.lawrencehallofscience.org/classes/camps/overnight/research)

UC Davis Summer Residential Research Program for High School Students (http://ysp.ucdavis.edu/)

University of Notre Dame Pre-College Program in Life Sciences (http://precollege.nd.edu/summer-scholars/programs-of-study/life-sciences)

University of Vermont/GIV Engineering Summer Institute (http://www.cems.uvm.edu/summer/2010/)

U.S. National Chemistry Olympiad Study Camp (http://portal.acs.org:80/portal/acs/corg/content?_nfpb=true&_pageLabel=PP_SUPERARTICLE&node_id=1020&use_sec=false&sec_url_var=region1&__uuid=88873d02-7816-4528-a452-ee038a1339db)

FILM, MEDIA, AND COMMUNICATION (SEE ALSO SUMMER PROGRAMS FOR ACADEMIC CREDIT)

Academy of Art College Pre-College Summer Program, San Francisco (http://www.academyart.edu/degrees/summer_artexperience.html)

Academy of Media Production at Boston University, with workshops in Film Television, Video Radio, and Editing (http://www.academyofmediaproduction.com/)

Columbia College Hollywood Summer Film Program (http://www.columbiacollege.edu/)

Discover the World of Communication at American University School of Communication: scriptwriting, video production, news and sports broadcasting, etc. (http://www.american.edu/soc/discover/)

InnerSpark, California State Summer School for the Arts (http://www.csssa.org/)

New York Film Academy Summer Film and Acting Camps (http://www.nyfa.com/summer_camp/)

New York University, Tisch School of the Arts Summer High School (http://specialprograms.tisch.nyu.edu/page/hsStudents.html)

School of Cinema and Performing Arts (http://www.socapa.org/)

UCLA School of Theater, Film and Television Arts Camp (http://www.usperformingarts.com/ucla-arts-camps.php)

University of Southern California School of Cinematic Arts Summer Film Program (http://cinema.usc.edu/programs/summer/)

FOREST ECOLOGY/GEOLOGY/CONSERVATION

Adirondack Woodsmen's School (http://www.paulsmiths.edu/woodsmenschool/)

Berry Botanic Garden Apprenticeships in Science and Engineering, Portland, Oregon (http://www.berrybot.org/administration/internships.html#high)

Environmental Studies Summer Youth Institute at Hobart and William Smith Colleges (http://academic.hws.edu/enviro/)

Mecklenburg Conservation Fellowships and Village of Cooperstown Conservation Fellowships (http://www.oneonta.edu/academics/biofld/INTERN/internships.htm)

Student Challenge Awards Program (SCAP) Grants, implemented by Earthwatch Institute (http://www.earthwatch.org/aboutus/research/scientistopps/scapgrants/)

Student Conservation Association National Conservation Crews (http://www.thesca.org/serve/national-crews)

UCLA Anderson School of Management's Center for International Business Education and Research's (CIBER) Global Green Business Week for Young Leaders (http://www.summer.ucla.edu/institutes/globalbusiness/overview.htm)

GOVERNMENT

American Legion Boys State and American Legion Auxiliary Girls State (http://www.boysandgirlsstate.org/)

Boys Nation (http://www.legion.org/boysnation)

Georgetown University American Politics and Public Affairs (http://scs.georgetown.edu/programs/101/summer-programs-for-high-school-students-american-politics-and-public-affairs)

Girls Nation (http://girlsnation-auxiliary.com/)

Presidential Classroom at Georgetown University (see Leadership/Service/Volunteer)

United States Senate Youth Program (http://www.ussenateyouth.org/)

LAW

Columbia University Constitutional Law and Leadership in Law (http://
ce.columbia.edu/Summer-Program-High-School-Students/Constitutional-
Law and http://ce.columbia.edu/Summer-Program-High-School-Students/
Leadership-in-Law)

Georgetown University Summer Programs for High School Students: Law and
Society (http://scs.georgetown.edu/summer-programs-for-high-school-
students)

University of Chicago Summer Program for High School Students: American
Law and Litigation (https://summer.uchicago.edu/minisite/index.html)

LEADERSHIP/SERVICE/VOLUNTEERING

Habitat for Humanity Experiences for students 14–25 (http://www.habitat.org/
youthprograms/ages_14_25/ages_14_25_default.aspx)

National Student Leadership Conference, including programs in subjects
ranging from Education to Forensics to Mastering Leadership to Law to
U.S. Policy & Politics (http://www.nslcleaders.org/)

Presidential Classroom, Georgetown University (http://www.
presidentialclassroom.org/)

LITERATURE/CREATIVE WRITING

Bard College at Simon's Rock Young Writers Workshop (http://www.simons-
rock.edu/young-writers)

Carleton College Summer Writing Program (http://apps.carleton.edu/campus/
SAP/writing/)

Columbia University Summer Program for High School Students; Creative Writing
(http://ce.columbia.edu/Summer-Program-High-School-Students/Creative-
Writing-Introductory-and-Advanced-Workshops)

Iowa Young Writers' Studio (http://www.uiowa.edu/%7Eiyws/tableofcontents.
htm)

Northwestern University College Prep Summer Program (http://www.scs.
northwestern.edu/collegeprep/)

University of St Andrews Creative Writing Program (http://www.st-andrews.
ac.uk/admissions/int/summerschools/creativewritingsummerprogram/)

University of Chicago summer program in creative writing (https://summer.
uchicago.edu/minisite/index.html)

MATH

American Mathematical Society Summer Math Camps and Programs for
Students (http://www.ams.org/employment/mathcamps.html): includes
most of the programs listed below

Avid Academy for Gifted Youth Math Olympiad Summer Camp (Grades 9–11)
(http://www.avidacademy.com/Summer/math-olympiad-summer-camp-
grades-9-11)

Hampshire College Summer Studies in Math (http://www.hcssim.org/)

Mathcamp, Mathematics Foundation of America (http://www.mathcamp.org/)

Program in Mathematics for Young Scientists (PROMYS) at Boston University
(http://www.promys.org/)

The Ross Mathematics Program at Ohio State (http://www.math.ohio-state.
edu/ross/)

Stanford University Math Camp (http://math.stanford.edu/sumac/)

Texas State University Honors Summer Math Camp (modeled after the Ross
Program) (http://www.txstate.edu/mathworks)

MEDICINE

Coriell Institute for Medical Research Summer Internships (http://www.coriell.
org/index.php/content/view/67/125/)

Drexel University College of Medicine, Mini-Med Summer Camp
(http://www.drexelmed.edu/Home/OtherPrograms/MiniMedSchool/
SummerCamp.aspx)

Magee Women's Research Institute, Summer Internship Program for High
School Students (http://institute.mwrif.org/viewcontent.asp?
sectionID=35537&subsectionID=354677)

National Institute of Arthritis and Musculoskeletal Diseases,
Summer Student Program (http://www.niams.nih.gov/Research/Ongoing_
Research/Branch_Lab/Career_Development_Outreach/summer.asp)

National Institute of Neurological Disorders and Stroke, Summer Program in
the Neurological Sciences (http://www.ninds.nih.gov/jobs_and_training/
summer/index.htm)

Stanford Medical Youth Science Program (http://smysp.stanford.edu/)

MILITARY

United States Naval Academy Summer Seminar (http://www.usna.edu/
Admissions/nass.htm)

West Point Summer Leaders Seminar (http://admissions.usma.edu/MoreInfo/
summer.cfm)

MUSIC

Boston University Tanglewood Institute for Young Musicians (http://www.bu.edu/cfa/music/tanglewood/)

Carnegie Mellon School of Music Pre-College Programs (http://www.music.cmu.edu/precollege/)

Interlochen Music Summer Programs (http://camp.interlochen.org/music-summer-programs)

Juilliard Pre-College Academic Year Program (http://www.juilliard.edu/precollege/general.html) and Juilliard Summer Percussion Seminar (http://www.juilliard.edu/summer/percussion.html)

Maine Summer Youth Music, University of Maine (http://www.umaine.edu/spa/YouthPrograms/MSYMseniorCamp.html)

Maryland Classical Youth Orchestras Summer Music Camps and Opportunities (http://www.mcyo.org/summer.htm)

National Symphony Orchestra Summer Music Institute (http://www.kennedy-center.org/nso/nsoed/smi/)

New England Conservatory Preparatory School Summer Programs (http://www.necmusic.edu/prep/summer)

New England Music Camp (http://www.nemusiccamp.com/)

NYU Steinhardt School of Culture, Education, and Human Development, Department of Music and Performing Arts Professions Summer Programs (http://steinhardt.nyu.edu/music/summer)

OCEANOLOGY/MARINE BIOLOGY

Acadia Institute of Oceanography, Seal Harbor, Maine (http://www.acadiainstitute.com/)

Marine Technology Society Summer Internship Program, San Diego, California (http://www.mts-sandiego.org/internship.php)

Newfound Harbor Marine Institute and Seacamp Association, Big Pine Key, Florida (http://www.seacamp.org/default.htm)

Project Oceanology, University of Connecticut, Avery Point Campus, Groton, Connecticut (http://www.oceanology.org/kidsprogram.html)

Shoals Marine Laboratory Programs for High School Students, Cornell University (http://www.sml.cornell.edu/sml_students_highschool.html)

PROGRAMS FOR GIFTED STUDENTS

Center for Talent Development (CTD) Summer Program at Northwestern University (http://www.ctd.northwestern.edu/summer/)

Center for Talented Youth (CTY) Summer Programs, nationwide, affiliated with Johns Hopkins University (http://cty.jhu.edu/summer/summer-programs. html)

Clark Scholars Program at Texas Tech University; includes a $750 stipend (http://www.clarkscholars.ttu.edu/)

Duke University Talent Identification Program (TIP), Summer Programs in leadership, the arts, law and sciences as well as overseas opportunities (http://www.tip.duke.edu/)

Education Program for Gifted Youth at Stanford University (http://epgy. stanford.edu/summer/)

Summer Institute for the Gifted (SIG), at Amherst College, Bryn Mawr College, Dartmouth College, Emory University, Princeton University, UC Berkley, UCLA, University of Texas at Austin, Vassar College (http://www. giftedstudy.org/)

Telluride Association Summer Programs (http://www.tellurideassociation.org/ programs/high_school_students.html)

SPORTS MANAGEMENT

Columbia University Beyond the Game: The Business of Sports (http:// ce.columbia.edu/Summer-Program-High-School-Students-NYC/Beyond-the-Game-The-Business-of-Sports)

Georgetown University Sports Industry Management (http://scs.georgetown. edu/programs/112/summer-programs-for-high-school-students-sports-industry-management)

SUMMER PROGRAMS FOR ACADEMIC CREDIT

Boston University Summer Term (http://www.bu.edu/summer/high-school-programs/)

Brown University Pre-College Programs (http://www.brown.edu/ce/pre-college/)

Carnegie Mellon University Summer Pre-College Program (http://www.cmu. edu/enrollment/pre-college/)

Colorado College Summer Session (http://www.coloradocollege.edu/ summerprograms/summersession/)

Columbia University Summer Program (http://ce.columbia.edu/Summer-Program-High-School-Students/Junior-Senior-Division)

Cornell University Summer College for High School Students (http://www.sce. cornell.edu/sce/high_school.php)

Georgetown University Summer College (http://scs.georgetown.edu/
   programs/113/summer-programs-for-high-school-students-summer-college)
Harvard Secondary School Program (http://www.summer.harvard.edu/2010/
   programs/ssp/)
Johns Hopkins University Pre-College Programs (http://www.jhu.edu/summer/
   precollege/index.html)
Skidmore College Pre-College Program for High School Students (http://cms.
   skidmore.edu/odsp/programs/precollegiate/index.cfm)
Stanford University High School Summer College (http://summer.stanford.
   edu/highschool/overview.asp)
A Summer of Excellence, University of Arizona (http://www.soe.honors.arizona.
   edu/)
Syracuse University Summer College for High School Students (http://www.
   summercollege.syr.edu/)
University of Pennsylvania Pre-College Program (http://www.sas.upenn.edu/
   summer/students/highschool/courses/precollege)
University of Virginia Summer Session (http://www.virginia.edu/summer/)
Yale Summer Session (http://www.yale.edu/summer/)

THEATER/DANCE PROGRAMS
American Ballet Theatre Summer Intensive Program (http://www.abt.org/
   education/summerintensive.asp)
Boston Ballet School Summer Dance Program (http://www.bostonballet.org/
   school/summer/SDP-Boston.html)
Boston University Summer Theater Institute (http://web.bu.edu/cfa/theatre/
   sti/)
The Juilliard School Summer Dance Intensive (http://www.juilliard.edu/
   summer/dance.html)
San Francisco Ballet School Summer Session (http://www.sfballet.org/
   balletschool/summersession.asp)
School of American Ballet Summer Course (http://sab.org/summercourse/)
Stagedoor Manor Performing Arts Training Center (http://www.
   stagedoormanor.com/)
Stratford Shakespeare Festival Shakespeare School (http://www.
   stratfordfestival.ca/education/students.aspx?id=1090&linkidentifier=id&it
   emid=1090)
UCLA Summer Acting and Performance Institute (http://www.tft.ucla.edu/
   programs/summer-institute/)

VETERINARY MEDICINE AND ZOOLOGY

Adventures in Veterinary Medicine (AVM) at Tufts University Cummings
School of Veterinary Medicine (http://www.tufts.edu/vet/avm/high_school.
html)

Zoo Careers Camp at the Fort Worth Zoo (http://www.fortworthzoo.com/
school/summer_career.html)

VISUAL ARTS

The Art Institute of Boston, Young Artist Residency Program (YAR) (http://
www.lesley.edu/aib/curriculum/yar_program.html)

Boston University Visual Arts Summer Institute (http://www.bu.edu/cfa/
visual-arts/summer/admissions/)

California College of the Arts Pre-College Program (http://www.cca.edu/
academics/precollege)

Carnegie Mellon Pre-College Experience—includes a Game
Academy (http://www.cmu.edu/enrollment/pre-college/apply-visit.html)

Fashion Institute of Technology, High School Summer Live (http://www.fitnyc.
edu/6512.asp)

Massachusetts College of Art and Design, Boston (http://www.massart.edu/
Continuing_Education/Youth_Programs/Summer_Studios.html)

Otis College of Art and Design, Summer of Art (http://www.otis.edu/
continuing_education/summer_of_art/index.html)

Parsons School of Design Pre-College Summer Programs (http://www.parsons.
newschool.edu/pre_enrollment/summer.aspx)

Pratt Pre-College Summer Program for High School Students (http://
www.pratt.edu/academics/continuing_education_and_professional/
pro_credit_programs/precollege/hs_programs/)

Rhode Island School of Design Pre-College Program (http://www.risd.edu/
precollege.cfm)

Savannah College of Art and Design Summer Seminars (http://www.scad.edu/
programs/community-ed-summer/summer-seminars.cfm)

The School at the Art Institute of Chicago (SAIC) ECP Summer Institute
(http://www.saic.edu/continuing_studies/high_school/summer_institute/
index.html#how)

Summer Academy in Visual Arts Studies, Roger Williams University (http://
www.rwu.edu/academics/schools/oldsaahp/summer_academy/)

The University of the Arts Pre-College Summer Institute (Philadelphia) (http://
cs.uarts.edu/precollege/si/index.php)

Selected Bibliography

Berger, Sandra. *The Ultimate Guide to Summer Opportunities for Teens: 200 Programs That Prepare You for College Success.* Austin, Tex: Prufrock Press, 2007.

Cohen, Katherine. *The Truth About Getting In.* New York: Hyperion, 2003.

Damast, Alison. "Pssst! Wanna Go to College for Free?" *BusinessWeek,* November 14, 2007, online edition.

Fiske, Edward B. *The Fiske Guide to Colleges 2010,* 26th ed. Naperville, Ill: Sourcebooks, 2009.

Franek, Robert, et al., eds. *The Best 371 Colleges, 2010 Edition.* Princeton, N.J.: Princeton Review, 2009.

Glater, Jonathan D. "Reed College, in Need, Closes a Door to Needy Students." *New York Times,* June 9, 2009, Business section, online edition.

Goldman, Jordan, and Colleen Buyers, eds. *The Students' Guide to Colleges: The Definitive Guide to America's Top 100 Schools Written by the REAL Experts—the Students Who Attend Them.* New York: Penguin, 2005.

Greene, Howard, and Matthew Greene. *The Hidden Ivies: 50 Top Colleges—from Amherst to Williams—That Rival the Ivy League,* 2nd ed. New York: Collins Reference, 2009.

Haigler, Karl, and Rae Nelson. *The Gap-Year Advantage: Helping Your Child Benefit from Time Off Before or During College.* New York: St. Martin's Griffin, 2005.

Hernandez, Michele A. *A Is for Admission: The Insider's Guide to Getting into the Ivy League and Other Top Colleges.* New York: Grand Central Publishing, 1999.

Hughes, Chuck. *What It Really Takes to Get Into the Ivy League & Other Highly Selective Colleges.* New York: McGraw-Hill, 2003.

Kravets, Marybeth, and Imy F. Wax. *The K&W Guide to Colleges for Students with Learning Disabilities*, 9th ed. Princeton, N.J.: Princeton Review, 2007.

Lewin, Tamar. "Going Off to College for Less (Passport Required)." *New York Times*, November 30, 2008, U.S. section, online edition.

Montauk, Richard, and Krista Klein. *How to Get Into the Top Colleges*, 3rd ed. Upper Saddle River, N.J.: Prentice Hall, 2009.

Pope, Loren. *Colleges That Change Lives: 40 Schools That Will Change the Way You Think About Colleges*, revised ed. New York: Penguin, 2006.

———. *Looking Beyond the Ivy League: Finding the College That's Right for You.* New York: Penguin, 2007.

Rimer, Sara, and Alan Finder. "Harvard to Aid Students High in Middle Class." *New York Times*, December 11, 2007, U.S. section, online edition.

Schwebel, Sara. *Yale Daily News Guide to Summer Programs*, 3rd ed. New York: Kaplan, 2001.

Schworm, Peter. "Passport to Higher Ed, Lower Cost." *Boston Globe*, December 25, 2008, News section, online edition.

Seghers, Linda, ed. *Peterson's Study Abroad 2008*. Lawrenceville, N.J.: Peterson's, 2007.

Spencer, Janet, and Sandra Maleson. *Visiting College Campuses*, 7th ed. Princeton, N.J.: Princeton Review, 2004.

Toor, Rachel. *Admissions Confidential: An Insider's Account of the Elite College Selection Process*. New York: St. Martin's Griffin, 2002.

Our Service

At Entryway, we provide both private and group consulting on college and graduate school admissions to students from all over the world. We counsel a broad range of students, from those with severe learning disabilities to those aiming for the Ivy League. Each student brings a unique set of strengths and weaknesses in both the academic and the extracurricular spheres, and we have placed students at many different types of schools, colleges, and universities throughout the U.S. and abroad. Our aim is to find the right fit for each student.

The strategy we have laid out in this book—"be alike but spike"— underlies all of our services. We guide applicants and families through each step of the application process, helping them assess choices from both a short-term and a long-term perspective. Above all, we try to remove the stress from college admissions by empowering families with reliable information and our proven strategy for success in college admissions and beyond.

We offer two categories of service in college admissions:

- One-on-One Consulting Service
- In! College Admissions Workshops

ONE-ON-ONE CONSULTING SERVICE

We work closely and intensively with students and families on all aspects of college preparation, including:

1. Ensuring that students are "alike" (that is, on a par with) other successful applicants in terms of the basics:
   - **Academic achievement** and course selection
   - **Standardized test** selection, preparation, and timing
   - **Leadership activities** and in-school extracurriculars

2. Helping students take the steps necessary to cultivate a "spike," or area of distinction, including:
   - **Identifying a passion**
   - **"Layering" that passion** through in-school, out-of-school, summer, and employment activities

3. Providing guidance on pre-application preparation, including:
   - Helping students determine the **right college fit**
   - Creating a **college list** that features safeties, probables, and reaches
   - **Visiting colleges** and making each visit count
   - Planning out the **application cycle** (early decision, early action, rolling admission, etc.)

4. Finally, providing guidance on the application itself, ensuring that it is both similar to and distinctive from those of the student's peers, including:
   - Completing all aspects of the **written application**
   - Creating and updating an **activity chart**
   - Outlining and editing **personal and short-answer essays**
   - Obtaining top **letters of recommendation**
   - Preparing for the **college interview** through mock interviews and sample question preparation
   - Creating and submitting **supplementary application materials**

All of these services are fully customized to the individual student.

IN! COLLEGE ADMISSIONS WORKSHOPS

We offer two workshops: Workshop 1: Preparing to Apply is tailored to sophomores and juniors, and Workshop 2: Creating Your Best Common Application is tailored to seniors.

WORKSHOP 1: PREPARING TO APPLY

This workshop is tailored to rising sophomores and juniors and ensures that students are strategically positioned to create winning and successful applications by the time they reach senior year.

In this workshop, we provide step-by-step guidance on topics including:

- Earning **top grades**
- Selecting the **right classes**
- Choosing which **standardized tests** to take and creating a **testing timeline**
- Recognizing extracurricular **leadership positions**—in and out of school
- Identifying a **passion**
- Developing strategies for cultivating that passion so that it becomes a true area of distinction—**a spike**—on the college application
- Determining which teachers to ask for **letters of recommendation**
- Maximizing each and every **college visit**

Each student comes away with a detailed timeline and actionable strategy that ensures that he or she is optimally positioned to create a winning college application.

WORKSHOP 2: CREATING YOUR BEST COMMON APPLICATION

This workshop helps seniors (and rising seniors) position, outline, and learn how to complete their Common Application in a manner that optimizes their candidacy, ensuring that they both fit in *and* stand out.

In this workshop, we provide step-by-step guidance on:

- Structuring and completing an **activity chart**
- Choosing the right topic and outlining **short-answer essay questions**
- Choosing the right topic and outlining the **personal essay**
- Developing strategies for obtaining optimal **letters of recommendation** from teachers, guidance counselors, alumni, and peers
- Conducting superior **interviews**—on campus and off campus
- Determining which **supplemental materials** to include or exclude
- Creating a **college list** comprised of safety, probable, and reach colleges
- Using early action, early decision first and second round, rolling, and regular **admissions options** to maximum advantage

Students come away with a detailed draft of their activity chart as well as comprehensive outlines of their personal and short-answer essays questions. They also understand how to optimally complete their applications so that they have the best chance of getting into their top-choice college.

Although it is most beneficial for students to participate in both workshops, it is not mandatory. Space is limited and workshops sell out. Each workshop is reserved with a deposit on a first-come-first-served basis.

For more information, please visit our Web site: www.entrywayinc.com.

Index

Cartoon Credits